IT'S A LONG STORY

Also by Willie Nelson

Roll Me Up and Smoke Me When I Die: Musings from the Road

A Tale Out of Luck: A Novel (with Mike Blakely)

The Tao of Willie: A Guide to the Happiness in Your Heart (with Turk Pipkin)

The Facts of Life and Other Dirty Jokes

Willie: An Autobiography (with Bud Shrake)

IT'S A LONG STORY

MY LIFE

WILLIE NELSON

WITH DAVID RITZ

sphere

SPHERE

First published in the USA in 2015 by Little, Brown
First published in Great Britain in 2015 by Little, Brown

1 3 5 7 9 10 8 6 4 2

Credits for song lyrics appear on p. 390.
All photographs are from the collection of Willie Nelson unless otherwise noted.

A CIP catalogue record for this book
is available from the British Library.

Hardback ISBN 978-0-7515-6175-3
C-format ISBN 978-0-7515-6174-6

Printed and bound in Great Britain by
Clays Ltd, St Ives plc

Papers used by Sphere are from well-managed forests
and other responsible sources.

FSC
www.fsc.org
MIX
Paper from
responsible sources
FSC® C104740

Sphere
An imprint of
Little, Brown Book Group
Carmelite House
50 Victoria Embankment
London EC4Y 0DZ

An Hachette UK Company
www.hachette.co.uk

www.littlebrown.co.uk

I dedicate this book to my beautiful wife, Annie,
my wonderful children, my great friends,
and all my loyal fans.

CONTENTS

IT'S A LONG STORY

INTRODUCTION

A SONG IS A SHORT STORY. It might have been my buddy Harlan Howard, a writer I met in Nashville in the sixties, who first said a song ain't nothing but three chords and the truth.

Well, songs come easy to me. I've written hundreds of them. I see them as little stories that fall out of our lives and imaginations. If I have to struggle to write a song, I stop before I start. I figure if it don't flow easy, it's not meant to be.

The truth should flow easy. Same for songs and stories. If you overanalyze or torture yourself to bring them to life, something's wrong. Just the way a mountain stream, bubbling with fresh clean water, keeps flowing, stories need to flow free and easy. The source of the water, like the source of the songs, comes from on high. It's a natural thing. It's a beautiful thing.

But what you're holding in your hands is something more than a simple song or a short story. *It's a Long Story* is the name of this enterprise. This time I've given myself a different task and a whole new challenge. And while I'll certainly need the truth to guide me, I'll need a lot more than three chords. I'll need more than three minutes and a few rhyming lines to convey the ideas in my head and the feelings in my heart. My head is filled with memories, and my heart, while filled with love, also retains the memories of loss and hurt.

My prayer is that, like the mountain stream, the memories flow freely. My prayer is that the memories, whether joyful or painful, refresh my spirit, and yours, by assuring us that the stream never runs dry.

Memories remind us that every moment of our lives, even the most tragic, have contributed to our strength. We've gotten through. We're still here.

I'm thankful that I'm still here. By the time you read this, I'll be eighty-two. I'm pleased to tell you that since turning eighty, I've written a couple of dozen new songs, recorded five new albums, and performed over three hundred live concerts. I don't say that to boast but only to reassert my belief that the essence of my work as a songwriter, singer, and performer is based on the simple task of telling stories. Telling those stories has kept me alive.

Now that it's time to shape all the short stories into one long yarn, I gotta admit that the job feels a little daunting.

Eight long decades of memories.

Eight long decades of successes and failures, heartbreaks and breakthroughs, miracles and mind fucks.

It's an epic tale. And to tell it right will require all the clarity at my command. But before I move on to glory and return in some reincarnated form, I'm determined to do it, determined to tell this story in my present form as Willie Hugh Nelson, a man who has lived a long and blessed life.

So if I view the task before me as just another song to sing—although a long one—I'll be fine. This isn't the Bible. This isn't the biography of a world leader or a great philosopher. It's just the story of a picker from Hill County, Texas, who got more good breaks than bad and managed to keep from going crazy by staying close to the music of his heart.

So let me just pick up Trigger, my trusty guitar that has comforted me through thousands of stormy nights and thousands of sun-filled days.

Let me find a melody.

Let me find the right words.

And in one fashion or another, I'll sing you this song.

PART ONE

MY BEGINNING

The End

A pal of mine recently pointed out a poem by T. S. Eliot that starts off by saying, "In my beginning is my end," and concludes with, "In my end is my beginning."

I'm no T. S. Eliot, but it reminds me of a song I wrote called "Still Is Still Moving to Me."

We're never still. When we think we're at the very beginning of a journey, we may well be at the end. Or when we're convinced we're at the end, we're really just getting started.

That was my situation in the early nineties.

Everyone was saying that I had reached the end. Everyone was saying it was all over.

The IRS had come down with the hammer. And those sons of bitches came down mighty fuckin' hard.

They said I owed $32 million in back taxes. They came in and took possession of everything I owned. And at that moment, in my late fifties, I possessed a helluva lot. Property in Colorado. A couple of ranches around Austin. A nine-hole golf course. A recording studio. Several homes, including a big beachfront house in Maui. Not to mention cars and jeeps and custom tour buses. There was talk that they were even going after Trigger, so they could auction it off to the highest bidder.

"The heat's not going to blow over," said a group of sophisticated and highly trained advisers. According to them, my tax situation was fucked up beyond repair.

How did that happen?

And why?

Man, I was at a loss. All I knew was that I bought a package of tax shelters I was assured would meet my tax obligations and assure my fiscal future.

When those shelters were disallowed, the walls came tumbling down. Now the world was saying that all the king's horses and all the king's men couldn't put Willie Nelson together again.

I became a punch line for TV comics:

"Heard the one about Willie Nelson? When the IRS served him with a lien for $32 million, he took the papers, sprinkled on some pot, rolled 'em up, and blew his troubles away. Next morning, ol' Willie didn't remember a thing."

Meanwhile, I was telling jokes of my own:

"What's the difference between an IRS agent and a whore? A whore will quit fucking you after you're dead."

The more I delved into the situation, though, I began to see an even bigger picture—a vast landscape made up of mind-boggling mazes. Like a character in some thriller novel, I saw myself trapped in that maze.

I began seeing some of the hows and whys that had gotten me to this point of no return.

Going back over the previous two decades, starting with my close friendship with President Jimmy Carter in the seventies and the political change in the Ronald Reagan eighties, I saw a seismic shift in cultural attitudes.

Jimmy Carter was a mighty good friend who saw me as a soul mate, a country boy who grew up, like him, in a backwoods church believing in the Holy Spirit. Jimmy Carter was good enough to have me spend the night at the White House. He and Rosalynn loved to come onstage and sing "Amazing Grace" and "Will the Circle Be Unbroken." That was the seventies, when there was a beautiful period of peace in the culture wars, when politicos, rednecks, and hippies were sharing the dance floor and maybe even an occasional joint, all in the name of love.

The eighties were a whole different deal. The eighties got dark. The eighties got crack-pipe evil. The eighties were all about secret arms deals and drug deals, the undercover Iran-Contra Affair. A time of speed, subterfuge, and hidden agendas.

I saw how the Iranian oil embargo had jacked up prices and how speculators were reaping the benefits. Millionaires were sprouting up like weeds on the West Texas prairie. Meanwhile, tax shelters were being packaged and sold like corn dogs at the state fair. Because I was an early buyer of those shelters, my mug was plastered all over those corn dogs. Because I was someone who'd been on the cover of *Time* magazine, sold a shitload of records, and acted in a bunch of Hollywood movies, the IRS saw me as a prime target.

Can't say for sure, but I have a feeling that in the eighties the federal government was upset by my increasingly public pro-pot stance. The men in charge didn't like how Farm Aid, the yearly event I'd cofounded, led to discussions about how the government continued to fuck the farmers.

By the end of the eighties and the start of the nineties, people were saying that I was a marked man. At first, I didn't take it seriously. I didn't feel important enough to be a marked man. But as the pressure mounted, I couldn't ignore what was happening. More and more, I felt like I was caught up in one of those old Roy Rogers or Gene Autry Westerns I loved as a kid. The posse of bad guys was coming after me. They outnumbered me. They had the horses. They had the guns. They had me cornered.

"If you want to get out alive," said one adviser, "your only hope is bankruptcy."

"But wouldn't that mean the IRS owning me for the rest of my life?"

"Afraid so, Willie."

"They'd be there at every concert, collecting the ticket sales. They'd get every nickel of every record I sell from now till I die."

"Sad but true."

I thought of men I admired, like the great boxing champion Joe Louis, who lived out his life in debt to the IRS. He became a wrestler and a referee before working as a greeter at a Vegas hotel.

They said Joe had been too generous with his family, friends, and colleagues. He had given away too much and trusted the wrong people. Now they were saying the same about me.

"Willie Nelson's glory days are behind him," one writer wrote. "Not only has he gone broke and squandered his fortune before reaching sixty, he's squandered his image as a man of integrity. For the rest of his career—or what's left of it—he'll be seen as little more than a weed-smoking tax dodger."

"Bankruptcy," the adviser kept advising. "Bankruptcy is your only way out. It's your only hope. If you don't declare bankruptcy, you're good as dead."

"You sure of that?" I asked.

"Positive," he said.

The man looked me in the eye.

"What are you thinking?" he asked.

"I'm not thinking," I said. "When it comes to something like this, I don't need to think. I need to feel."

"And what are you feeling?"

"I'm feeling fine."

"Then you'll declare bankruptcy?"

"Hell, no. It's the last fuckin' thing in the world I'd ever do."

"Then what are you going to do?"

"Have a little toke, play a little golf, take a little nap, and play a little dominoes."

"All you're doing is postponing disaster."

"All I'm doing," I said, "is keeping a positive thought."

"That's not enough," said the man. "That's crazy."

" 'Crazy' is the name of a song that made me quite a bit of change."

"That was a long time ago, Willie. That was a different day, a different world. This is today, and today your world is about to collapse."

I thought about what the man said. No doubt he had a sharp mind. He'd been to a distinguished college, earned several graduate degrees, and was well versed in the nuances of high finance.

I asked myself the question, who am I to so blatantly ignore his sage advice?

To answer the deepest question of all—who am I?—won't be easy. To do so, I need to reinvoke the poet who said, "In my end is my beginning."

I need to tell you about my beginning.

1

HOME

MUSIC IN THE BLOOD. MUSIC in the house and music in the fields. Music in the air, in the songs sung by the birds flying through the clear blue Texas sky, in the sound of the wind and the thundering rain. Music in the heart of my father, a fine fiddler, and my mother, a beautiful singer, who gave birth first to my sister, Bobbie, a wonder child of music, before two years later giving birth to me.

Mother was Myrle, three-quarters Cherokee Indian, who'd traveled down from dirt-poor Arkansas with Ira, my father, who had followed his father, Alfred, and his mother, Nancy, to Abbott, Texas, where the land was dark and fertile and the farmland offered a degree of hope.

When I came into this world on April 29, 1933, hope was a sparse commodity. The Great Depression had hit the homeland hard. As an adult, I realized that I had grown up in rural Texas during one of the worst periods in American economic history. But that was something I learned out of books. What

I learned out of life was something entirely different. What I learned was love. Like music, love was everywhere I looked and everything I felt. Fact is, I equated music with love, 'cause to hear or play or sing a song put me in a loving mood.

Myrle and Ira married when they were sixteen. They divorced when I was six months old. Other than giving life to me and Bobbie, I don't think they were ever meant to be together.

Myrle was a Greenhaw, a big family spread out between Arkansas and Tennessee that included a number of moonshiners and musicians. My mother had a wild side, no doubt, and an exotic allure that had Texans believing she was Mexican and Oklahomans believing she was Indian. She was a card dealer, a dancer, a waitress, a woman who sought adventure and the open road.

Ira's people, being from the Ozarks, grew up among the Irish and English who carried with them the tradition of Old Country storytelling, folk singing, and fiddling. More than a fiddler, though, my father was a first-rate mechanic. In fact, his main gig turned out to be chief mechanic for Frank Kent Ford Company in Fort Worth. He had a lot less wanderlust than Mom and was happy to fiddle around the honky-tonks along the highways and byways of north central Texas.

You'd think the absence of a mother and father would cause little kids like me and Bobbie all sorts of emotional damage. Well, I'm here to say that it didn't. It didn't because my grandparents—whom we called Mama and Daddy Nelson—took over. They were unflinchingly responsible. In addition to watching over me and Bobbie, they took in my older cousin

Mildred. They devoted their lives to our care. Hell, in my case, they spoiled me rotten.

So there I was, in the middle of the Depression in the farmland of Hill County, Texas, in this tiny town of Abbott, population somewhere around four hundred, seventy miles south of Dallas and thirty miles north of Waco. Closest towns were West, population three thousand, six miles to the south, and Hillsboro, population eight thousand, twelve miles to the north.

You might say that I was born in the middle of nowhere, but I feel that I was born in the middle of everywhere. I was born in the middle of what I look back on as a musical miracle. I call it a miracle because so many different kinds of music were coming at me strong and sweet. My heart was being filled up by melodies, just as my body was excited by rhythms—maybe the rhythms that got my father and my mother to run off into the night, rhythms that would soon have me running in a hundred different directions. But mainly the music kept me home because home—the home of Mama and Daddy Nelson—was where the music was strongest. That's where the music was not only played and sung, but where it was taught.

I'm thankful for being born in the heart of Texas in the care of loving grandparents who were also dedicated music teachers. I'm grateful and amazed when I think about the passion these two people had for music. They passed that passion on to me and Bobbie and let us know that there was nothing more beautiful in this world than to make music.

Bobbie became accomplished at an early age. I lagged behind—and remain so to this day. Bobbie is a musician in the true sense of being able to play with great facility in any style. She learned to read beautifully and was known far and around Hill County as a genuine piano prodigy.

That had a lot to do with my grandparents ordering music books that came all the way from Chicago. The method of symbolization was called "shape notes" — "do re mi fa so la ti" each had its own configuration. Many churches used this method to help the whole congregation sing along. Mama and Daddy Nelson were principally church musicians.

Our church was the Abbott United Methodist, but there were also the Baptist, Catholic, and Church of Christ congregations, all right close to each other. Maybe there were differing opinions among the church members about which one had the true line to God, but I'll be damned if I remember a single day of disagreements among the Christians in Abbott. We all went about our religious business in our own way.

There was love in our little church. That love was first expressed to me by the Women's Missionary Society, which decided, when I was only six months old, to christen me and make me a lifetime member. That meant God had told them that this child was going to be a missionary. Well, I did find a mission early in life. It was a musical mission, born in that Methodist church. If you look broadly at what it means to be a missionary, at least as I look at it, I'm reasonably sure their prophecy proved true.

I was a believer as a kid, just as I am a believer as a man. I've never doubted the genius of Christ's moral message or the truth of the miracles he performed. I see his presence on earth and resurrection as perfect man as a moment that altered human history, guiding us in the direction of healing love. As I've gotten older, I've augmented my belief in Jesus with other philosophies that complement his. The basis of my faith, though, was formed in that little country church where we sang hymns about "amazing grace, how sweet the sound, that saved a wretch like me," and "just as I am, without one plea, but thy blood was shed for me," and "in the garden where he walks with me and he talks with me and tells me I am his own."

I didn't know that those hymns had been written in earlier centuries in foreign lands. To me, they were as new and fresh as the corn and cotton growing in the fields just outside church. These songs grew out of the rich fertile faith that was the sum and substance of Mama and Daddy Nelson. With Bobbie playing her little heart out on piano, church was, for me, both a joy and the source of a musical expression that has lasted a lifetime.

Church, however, did not calm my restless and rambunctious soul.

Mama Nelson had to tether toddler Willie to a pole in the yard to keep him from wandering off. Don't know where I'd have gone if I could have, but I had the itch early on—the itch to look beyond the bend in the road.

The Methodist church preached that straight is the gate. Liquor and smoking were seen as first-class tickets to hell, and while I heard those exhortations, even as a small child I never absorbed fear of the fiery pit. I can't remember being afraid of venturing beyond that straight gate. My natural curiosity overwhelmed my religious piety.

My first foray out of the tiny world of Abbott into the larger world of Texas was a six-mile bike ride to West, where there was a large community of Czechs. They spoke in different accents, attended the Catholic church, and had nothing against drinking beer. I was fascinated by the presence of these people who had crossed a great ocean and somehow wound up in Hill County.

I was fascinated by the very fact of being alive—that my heart beat to the rhythm of life under the sun of the huge Texas sky, that my eyes took in the amazing sights of cotton gins and horse-drawn plows and far-off fields scorched brown under the summer heat or blooming green grass in the early days of spring.

My eyes were even more amazed by what I saw on the screen of the Best Movie Theater in West—an even wider world whose heroes were more than mere men in white hats who shot straight and caught the bad guys. They were men who cradled guitars in their arms and sang the stars down from the heavens. They moved through the world serenading away the sinister side of life. Even though they were macho men who feared no rustler, they sang sweetly, effortlessly, and proudly. I saw that a cowboy hero is a romantic lover of life with a song on his lips, a funny sidekick close by, and a beloved horse on whose back he rides the trails of life.

First viewed in the small movie theaters of West and Hillsboro, Texas, the Western became an early and beautiful obsession. The Western was all about daring and danger. Up on the big screen, these fearless cowboys were my first heroes. Their moral lessons, like the lessons of the Methodist church, were clear. You live life based on loyalty. You stay on the right side. You protect your own. And when the going gets rough and the day grows dark, you pick up your guitar and soothe your soul by singing the pain away.

Their songs—eternal anthems like "Happy Trails to You" and "Back in the Saddle Again"—weren't sung in church, but they entered my soul and informed my heart with the impact of the holy hymns taught by Mama Nelson. They were all about the great adventure. Early on, I yearned for a great adventure of my own.

Years later I learned that these songs, whether written by Gene Autry or tunesmiths out in Hollywood, signaled the start of a category called country western music.

Like most every little boy in the America of the late thirties, I wanted to be a cowboy, whether Wild Bill Elliott, Lash LaRue, Eddie Dean, Whip Wilson, or Hopalong Cassidy. But how can you be a cowboy without a horse? And living in a one-horse town like Abbott, that can be a problem. Fact is, Abbott was a *no*-horse town 'cause the only steed belonged to Mr. Harvel, who lived two miles outside town.

On a sunny day in summer, I'd walk out to his place and ask if I could take a little ride.

"Sure thing, little Willie," he'd say. "Just don't go too far."

Sitting on top of that old nag, I pretended to be Tex Ritter riding the plains of Wyoming until a friend spotted me and called out, "Hey, Willie. You look like you 'bout to fall off that thing."

"Not gonna happen," I said. And it never did. Been a comfortable rider all my life.

From an early age, I was also comfortable writing poems. I liked stringing words together and telling little stories. I liked the fun of rhyming, the easy flow of expressing my feelings.

Mama and Daddy Nelson were big on proper speech. In addition to giving us music lessons, they taught us elocution. And though Bobbie and I were essentially shy country kids, they encouraged us to perform before the public, especially when the appearance was part of a religious event.

The seminal event happened when I was four or five. My grandparents had given me a poem to read in front of a gala outdoor tabernacle meeting in Brooking, Texas. The day was part revival, part picnic. You'd eat, you'd pray, you'd hear some preaching, you'd do some singing. This went on all afternoon. Mama Nelson had dressed me up in an all-white sailor suit. The outfit brought me pride, but the idea of reciting a poem in front of this huge audience gave me jitters. Just before I was set to go on, I started picking my nose. I was nervous and didn't realize how deeply I had dug into my skin. When I hit the stage, red blood was pouring all over my white suit. Right then and there, I ditched the poem and improvised a new one on the spot.

What are you looking at me for?
I got nothing to say
If you don't like the looks of me
You can look another way

That's how I got the nickname Booger Red.

* * *

What kind of kid was Booger Red?

I was scrappy. I was physical. I played all the sports. I loved to compete. Winning was important. Winning felt good. I wouldn't call myself a sore loser, but I did all I could to avoid defeat.

And even though I'd get into fights now and then, I got along with everyone. I had a naturally easygoing nature.

Felt natural, for instance, to be living across the street from a Mexican family. We accepted them and they accepted us. Our Mexican neighbors worked out in the fields right alongside us. Before I was old enough to pull my own cotton sack, I'd ride on Mama Nelson's sack while she picked cotton. I loved that puffy white landscape of cotton plants bursting with blossoms. I also loved listening to the black workers making music of their own. They weren't singing songs of complaint. They were singing songs of hope driven by a steady beat and flavored with thick harmonies made up on the spot. I couldn't help but sing along. These were songs that praised the Lord.

So once again I got the notion that God was everywhere. Even in the midst of backbreaking labor, God was inspiring his children to sweeten the air with melodies of joy. The field workers knew that they were being exploited with tiny pay for heavy labor. And yet they sang. They used music to turn their mood from dark to light. Music was offered up to the sky. Whether they were picking cotton, baling hay, or shucking corn, music was part of the work. As music expressed the pain, it eased the pain.

For a young kid to absorb that idea was both a heavy and heart-lifting experience.

Wherever you go, take music with you.

Music never has to stop.

Let the music keep coming through you.

Keep singing and playing and telling your story—no matter how happy or sad—through music.

Music will protect you.

Music will keep you going.

Music surrounded me, and rhythm was everywhere, too. Daddy Nelson was a blacksmith. His work fascinated me. I hung out in his shop every day and acted like his little assistant. I loved watching him take the metal from the fire before hammering the horseshoe into shape. I didn't really have the strength to handle the anvil myself, so he'd put his hand on mine and together we'd start pounding.

"You're strong, little Willie," he'd assure me, "and getting stronger every day."

Daddy Nelson was enormously strong himself, a heavyset man who wielded the heavy tools in his blacksmith shed like they were toys. I saw him as the strongest man in the world. On those occasions when I disobeyed him by running down the road and not returning till dinnertime, he'd spank me, but the spanking was never severe. It wasn't in the man's nature to hurt me. But when he did, he'd say, "If you don't obey, son, we'll never trust you." Hearing those words hurt me—and, at least for a while, I stopped running off.

Might sound corny, but the truth is we were dirt-poor in material possessions but rich in love. Along with our garden and animals, love was our sustenance. I had calves and hogs. These were creatures that I fed and raised. I remember when one baby calf was so small I could stand him on my chest. That thrilled my heart. I spent hours watching the hogs sloshing around their pen. I saw that they had their own kind of keen intelligence. I saw that animals, like people, responded to love.

I loved watching the vegetables grow—the tomatoes and the lettuce and the carrots, the turnips and the green beans. We'd throw our potatoes and onions under the house to store them for winter. Even though I didn't use fancy words like "horticulturist" or "breeder," I was developing skills at farming, not only because of my grandparents' instructions but because I was a member in good standing of the Future Farmers of America, a proud organization that was strong in the rural cities of Depression-time America.

At night we came together in front of the little Philco radio, where we heard about the suffering caused by the economic calamity. But I wasn't old enough to understand. All I knew was that I was protected by a man and a woman devoted to making me feel safe.

There was gospel music coming out of the Philco radio—music already close to our hearts—but also music from the Mexican station, the same kind of spirited guitar-and-marimba music we'd heard our neighbors playing late at night. We heard music from powerful faraway stations like WLS in Chicago and XERF in Mexico and KWKH in Shreveport—

mariachi music or the big band music of Benny Goodman and Glenn Miller or, closer to home, country music by masters like Ernest Tubb, whose songs like "Walking the Floor Over You" made a deep impression. They called him the Texas Troubadour.

I loved that word "troubadour" and wondered what it meant. When I was told it referred to a wandering singer of songs, that seemed like the greatest job in the world.

The greatness of Tubb had to do with the ease with which he performed. His appeal was naturalness and sincerity. He didn't hide his heart. A woman had left him and he had no shame about letting you know how much it hurt. He had the blues. I didn't know the name "blues" yet, but I knew the feeling. It was the feeling of loneliness and loss.

The blues hit me—a deep and gut-wrenching case of the blues—in 1939, when Daddy Nelson passed away at age fifty-six. He had caught pneumonia and stayed sick for a week before he died at home in bed. I was devastated the way any six-year-old boy losing the most important man in his life would be devastated. This was my first encounter with death, and the encounter could not have been closer. I wish I could tell you that I cried for days on end because I believe crying is healthy. There's healing in tears. But my memory is foggy. Maybe I just suppressed all the scary stuff going through me. Maybe that was my way of surviving the ordeal.

No one expected this. Daddy Nelson was a healthy giant of a man, the man with the anvil, the man with the golden voice, the man with the courage to move his family from Arkansas to Texas so that we might live off the fruit of the land, the man who sat in the first pew in the Methodist church, the man adored by his wife and his grandchildren, the man who kept it all together.

Our rock solid world was suddenly ripped apart. Like a thief in the night, death broke down the door and stole Daddy Nelson away.

And yet...

I did not fall apart.

Sister Bobbie did not fall apart.

And, most certainly, Mama Nelson did not fall apart.

Mama Nelson gathered her strength, gathered us to her side, and assured us, no matter what, that this family would not be broken. This family was staying together. Even though Mother Myrle and Daddy Ira were still not in a place where they could care for us, Mama Nelson could. And would. And did. And God bless her beautiful loving soul for doing just that.

After Daddy Nelson's death, Myrle and Ira came around. They loved the man and paid their respects. When they left us again, after services, they knew full well that we were in good hands. They realized that Mama Nelson possessed the strength and fortitude to raise us right.

If we were poor before, without Daddy Nelson's blacksmith trade we were that much poorer. We had to move from our two-story house to something I'd call a cottage or even a shack. Sometimes we pasted newspaper on the walls to keep the wind from blowing through. It wasn't much. And yet...

We tended our garden, we raised our animals, we worked the corn and cotton fields alongside the whites, blacks, and Mexicans who were in the same shape as us—folks looking to survive. We went to church, we praised the Lord, we sang his holy hymns. Bobbie kept playing that church piano and got better by the day. Music kept providing me with nourishment and bulking up my spiritual muscles.

I don't think it was any accident that I received my first guitar only months before Daddy Nelson passed. It was a Stella fresh from the Sears catalog. My grandfather was there to give me my first lessons. This would be the instrument that would enable me to survive life without him and endure a whole mess of heartbreaks to come.

Like the heavy metal shoe forged to fit the horse's foot, the guitar allowed me to trudge ahead. The guitar also awakened me to the wider world. It was the instrument I heard played when Ernest Tubb was walkin' the floor, the instrument that, because of its simplicity, spoke to me. Sister Bobbie's vast musical mind could deal with all those white and black keys on the piano. She knew what to do with them. Six strings was about all I could handle. Six strings made sense.

The flood of music coming out of the Texas of my childhood made complete sense, too. And the guy who made the most sense was Bob Wills and his Texas Playboys. Later I learned that his brand of western swing changed the nature of country music. As a kid, all I knew was that I loved every song he put out. He was a fiddler and a singer and a bandleader located in neighboring Waco before he moved up to Oklahoma. He was always close by. In 1940, the year I turned seven, his "New San Antonio Rose" was a million seller. You'd hear it on the radio every ten minutes. They were calling Wills the "King of Western Swing."

I felt the "swing" deep in my soul. Because I had been listening to and loving the jazz of Louis Armstrong and Duke Ellington coming out of the Chicago station, I knew Bob Wills had been doing the same. There was the syncopation of jazz in his music. That was the swing, the part that got folks to dancing. And because I had been so close to black people, hearing them sing in the fields and on those faraway radio stations, I also heard blues in Bob Wills. Like Ernest Tubb, he sang of loss and loneliness.

I'm not here to psychologize, but maybe because I had just suffered the loss of Daddy Nelson, maybe because I understood how lonely Mama Nelson was without her loving husband, I related to those emotions.

This was the time when I started writing poems. I was getting more comfortable moving my fingers up and down the strings of the guitar and able to marry words to melodies. I did all this with great confidence.

Convinced that both Bobbie and I would make our way through music, my grandmother bolstered that confidence. Every little song I invented—no matter how lame—gained her approval. There was never harsh criticism. And even though she was a God-fearing woman who loved praising the Lord, she never frowned when the secular music of Ernest Tubb and Bob Wills started stirring my heart.

As much as this book is the history of my heart—and especially the ways in which my heart has been shaped by music—the seventh and eighth years of my life were a turning point.

The arrival of that little Stella guitar, the death of Daddy Nelson, my introduction to suffering loss, my introduction to the joyous sound of western swing, my willingness to commit words to paper, my understanding that emotions and music could be—*must be*—combined...these were elements that forged a mighty motivation deep within my soul.

The mighty motivation was to move forward.

To write another poem.

To learn to pick that guitar with crazy precision.

To keep those melodies swirling inside my head.

To let these songs help me overcome my shyness.

And—if I'm really honest—to use these songs to get closer to the girls at school.

And oh man, did I want to get close to the girls at school!

2

TO ALL THE GIRLS AT SCHOOL

MY RELATIONSHIP TO THE FEMALE sex is a major theme. I'd like to think it's a good theme, a strong theme, and one that has resulted in a great happiness. Because I'm a man who doesn't like conflict, I'm not going to dwell on every last conflict I've encountered in the area of romance. But because I'm a guy writing a truthful memoir, I know that there are certain conflicts—hell, *many* goddamn conflicts—that I can't ignore. All that will come later. But here, in my grade school years, such conflicts didn't exist at all. I thought that the girls in Abbott were the prettiest flowers in all of Texas. They charmed me and, at the risk of boasting, I think they saw me in a favorable light.

When it came to girls, I got off on a good foot. Fact is, I got along beautifully with members of the opposite sex my entire life—until I started marrying them. But that's a different story for a different chapter. In this chapter, Booger Red, at age eight or nine or ten, began seeing the sweet correlation between music and romance. Booger Red was fascinated by the workings of the guitar and the composition of simple little songs, but it was a fascination fueled by the knowledge that a kid with a guitar in his arms and a song on his lips had a better chance of coaxing a pretty young thing into a moonlight stroll and maybe stealing a kiss.

At school, Bobbie and I were seen as musical prodigies—she still far more than me. We were asked to perform at the assemblies and were always greeted with warm appreciation. That, along with Mama Nelson's undying support, made us feel special and helped melt away our natural shyness. Bobbie took in the praise gracefully. I got spoiled.

I was getting more interested in what was coming out of that Philco radio, our central source of information. These were the years when I delivered the *Hillsboro Mirror* on my bike, but when it came to news I was more of a listener than a reader.

We'd gather around the radio to hear President Roosevelt deliver his fireside chats. Those were moments of comfort. He was a father reassuring his children. He exuded an authority and confidence that made these dangerous days less scary. When the war broke out just around the time of Daddy Nelson's death, we saw young men from Abbott enlist. We prayed for their safe return. The radio broadcast news reports from foreign battlefields, yet it was hard to grasp the severity of the situation. At my age, I was more attuned to the entertainment floating over the airwaves.

Naturally I loved the cowboy adventures like *The Lone Ranger,* but also the comedies—Jack Benny, Fred Allen, and Burns and Allen. There were the mysteries like *The Green Hornet* and *The Shadow,* and the soap operas like *Stella Dallas* and *Our Gal Sunday* that Mama Nelson never missed.

In 1943, the year I turned ten, another radio personality caught my ear. Frank Sinatra joined *Your Hit Parade.* And though he was a million miles from western swing, he had a sweet swing of his own. There was a tenderness to his voice, a purity and ease of phrasing. When he sang the popular songs of the day, I marveled at the natural way he told the story. When he sang with trombonist Tommy Dorsey, I heard how he used his voice like an instrument. And when Dorsey played his mellow trombone, I heard how he used his instrument like a voice.

I also loved Louis Armstrong, who sang like he played and played like he sang. There was this same naturalness in the sound of Bing Crosby's voice, a singer who made you feel that he was right there in the room telling you a story. I didn't know the word "intimacy" then, but I felt it. Even in Abbott, where it hardly ever snowed, "White Christmas" had me dreaming of a winter landscape. Like Sinatra, Crosby turned singing into more of a conversation than a performance. He put you at ease. He spoke right to you. He made you feel he truly cared about you.

Same year Sinatra came on *Your Hit Parade,* Ernest Tubb came on *The Grand Ole Opry.* Because Tubb was a Texan, I related to him as a neighbor. Like Sinatra and Crosby, he sang conversationally. I also learned much from his writing.

Along with Ernest Tubb, Floyd Tillman and Roy Acuff were artists who touched my heart. I have a precious memory of Mama Nelson singing Acuff's "Great Speckled Bird." It's a mystical song about a bird descending from heaven to carry us up to meet the Lord. The bird has enemies—forces that would devour him—but the bird prevails because of his faith.

"God always prevails," Mama Nelson never tired of telling us, "because God is good and goodness can never be defeated."

All this music, sung on the radio, sung by my grandma, and played on the piano by sister Bobbie, was haunting my imagination. I didn't take it in critically; I took it in viscerally.

Because I was surrounded by such a richness of sound, I felt myself part of these sounds. I never approached music as an outsider. I never thought that Roy Acuff or Ernest Tubb or Bob Wills or even Frank Sinatra and Bing Crosby were doing something that I could not do. It wasn't that I was conceited. Nor did I have delusions of grandeur. It was simply that I was a kid who enjoyed a natural and familiar relationship with music. Early on, I saw that I could play it, sing it, and—maybe easiest of all—write it.

How else can you explain ten- or eleven-year-old Booger Red putting together something he called the Willie Nelson Songbook?

I designed the booklet myself, using a cowboy motif and roman numerals to index the twelve lyrics I had written. Songs had names like "I Guess I Was Born to Be Blue," "Faded Love and Wasted Dream," "The Storm Has Just Begun," "I'll Wander Alone." I guess the melancholy was already there. On the back I drew a lariat composed of the phrase "Howdy, pard." It's also telling that I did not write "Willie Nelson Songs, Abbott, Texas," but instead wrote "Willie Nelson Songs, Waco, Texas." I suppose I wanted to give the book a big-city boost, and Waco was the closest big city to tiny Abbott.

Around town I had seen the various songbooks of the day—songbooks by Hank Williams and Jimmie Rodgers, Roy Acuff and Hoagy Carmichael. To put myself in their company, it seemed only logical that I would have a songbook of my own.

When Mama Nelson leafed through my little book and looked over the lyrics, she saw that there were mainly songs about loss. She wondered why there weren't songs about loving the Lord.

"There will be," I promised her. "I'll write those kinds of songs, too."

She couldn't help but smile. She saw that her young grandson had ambition and a modicum of talent.

"This is good work, Willie," she said, "and I'm proud of you. But just don't forget that, while you are creating beautiful songs, God is the real creator. He created you, just like he created the music inside you."

Through the influence of Daddy and Mama Nelson, I had great love for my creator. But I can't say that I abided by the rules of the churchgoers who claimed—in the hard-core culture of Hill County, Texas—that smoking and drinking would send me straight to hell.

As a kid, I'd sneak off and smoke anything that burned. Loved to smoke. Would even smoke strips of cedar bark. The various substances have changed over the years, but the act itself has never ceased to satisfy me.

Smoking might also relate to my strong mischievous streak. I loved to stir things up. When I was a boy, farmers, whose plowing was impeded by the presence of bumblebee nests, would have me and my pals go out there and stir the nests. To get some air going, we'd drill holes into Ping-Pong paddles, take one in each hand, and start whacking the nests. We'd wind up killing dozens of bees, but not before dozens of other bees stung our eyes to where we'd walk home half blind. The adventure was worth the pain.

I didn't mind physical pain. I was taken in by those Charles Atlas ads in comic books that talked about "the Insult That Made a Man Out of 'Mac.'" There was the bully kicking sand in the face of the skinny guy. *Send off for Atlas's "Dynamic-Tension" method of bodybuilding and learn to fight back.* Well, I did send off, I did start bulking up, and, while I didn't win every fight, I did manage to get a reputation as a formidable scrapper. That began my lifelong interest in training and eventually a passion for martial arts.

I played all the sports, and played them hard. Throughout my school years in Abbott, I was on the Fighting Panthers track, baseball, basketball, and football teams, where at various times I started at quarterback, halfback, and center. We played on a dirt field that was rocky as hell. Because I was small, I got the shit kicked out of me. Wound up with a broken nose and busted collarbone, but nothing stopped me. The drive to compete overwhelmed any fear of injury. When the injuries did come, I didn't feel defeated or depressed. The minute I healed up, I was back out there.

In my childhood memories, the rugged athletic battles loom large, but no larger than moments of sacred song. Close to our little house and the corner where the Methodist church sat directly across from the Baptist church was an outdoor tabernacle made of wood and covered in vine. When the weather was good, folks from all over Hill County would sit on benches and, as afternoon turned to evening, listen to the singing and preaching. There were times when, distracted, I'd go off and play marbles with the other kids. But other times, especially when the holy hymns came down from the heavens, I felt drawn to the miracles described in the music.

There was also the draw of the city, via miraculous transportation provided by Interurban, an electric train that went from Waco to Dallas, with stops in towns as small as Abbott. This was the era before interstate highways. I could jump on the Interurban and, for just a few cents, be transported to these big cities. The Interurban allowed me to take my first girlfriend, Ramona Stafford, to the Texas State Fair in Dallas, where we rode through the tunnel of love and I dared to put my arm around her. That took some guts.

It took less guts to start playing at the school dances. I could watch the dancers from the stage—always my preferred position—and not worry about being rejected by some girl who might not like the way I danced. Music was my protection.

Music was also my provider. The Interurban station stood close to the cotton gin, the town's only café, the churches, and the barbershop. I got the brilliant idea of convincing Mr. Clements to let me set up a shoeshine stand in his barbershop. After shining shoes, I'd ask the customer his favorite song—and I'd sing it, right then and there. With passengers coming off the Interurban, I was certain that the sound of a song would bring them into the shop.

I did this for a day, shining a dozen pairs of shoes and singing a dozen songs.

"You did good," Mr. Clements told me. "Here's a quarter."

I was expecting at least a couple of dollars.

"A couple of dollars," said Mr. Clements, "is all I make in a day."

Knowing Mr. Clements to be an honest man, I accepted the coin and thanked him. But I also closed up shop. There had to be a better way to make money making music.

Other than by teaching music, Mama Nelson, too, was looking for another way to make money. Always thinking of her grandkids, she got a job in the kitchen of the school cafeteria. This was a blessing because, beyond what we grew in our garden, we were guaranteed an abundance of leftovers. My grandmother's ability to sustain us in all ways was a source of great security.

Ironically, it was that same sense of security that allowed me to do something that Mama Nelson strongly disapproved of. It happened in the sixth grade. I was ten, a member in good standing of the Methodist church and a devoted grandson. At the same time, when I was invited to play music in a beer joint, I said to hell with all the objections raised by the Bible-thumpers.

I took the job and found myself on a road—a raucous, rocky, crazy road—and the same road that, to this day, I'm still traveling.

3

FIRST FAMILY BAND

My sense of music as family was there from the get-go. After all, music was presented to me as a family affair.

So it makes perfect sense that my professional debut came in the form of a fifteen-person family band led by John Rejcek. It was a polka band that also played waltzes for the Czech community that flocked to dance halls around West and Waco. Rejcek's family members were horn players, fiddlers, bass players, drummers, and singers. The last thing they needed was a kid strumming a Stella guitar. But I guess ol' John took a liking to me. He sensed how much I loved the dance music he played and invited me into his group.

Up on the bandstand, I was in heaven. I didn't do much to add to the overall sound. But I was in the mix. I got to play those polkas and watch the beer-drinking crowds stomp on the dance floor and have a ball. Even though its origins were European and a world away from Hill County, Texas, the music had a spirit I could feel. Just being part of the band made me feel that I was accepted. As a preteen picker, I felt that I had already made it.

That powerful feeling came early in my musical life. For me, it was enough to see that the music being made by me, no matter how small my contribution, pleased a crowd. More and more, I was driven by one thought: music makes people happy.

Mama Nelson was hardly happy when she learned that I was playing beer joints with the Rejcek band.

"I don't want you in places where there's smoking and drinking," she said.

"Yes, ma'am. I understand. But the music is good."

"The music I've taught you, Willie, the music you're singing at church, is more than good. It's holy. It's sacred."

"I realize that."

"And you'll honor that?"

"Always. But I also have to say something else, if I may."

"Go on, son."

"In the summers, I can work in the fields all week for eight dollars, right?"

"Yes."

"Well, that's what Mr. Rejcek paid me for only one night in Waco."

For all her love of the Lord and the Lord's music, Mama Nelson was a practical woman. She had a family to raise on her own. And when I took the eight dollars out of my pocket and handed it to her, I could see the surprise on her face. I could see her disposition change. She didn't say anything. She didn't have to. From then on, she never complained about her little Willie playing dances where folks were smoking and dancing and having a natural ball.

As I grew up, my father, Ira, and mother, Myrle, continued living their separate lives. Ira had moved to Fort Worth, married a nice lady named Lorraine, and started a new family. Mother Myrle had also married again, but not for long. About the same time I started with John Rejcek, Mom showed up in Abbott with her third husband, Ken. By then she'd been out to California and was on her way to the state of Washington.

Mama Nelson didn't approve of her daughter-in-law's drinking and partying ways any more than she approved of my playing in a polka band. Yet she had the wisdom to accept reality. My mother would always be something of a wild child. Mama Nelson saw that same streak of wildness in me. She saw that, given their nature, Ira and Myrle were doing the best they could. She understood that, in their own way, they loved me and Bobbie. She never tried to poison our minds against our parents. Her openhearted attitude allowed us to keep our hearts open as well. Mother and Father would continue to run in and out of our lives for decades to come. And that was just fine with us.

We were about to get a new family member, besides.

Time to introduce the next major character in my musical life:

Meet Bud Fletcher.

A charmer and a hustler, Bud had charmed his way into our

family by courting sister Bobbie. He was in his early twenties and Bobbie was sweet sixteen. Bud was a handsome guy, Bobbie a gorgeous gal, and cupid struck with lightning speed. They met in March and married in April. But Bobbie, the most popular girl at school, wasn't about to shortchange her education. She stayed on for her senior year, played basketball, played piano at all the big functions, and became the first married student to attend and graduate Abbott High.

Seeing Sister's talent—and a little bit of mine—Bud took it upon himself to form a band. Using Bob Wills and his Texas Playboys as a model, he put together Bud Fletcher and the Texans. There was one problem, though. Bud couldn't sing or play any instrument. But that didn't bother Bud. As Bobbie said, "Bud stuck a broom handle into a bucket of sand and whacked it like a bass." His main job—his only job—was to act as the joke-cracking, fun-loving bandleader. He'd coax the crowd into dancing, call off the names of the tunes, and then let me and Bobbie lead the way.

I was the picker and singer, but I was really shadowing everything Sister did. She knew every song in every style. She covered up all my mistakes.

Bud's ability to get us booked, even with our ragtag sound, was a godsend. We played joints in Waco like the Avalon Club and the Scenic Wonderful. We also had gigs in West and Hillsboro. Sister and I gave all our earnings to Mama Nelson, who wasn't thrilled about Bobbie's marriage to Bud but was thankful for the money.

Bud Fletcher and his band also opened another huge door for us: radio.

Not only did Sister and I get to go on the air for the first time during a talent show on station WACO, but we—in the guise of Bud Fletcher and the Texans—actually got a quarter-hour show of our own on KHBR, the little station operating out of Hillsboro.

If you can believe it, some of the gals at Abbott High even formed a Willie Nelson fan club. So if I tell you that, at age fourteen, I already felt as though I had hit the big time, you'll understand. Didn't matter that I hadn't left Hill County. Didn't matter that most of our gigs were at run-down beer parlors and sawdust-on-the-floor roadhouses. All that mattered was that I was up there with my guitar, singing my heart out.

I was connecting.

I was also promoting. With the help of Bud Fletcher, the fearless hustler, I figured I could do a little hustling of my own. And rather than start at the bottom, I figured I might as well go for broke. I decided I'd promote a show with Bob Wills and his Texas Playboys.

May not sound like much to you, but it was as if the mayor of Abbott was inviting President Truman to come down and address our five-member city council.

To a starry-eyed wannabe like me, Bob Wills was the president of music. He represented supreme accomplishment. Not only had he helped create and carry his western swing out to California and back across the country to Chicago and New York, but he'd written songs that all the other popular bandleaders, like Adolph Hofner and Dewey Groom, were quick to cover. When he started using two fiddlers, everyone followed suit. When he added a third, you can bet that the rest of the boys did the same. When he hired the great Johnny Gimble to play electric mandolin, you suddenly saw electric mandolins popping up everywhere. When he had gals singing ballads or yodeling or belting out dance tunes, every other country music bandleader copied his formula.

What gave me the guts to think that I, a fourteen-year-old, could book Bob Wills at an outdoor pavilion by Lake Whitney, some twenty miles from Abbott?

Just seemed like something I should try. At the very least, it was a way to see Bob Wills and his Texas Playboys live and in person. That was even more important than the potential profit.

Fact is, I didn't make any money. I did put up posters all over Hill County, and I did go on the Hillsboro radio station to tell the folks about this once-in-a-lifetime opportunity to see the King of Western Swing. And folks did show up—maybe four or five hundred strong. But the gate receipts barely covered Wills's fee—around a thousand dollars—with nothing left over for me.

Didn't matter. The summer night was magical. After a scorching hot Texas afternoon, the temperature had cooled down. Moonlight glistened on the silky-smooth surface of Lake Whitney. The sky was crowded with a thousand stars. Fireflies flickered over the heads of the happy dancers. I didn't dance. I couldn't even move from my spot at the foot of the bandstand.

I studied Wills's performance. That's the night I learned what it meant to entertain a big roomful of folks. It meant nonstop music. It meant being the man in charge who wasted no time with flowery remarks or long-winded introductions. I marveled as Wills seamlessly moved from one song into another. I saw him continuously measuring the moods of his fans. He switched from having Tommy Duncan sing bluesy-slow songs like "Trouble in Mind" to fiddle-friendly rompers like "Stay All Night" to lonely laments like "Bubbles in My Beer."

Standing there over the course of four hours, I was not only transfixed by the waves of music washing over me, but I witnessed a living example of a lead musician in total command. There, by moonlit Lake Whitney, Bob Wills was telling me, not in words, but in spirit:

"Young Willie, if you wanna make your way with music, just keep the music coming, song after song after song. Forget about stopping to say something clever. Forget about jokes. Forget about taking breaks. Forget about whatever was on your mind before you came to play. The job is to play like your life depends upon it. The job is to put the pedal to the metal and drive this music machine a hundred miles an hour through every dance hall and beer joint and honky-tonk from here to hell. The job is to give the people what the people want and what the people need. And that ain't nothing more than songs that will let them dance their troubles away. Do that, young Willie, and you'll have yourself a career. You might make a fortune or you might go broke, but it won't matter because you'll have a ball—and so will the fans who'll flock to hear you play."

Before I'd heard Bob Wills that night, I knew the music of immortals like Jimmie Rodgers and Hank Williams. I loved them all, just as later I would love Lefty Frizzell. These were figures carved out on the Mount Rushmore of country music. Each had an individual sound and an intimate voice that contributed to my own developing voice.

Wills, though, showed me how a band, far more than a single singer, could convey a voice of its own. He and his Texas Playboys showed me that a collective voice, capable of expressing every mood from sky-high joy to low-down pain, can captivate the raunchiest crowd from eight in the evening to deep in the midnight hour.

Going deeper into the music, I would soon discover a guitarist, far from the fields of western swing, whom Bob Wills had also discovered. I'm talking about the great Django Reinhardt. This was a man who changed my musical life by giving me a whole new perspective on the guitar and, on an even more profound level, on my relationship with sound.

In the aftermath of World War II, when I was a teenager, Django's music began to surface in America on a regular basis. They had some of his records at the Hillsboro radio station. Over the coming years, in bits and pieces I learned about his myth. He was born in 1910 into a family of Romanian gypsies in Belgium, where his name was Jean. In the dialect of his people, his nickname, Django, meant "I awake."

Django awoke in me a new and joyful appreciation of swing and jazz. The appreciation deepened when I learned that, at age eighteen, he was injured in a near-fatal fire that burned two fingers—the fourth and fifth—of his left hand to the point of paralysis. He was told he could never play the guitar again. He was also told that one of his legs, also badly burned, would have to be amputated. But he refused the surgery. He also refused to believe the doctors when they told him he'd never walk again.

Yet he did walk and, man, did he ever play! He found a way to negotiate his guitar solos with only two fingers, using his two injured fingers for chording. That negotiation—that act of defiance, bravery, and practicality—yielded astounding results.

In 1933, the year of my birth and of the death of Jimmie Rodgers, Django began recording in Paris. He was promoted by the Hot Club de France, a group of Parisians devoted to spreading what they considered to be genuine American blues-based jazz. That's when he joined forces with French violinist Stéphane Grappelli, who became Django's artistic soul mate. The music they made together—light, sweet, easy, breezy, imaginative, and always pretty—ranks as some of the most original jazz ever created.

I followed Django's fortunes. In 1946, he came to America, where he was invited by Duke Ellington to appear with Duke's famous orchestra. I began reading music magazines that reported the controversy surrounding him. When he played clubs in New York and was asked whether he belonged to the camp of traditionalists like Louis Armstrong or modernists like Dizzy Gillespie, he simply said, "Both. I hear it as all one thing. One music expressed in different ways, but always connected to each other."

He said that various schools and genres should never fight but reflect the harmony that is, after all, the moral message of all music.

That lesson was not lost on me. During my formative years,

as I listened to Django's records, especially songs like "Nuages" that I would play for the rest of my life, I studied his technique. Even more, I studied his gentleness. I loved the human sound he gave his acoustic guitar. I loved how he integrated so many foreign feelings into his music: Spain and France, the gypsy camps, New Orleans Dixieland, blues singers like Big Bill Broonzy, the big bands of Chicago and New York.

Django wasn't a show-off or a look-at-me kind of star. His star shone with an inner glow. He loved to softly chord while his cohort Stéphane Grappelli soloed. He wasn't greedy for the spotlight. His delight came in quiet creation. In this way he influenced me perhaps more profoundly than any single musician.

In my mind, the guitar-and-fiddle counterpoint of Django and Grappelli mirrored the guitar-and-fiddle style of country music. Two different string instruments doing a dance. They never got in each other's way. They never stepped on each other's toes. They brought out the best in each other while swinging hard and having a ball.

Other musical avenues would open to me—big wide boulevards on which I happily traveled. But no one opened my heart like the gypsy jazz guitar of Django Reinhardt.

"Absorb everything," his spirit said to me. *"Love every style. Love every musical thing. No matter its place of origin, you will find yourself in that style. You will become part of everything. And everything will become part of you."*

Late at night, my ear close to the Philco radio, the music would float in on a dream. The dream had a name. One night it was

"Body and Soul." One night it was "Laura." One night it was "Fools Rush In."

The dreamy sound of Frank Sinatra's voice.

The dreamy sound of Django's guitar.

Two artists who could not be any more different from each other or from me—a gypsy jazz guitarist and a New Jersey pop crooner—impressed themselves on my soul.

And in between here's Eddy Arnold singing "Texarkana Baby."

And here's Gene Autry singing "Buttons and Bows."

And here's Roy Rogers singing "Blue Shadows on the Trail."

Blue shadows, blue singing, blue moon over Abbott, Texas.

Just a kid, like millions of other kids, falling deeper and deeper in love with music.

4

ZEKE

NOT LONG AGO I WAS telling a friend about my childhood in Hill County. After hearing me describe how I lettered in all the sports, learned music from my grandparents, played in local bands, and subscribed to all those Charles Atlas self-defense programs, the friend said, "Hell, Willie, you were the all-American boy."

"Not all-American," I said. "All-Abbott."

"What's the difference?"

"All-American," I said, "has me thinking of Jack Armstrong, the hero of the radio program that everyone listened to in the nineteen thirties and forties. Jack was the all-American because he ate his Wheaties and had all these adventures where he always came out on top. He didn't drink, cuss, or smoke."

"And what's all-Abbott?" asked my buddy.

"All-Abbott was a kid like me who did it all, the bad and the good. Sure, I was a good competitive athlete, and sure, I sang in church, and sure, I started learning how to play the guitar. Sure, I was something of a poet, and sure, I had girlfriends. But unlike Jack Armstrong, I was also drawn to the wild side."

"Who drew you there?"

"Probably just nature," I said. "Probably just my DNA. But it also had to do with the company I kept."

"You hung out with some bad guys?"

"I didn't see them as bad. I saw them as fun. And no one was more fun than Zeke Varnon."

I met Zeke during my formative teen years. I liked him immediately and we stayed friends for life.

Just as Django Reinhardt and Bob Wills had a lasting influence on my musical life, Zeke exerted a big influence on my personal life. He showed me a different way to live, and I liked it.

It wasn't that I rejected the way of Mama and Daddy Nelson, the way that praises the Lord and puts family first. At the same time, though, I adopted Zeke's way. You might argue that these two ways are incompatible, but that's an argument I never bought. I wanted it both ways.

Zeke liked to drink. He liked to smoke. He liked to play poker and pool. He was a world-class dominoes player. He liked chasing women. He liked telling tall tales. And if he could pull off a little con now and then, well, so much the better. From where I sat, it seemed he did all this without hurting a soul.

If I was sixteen when I met Zeke, he had to be twenty-one or twenty-two. He'd just come out of the service and had far more worldly experience than me. He often dropped by the Nite Owl, a beer joint on the county line where Bobbie and I played in Bud Fletcher's band. Zeke never tired of telling me how much he liked the way I sang and played. He was among my earliest fans.

He was also a daredevil. He showed me, for instance, that gambling was more than a matter of learning the game; it was also a question of daring—daring to call your opponent on a bluff, daring to bet money you don't have, daring to put your ass on the line. Why was I excited by Zeke's sense of daring? Because it involved danger. Because it gave ordinary life a sharp edge. Because it welcomed the unpredictable and invited the unknown.

Zeke's creed—that life is a gamble and you might as well enjoy it—was an attitude I found irresistible. Beyond the attitude, I fell in love with the very act of gambling. I was drawn to the strategizing. You had to be cunning and ruthless, patient and insightful. I already knew the thrill of fierce competition in sports. I was similarly thrilled when I found myself in a poker or a dominoes game. And when Zeke started taking me around to his barroom hangouts, where he and his cohorts played killer card games late into the night, I studied the players. I saw that they not only read the cards, but they read each other. Psychology was always in play. Some players were nonstop talkers; others wouldn't say a word. Often the mood was jovial. The guys told dirty jokes, they put each other down unmercifully, they used wit and ridicule to lighten the mood or to intimidate an opponent. Every hand was high drama. That drama hooked me for life.

In the behind-the-barroom gambling world of my misspent youth, Zeke Varnon was top dog. In his hometown of Hillsboro, he eventually bought a trailer house where he ran a poker game four nights a week. He conducted a bookie operation where you could place bets on local and national football games. He also loved running out of town on a minute's notice.

Zeke was always ready to hit the road, and when he jumped into a boxcar of a slow-moving freight train, I'd be foolish enough to jump in after him. The destination didn't matter as much as the journey itself. If that sounds a little Zen, well, in his own Hill County way, Zeke was something of a Zen master.

Over the years, Zeke got good at telling stories about my coming-of-age. He told them so often and so well that, whether they really happened or not, I began believing them as the gospel truth.

He loved telling the one about how, late one night in Fort Worth, he dared me to jump a freight headed to California. I took him up on the dare. We got in the boxcar and promptly fell asleep. When the light of day woke me up, I expected to look outside and see the palm trees of Los Angeles.

"We on the coast, Zeke?" I asked.

"Afraid not, Willie," he said.

"Where are we?"

"Weatherford, Texas."

Weatherford is barely twenty-five miles west of Fort Worth.

It was the end of the line for this particular freight. Zeke and I wound up out on the highway, thumbs out for hours, until some guy in a rusty ol' pickup had the heart to stop and haul us back home.

A little further down the road, I was able to scrape up enough money to buy a beat-up '46 Ford. Zeke and I were riding around Hillsboro. I'd just gotten gas for the car. Twenty cents a gallon seemed like a lot of money. Maybe the two bucks it cost to fill it up distracted me. We didn't know it, but while we were driving to my girlfriend's house, gas had spilled over the side of the car. I'd left the cap off the gas tank. While I went in to fetch my honey, Zeke waited in the passenger seat.

A kid came by and asked, "What would happen if I lit a match to all this gasoline on the side of the car?"

"The fuckin' car would blow up, you dumb son of a bitch."

That's all the kid needed to hear. He lit the match. Zeke jumped out in time to save his ass, barely avoiding the explosion.

That definitely happened, but here's where Zeke and I have different memories.

I remember trying to chase down the kid. I was ready to beat him to a pulp.

Zeke remembers my girlfriend asking me, "What are we gonna do now, Willie?"

And me answering, "We're gonna wait around like everyone else and watch this car burn. And then go get drunk."

Both versions sound like me.

By the time I reached my senior year in high school, I was on top of the world. The fact that my world was small hardly mattered. It was the only world I knew.

Along with Bud and Sister, I stayed on the air. Thanks to the Hillsboro radio station, I saw that I had a gift for self-promotion.

Even at the tender age of seventeen, sitting behind a mic felt natural. Felt good having a vast invisible audience listening to my every word. I never worried about what I was gonna say. I just said it. It wasn't that I was super-articulate or blessed with a vast vocabulary. I was plainspoken. Didn't have much to say beyond, "Here's a little tune I hope y'all like." And I didn't have much to sing except hit songs by the big artists of the day. Might be "Lovesick Blues" by Hank Williams with his Drifting Cowboys. Might be "One Kiss Too Many" by Eddy Arnold or "Slipping Around" by Ernest Tubb or anything by Tennessee Ernie Ford, Floyd Tillman, Hank Thompson, or Bill Boyd and the Cowboy Ramblers.

I loved operating a turntable and carefully placing a needle on a piece of shellac. I came to radio just at that moment when shellac was on its way out and the new formats—45 rpm vinyl singles and 33⅓ rpm long-play albums—were coming in. That was another thrill. Right there in Hillsboro, Texas, I was privileged to have a hands-on experience with modern technology in recorded music.

As the only singer/picker/radio personality in all of Abbott, I was lucky as hell—lucky to have a grandmother who let me perform outside the church, lucky to have a brother-in-law who kept me gigged up, lucky to land a spot on the air, and luckiest of all to have this loyal band of fans, these great gals who put their money together to buy me a Western outfit and made me feel like a star.

But like I said, small world. Next question:

What does a local-yokel star do after high school?

Answer:

He has no idea.

So he turns to his friend Zeke, who has an answer for everything, and is told, "We're going to Tyler."

"What's in Tyler?"

"Trees."

"And what are we gonna do with the trees?"

"Trim 'em. What the hell else are you supposed to do with trees?"

So we made our way to Tyler, about 115 miles east of Abbott, where we were set to make some quick money. Zeke, who knew everyone everywhere, knew a guy who owned a tree-trimming outfit.

My job was to run the chipper, a bright orange machine that ground up the fallen branches and brush. Once the chipper was full, I hauled off its contents to the trash. Easy work.

The hard work was left to the guys who worked on high.

One day one of those guys yelled down to me.

"Hey, kid," he said. "I need a rope."

He was at the top of this giant elm, forty feet off the ground. There were various ways in which I could get him the rope. But being young and proud and eager to show off my athletic skills, I said, "No problem. I'll bring it right to you."

The veteran tree trimmers stopped what they were doing so they could watch my ascension.

My ascension was quick. With the rope over my shoulder, I scurried up the tree like a chimp. It didn't take long, though, for the chimp to turn into a chump. After I handed the trimmer the rope, he tied it to a limb. That's when I decided to show off a little more. Several feet above the electrical high wire, I made a daredevil move. The smart move would have been to carefully climb down, hugging the trunk all the way. Not this boy. I was going to put on a little show for the assembled workers and play Tarzan.

So there I was, flying high forty feet above the earth, grabbing the rope and swinging in the breeze, determined to get down the fast way. Well, Tarzan fucked up. Before I started my descent, my hand got hung up in the rope. The rope got twisted in my fingers and caught on a branch so I could neither go up nor down. I was stuck all the way up there. The guys started yelling instructions at me, but, given my predicament, I couldn't focus on what they were saying. All knew was that I wanted down—and quick.

"Just cut the rope!" I told the trimmer.

A wiser trimmer would have ignored my demand, but this guy, reacting to my previous cocksure attitude, fulfilled my foolish request.

The result was a free fall from on high. On the way down, I could have easily hit the electrical wire and left this world as a seventeen-year-old. Somehow the good Lord or good fortune or blind luck let me brush by the wire as I awkwardly tumbled downward, crashing through leaves and breaking branches all the way down, down, down.

It was a wonder that I didn't break my ass—or my back, which was already messed up from the hay baling I'd been doing all my young life.

I got up from the ground, hiding the pain shooting through my limbs and acting like I was okay.

I wasn't.

My body was injured, my pride injured even more.

I turned around and started walking.

"Hey, Willie," said Zeke. "Where you going, boy?"

I didn't answer.

"You ain't quitting, are you?" asked Zeke.

I still didn't answer. I just kept walking. If my butt and my back hadn't been screaming in pain, I would have walked all the way back to Abbott.

I just knew one goddamn thing: no more tree trimming for this boy.

5

FALLING INTO THE 1950s

Somewhere between the end of the forties and the start of the fifties, the boy known as Willie Hugh Nelson became a man.

Can't tell you the exact time or date, but it did happen. Can't tell you that, having reached adulthood, I put childish things behind me, because I didn't.

But I did grow up and grow out of that small Hill County corner that I loved so well. I did venture forth into a larger world. And I did enter the new decade with a genuine hope for the future.

In 1951, I was an eighteen-year-old and classified 1-A for the draft. The Korean War was raging. Rather than wait to be called, I figured I best make a move of my own. So with the romantic notion of becoming a jet pilot, I signed up for the air force.

"Report to Lackland in San Antone," I was told.

A week after enlisting, I was sitting in a barber's chair on base, getting my red locks clipped. They had me looking like a shorn chicken.

During my physical, the doctor noticed my bad lower back.

"How'd it happen?" he asked.

"Baling hay."

"All right, country boy. Let's see if you can get through basic training."

I got through it fine.

Because I'd been a high school athlete—a proud Fighting Panther—I could run with the best of 'em. I could deal with the obstacle courses. I could crawl under those barbed wires and, despite my trauma in Tyler, I could climb up a rope faster than anyone. I thought I was fit.

So did the air force. They promoted me to first class and gave me a stripe. That lasted a day. One wiseass didn't think I deserved the promotion and gave me lip. So I busted him in the mouth. There went my stripe. I really didn't give a shit because by then I knew that the authoritarian ways of the U.S. Air Force were not to my liking.

It also wasn't to my liking to be sent to Sheppard base in Wichita Falls for more basic training and then to Scott base in Illinois, where I was in a holding pattern. They were trying to figure out my next "relocation." The holding pattern principally had me holding cards. I spent most of my time playing poker.

Then on to Biloxi, Mississippi, and radar school, where I tripped over the math and washed out. I landed in the shipping room loading heavy boxes. That wrenched my back even more and landed me in the hospital for two months.

They said they needed to operate.

I said, "Hell, no."

They said if they didn't operate they'd have to send me home with a medical discharge.

I said, "Hell, yes."

After nine months, I was out of the air force and back in Abbott.

Now what?

Time for a little soul-searching.

Sure, I was a pretty good athlete. Sure, I was a pretty good farmer—a Future Farmer of America. Sure, I was learning to be a pretty good gambler.

I loved working the land. I loved dealing with animals and crops. I loved playing poker and dominoes late into the night. These were passions that would serve me—and sometimes unnerve me—for the rest of my life. But would they sustain me?

No. Only music could do that. Only music opened my heart and let the poetry flow from my soul. Without that flow, I was no good. I was always writing songs. Some were okay, some awful, but good or bad made no difference. I didn't judge them. I just let 'em happen. I wrote early in the morning or late at night, in the middle of dinner or walking around town. I was always scribbling down ideas on the back of matchbooks or cereal boxes, little pieces of poetry that eventually became lyrics. Dozens of promising ideas got lost. Others were turned into tunes. And once the tunes were written, I had to play them.

When I returned to Abbott from the air force, I realized I

had to get back to my music. Along with my buddy Zeke, I was staying at a low-rent motel. I managed to put together a ragtag unit that played beer joints around Waco. The local station, WACO, had been the launching pad for local singer Hank Thompson, first called Hank the Hired Hand. In the early fifties Hank had a huge hit with "The Wild Side of Life," a song with a line that became immortal: "I didn't know God made honky-tonk angels."

If Hank could break out into bigger things from Waco, well, I figured maybe I could, too.

"It isn't a question of *if* you gonna break out, boy," said Zeke. "It's only a question of *when*."

I needed that encouragement 'cause I had a bad case of the empty-pocket blues. The little gigs didn't cover my costs. I'd have to pawn my guitar during the week. If Zeke had a good week at poker, which was usually the case, he'd loan me—or flat-out give me—money to get my instrument out of hock. And although we were scrambling financially, that didn't stop our pursuit of the fairer sex. Zeke and I were always on the hunt.

Spring night in Waco. Big Texas sky lit up with stars.

Me and Zeke, driving around in his old jalopy, were a little liquored up.

"Hungry?" asked Zeke.

"Starved," I said.

"How 'bout a cheeseburger?"

"Great."

We pulled into a drive-in, the kind where carhops take your order. The carhops were teenage girls in halter tops and shorts.

Our carhop wasn't just cute. She was gorgeous—slim, tall, sexy. Beautiful black hair. Beautiful dark eyes. Beautiful olive complexion.

She knew who I was.

"You're Willie Nelson," she said. "I've seen you play at some of those dances."

"I know who you are," I said. "I've seen you dancing at some of those dances."

"What can I get you boys to eat?" she asked.

"A couple of double cheeseburgers with fries," said Zeke.

"Coming right up," she said.

"You can't leave me now," I said.

"Why not?" she asked.

"Don't know your name."

"Martha. Martha Jewel Mathews."

Martha went off to put in the order. As she walked away, I couldn't keep my eyes off her.

"She's Martha," I told Zeke, "and she's a jewel."

"A very young jewel," said Zeke.

When Martha returned with the food, I thanked her and said, "Zeke was saying you're a pretty young jewel. I was wondering how young."

"Sixteen."

"Sweet sixteen," I said. "The perfect age. And this is the perfect night. I'm just hoping that when your night is over you can let us take you home."

"You boys been drinking, haven't you?" she said.

"These burgers and fries are sobering us up right quick. So what do you say? What time you get off?"

"My mama is picking me up. But thanks again. Nice seeing you, Willie Nelson."

"I'll be back, Martha Jewel."

As she smiled and walked away, my eyes stayed focused on her every move.

Next night I was back in a borrowed car. Alone.

"I am not drunk," I said, "but I *am* persistent. You gotta let me take you home, Martha."

She let me. And then she let me some more. And the more she let me, the happier we both became.

It was love—my first full-blast love, the kind of love where you lose your mind and let your heart lead the way. Martha was a spectacular woman. She was a full-blooded Cherokee who possessed the striking features of an Indian princess. Like a princess, she was spoiled. But hell, so was I. Two intractable forces about to clash.

Just like that, we were seeing each other every day. The sex was superhot, but even hotter was the deep love that swept over us. And then—you guessed it—we got married in a fever. Ran off to Cleburne, where a justice of the peace did the deed. Martha had a letter saying she was of legal age. In truth, she was still sixteen. I was nineteen.

We were so hot to trot, we didn't bother to ask anyone's permission—not her folks, not mine. We had no money, we had no plans. Just each other.

God bless Mama Nelson, who, although she wasn't thrilled to see me married in this lickety-split manner, said we could move in with her.

"But you're gonna have to get a job, Willie, and help with the bills. Both of y'all are gonna have to work."

To supplement the few dollars I was getting in the beer joints, I found a day job in a saddle factory. Loved the smell of leather and loved the handiwork involved. Loved anything having to do with horses. But didn't love sewing those stitches when the needle started cutting up my fingers. Next to his pecker, a picker's fingers are his most precious body parts. To protect my future, I had to quit.

Martha, who always found waitressing work, was itching to get out of Hill County. Me, too. So we started thinking of possibilities.

While we were thinking, we were also fighting. With Martha and me, fighting and loving went hand in hand. She was as feisty as me, as stubborn, as jealous, and as flirtatious. Jealousy raised its ugly head early and often in our relationship.

"You been eyeing that girl all night," she said after a gig at a club on the county line.

"How would you know, Martha? You were too busy dancing with that cowboy from West."

Add a mess of beer and liquor to the mix and you have a heady brew of mistrust.

Martha was an adventurer and a teaser, and so was I. We didn't mind showing each other how popular we were with the opposite sex. At the same time, we were powerfully drawn to each other.

"Look," I said one day after a particularly nasty fight. "We need a change of scenery."

"I've been saying that for months," said Martha.

"Let's go see my mother. She's going to love you."

"Where's she living these days?"

"Eugene, Oregon. What do you say?"

"I say let's go."

I was ready to see my mom. It had been too long.

Dad was close by in Fort Worth. That was a comfort to me. In fact, he'd often show up in Hill County and sit in when Bobbie and I were playing with Bud Fletcher. I loved hearing how he made his fiddle sing.

But Mom hadn't paid a visit to Abbott in years. I missed her wild spirit. Because Martha projected a wild spirit of her own, I knew they'd get along.

But how do you get from Abbott to Eugene when your net worth is twenty-five bucks?

You hustle up a driveaway car and head up to the great Northwest.

The long trek wasn't easy. We were fighting and fucking all the way. Maybe the fighting made the fucking even better. Martha was a pistol. In both fighting and fucking, she gave as good as she got. She was all passion, all the time.

Alone with me in that car for two thousand interminable miles, she had time to vent her complaints. She was sure I was cheating. I wasn't. Before long I would be, but in this early stage of our marriage I was still walking the straight and narrow.

But that didn't keep us from fighting. We knew how to push each other's buttons.

"I'll tell you one goddamn thing, Willie Nelson," said Martha. "You can't play out in public without fixing your stare at the prettiest girl in the place."

"That would be you, Martha."

"Don't bullshit me. I've seen you time and again. You start singing and lock eyes on some honey who follows you when you leave the bandstand."

"I'm a showman putting on a show. I gotta connect with the audience. That's my job, Martha."

"That's an excuse. You're not fooling nobody."

Later, when Zeke asked why we fought so much, I said, "Martha's a full-blooded Cherokee, and every night is Custer's last stand."

When we finally arrived in Eugene, we were all fought out. Myrle was glad to see me and delighted to meet Martha. The two got along famously.

Western swing happened to be big in Oregon. I got a little gig with a country band that played a show called *The Hayloft Jamboree* on KUGN. Loved being back on the air. Working in a radio station was always good for my soul. It was where I belonged—access to a thousand and one records and, more importantly, access to the fans.

In truth, though, I hardly had any fans in Eugene. The gigs were few and short-lived. I had to find work as a plumber's assistant. I don't have to tell you that I was not made out to be a plumber's assistant.

Martha worked as a waitress. No matter where we were, restaurants and bars hired Martha in a hurry. With her long dark hair and exquisite features, she always drew customers.

When she brought home good tips, I was convinced that they came as a result of her flirting. Or worse. More brawling ensued. And then, if I was lucky, more balling.

This went on, but not many months after arriving in Eugene, I knew it was time for us to bail. When I said good-bye to Mom, she understood. She recognized her restlessness in me. It was in the blood.

So me and Martha headed home to the Lone Star State, where surely my star would rise. We settled in Waco for a short while.

In my only nod to higher education, I went to Baylor University for a few months, until I ran out of GI Bill money. Can't remember a damn thing I was taught. That's probably because, when all was said and done, I really majored in dominoes.

Then good news: Martha was pregnant. We both wanted kids. Even with my unconventional upbringing, I always felt connected to a strong and loving family. That sense of family was something I needed—then, now, and always. So the realization that I was starting a family of my own, even before I was twenty-one, brought me great joy. I loved the idea of being a dad, loved looking at a future with Martha and a brood of little ones.

On May 11, 1953, though, my future was nearly upended. It was Monday and, true to form, I spent a few pleasant hours at the dominoes hall in downtown Waco, where I took on some of the town sharpies. In the afternoon I wandered off to Jim's Tavern, located right along the Brazos River Bridge. I was enjoying a beer with a buddy when it started raining. When I poked my head outside, I saw that the sky was aglow in a strange light, followed by a sudden darkness and heavy hail. These were the telltale signs of a tornado. Then someone ran in and said a twister was heading our way from Middleton, a town just west of us. We decided it was time to go back to drinking. Drinking probably gave us the crazy idea that it might be fun to chase after the tornado. By then the storm felt mighty goddamn close. We wanted to see it.

When we went outside, all sorts of shit was flying around. But, brave on booze, we were going to enter the fray. We were going to run across the Brazos River Bridge and see what the damage looked like. Except the bridge wasn't there. The twister had eaten it up and spit it out. That's how close the tornado came—no more than fifty yards—to demolishing Jim's Tavern and killing everyone inside. This was my closest brush with death. I found it exhilarating.

Exhilaration quickly turned to deep sadness. The twister had torn up downtown Waco. The five-story RT Dennis building, right across the street from the dominoes hall, had been flattened. Scores of people had died. Hundreds of homes lost. It was being called one of the deadliest tornadoes in Texas history.

My struggles in Waco weren't over. Because I couldn't find enough gigs to cover our costs, I went to work selling encyclopedias. The commission was low but, as always, my hopes were high. I was a good salesman. I could put my foot in the door and say my piece with easy confidence. I could call upon my charm. I could bullshit with the best of them.

And even though I glibly expounded on the wonders of these books of knowledge and enjoyed modest success, I didn't enjoy the one time when a man, angry that I had disturbed his day, turned his rottweiler on me. I had to run for my life.

But running was nothing new. It's what I did.

Run here, run there, run to wherever the possibilities seemed brightest.

As fall turned to winter, possibilities appeared less and less bright in Waco. I figured I had to go farther afield to find a break. I needed a bigger arena with more action.

San Antonio, a bigger city 180 miles away, seemed like a reasonable bet. And since I was a betting man, why not give it a try?

6

MISSION CITY AND OTHER STOPS ALONG THE WAY

THE MOMENT I LAID EYES on my daughter De Lana, born November 11, 1953, the world turned more beautiful. I offered gratitude to God for the safe deliverance of his creation. She was exquisite, perfect in every way. My heart sang with joy. I took fatherhood seriously.

Even though my time with Daddy Nelson was brief, he left an indelible impression. He was a strong and steady presence in the life of his children and grandchildren. Marveling at my firstborn, I wanted to exert the same strength and steadiness. I wanted to be there for her.

I tried to be there, and in many ways I succeeded. In other ways I didn't. Martha and I weren't capable of forging a calm home life. After Lana's birth, we went back to battling. And it was more than verbal. Martha could get physical. I'm glad to say that I never swung back, but how could I when, while

I was asleep, she tied me up in ropes and beat me with a broom? She probably had good reason. I probably hadn't been home in a day or two. The reason was obvious—at least to me. The nightlife was calling.

Our move to Mission City charged me up. The city had a buzz. Five military bases gave the nightclubs a steady stream of customers. The sound of enticing Mexican music was everywhere. The huge Mexican population gave the place a special flavor. And there were also Indians. They wore the headbands of their native tribes and held ceremonies in the ballrooms of the downtown hotels. I loved the Mexicans, I loved the Indians, I loved the whole colorful ethnic mix.

Because I hadn't made my mark in Eugene or Waco, I greeted San Antone with renewed hunger. All these nightclubs with all this music meant that I'd surely prevail. My ambition heated up. I'd always seen myself as a winner. Now it was time to claim the victory.

I met a number of great musicians, but none made a bigger impression than Johnny Bush. When I ran into him in some beer joint downtown, I immediately knew he was a winner. He had a tremendous voice filled with feeling. Later they'd call him "the Caruso of country." First time I heard him sing "Stardust" I fought back tears. A country singer interpreting Hoagy Carmichael! Made me see that a great singer can sing any song in any genre. Johnny Bush was a great singer.

He said that he was playing drums because there were more gigs for drummers than singers. He reinforced my belief that a good sideman can always find work. And he and I worked great together. With Johnny on drums and me on guitar, we played in the Pearl Wranglers, a well-known country swing band led by Adolph Hofner. Hofner named his group after his sponsor, Pearl Beer, one of the breweries headquartered in San Antonio. Early on, I learned about the link between big business and music. I liked that link.

I also liked how Johnny reminded me of Zeke—both good guys who never shied away from a wild adventure. Neither did Johnny shy away from expressing an opinion about my singing.

"I'm forming a band and I want you in it, Willie," said Johnny, "but I want you playing, not singing."

"What's wrong with my singing?"

"It ain't on the money. You got no time. You're either ahead or behind the beat. Besides, this band don't need more than one singer—and that's me."

"Can't argue with you, Johnny. You're a belter."

So Bush formed the Mission City Playboys—with him singing and me playing. It was a band that went nowhere fast, but we had fun going there.

I was fast to answer an ad saying that KBOP, a radio station in Pleasanton, some thirty miles outside San Antone, needed a disc jockey. I ran over and, as luck would have it, met a man who'd have a mighty influence on my life.

"Name's Parker, Dr. Ben Parker, but people call me Doc," he said when I arrived at the station.

"Pleasure to meet you, sir. I'm Willie Nelson."

"Well, Willie, first thing I must ask is whether you've had experience on the air."

"Yes, sir. Worked at KHBR in Hillsboro."

"I know KHBR. A fine little station."

"We played live music on the air as well."

"And you worked the board?"

"You bet."

"They use an RCA board up there?"

"No, it was a Gates board."

"We use RCA. It's a lot different. Are you familiar with it?"

"Can't say I am."

Dead silence. I wondered if this meant the interview was over. If I couldn't operate the board, what good was I?

"Tell you what, Willie. I see something in you that I like. Something I trust. Let me take a little time and show you how the RCA board works."

"I'd appreciate that."

And I did. I paid close attention and was hands-on in short order. Doc Parker was impressed and decided, right then and there, to give me an on-the-air test.

"Part of the job is to read live news and commercials. You have a problem with that?"

"None whatsoever."

"You ready?"

"Sure thing," I said with forced confidence.

"In five minutes you'll be going live."

Doc Parker handed me a few sheets of copy. The news off the ticker machine was easy to read. But the commercial was hard. It said, "The Pleasanton Pharmacy's pharmaceutical department accurately and precisely fills your doctor's prescriptions."

Somehow I got all those words out. The boss smiled.

"Excellent, young man. You have a job."

That made my year. I was back in my element. And to make matters sweeter, I had a mentor, a man only too happy to school me.

Ben Parker was "Doc" because of his practice as a chiropractor. He was also a college dean, a pastor, and a sharp businessman who owned seven radio stations. I saw him as a kindhearted human being with great wisdom.

"Take people for who they are," he once said to me. "Everyone requires respect. The less you judge people, the more successful your dealings with them. Don't preach. Don't be harsh. Don't be arrogant. When it comes to working with others, understanding is the key. You can't be too compassionate. Compassion leads to cooperation, and cooperation leads to accomplishment."

Compassion and understanding were the two qualities Doc exhibited on a daily basis. He was never too busy to stop and offer me praise when I deserved it and a critique when I needed it.

"What I like about you, Willie," he said, "is that you let your easygoing personality come out. Listeners like someone who's not trying to impress them with his importance. What they don't like, though, is when they turn on their radio early in the morning and discover that the deejay isn't there. They don't like that at all."

Doc was referring to the fact that, due to late-night gigs I had with Johnny, I had arrived late for a couple of my early morning shifts. Another boss would have fired me. Not Doc.

Doc said, "Look, Willie, I know you're looking to find yourself as a singer and a songwriter. No doubt you have talent, boy. I wouldn't do anything to discourage that work. In fact, if it's easier for you, I'll move you to an afternoon shift."

"Thank you, sir."

"I'm looking for you to do big things, Willie. You and that Johnny Bush as well."

Doc also gave Johnny a deejay shift.

"Both you guys are characters," he said, "but the kind of characters our listeners like. Our listeners are getting a kick out of you."

One morning, rushing to KBOP, I could have kicked my own ass when I ran out of gas. Making matters worse, I was hungover. Had no choice but to hitchhike.

I'd be goddamned if the first person to stop wasn't Johnny Bush.

"You're one sorry son of a bitch," said Johnny, also on his way to the station. "Get in. Good thing I happened by."

We started shooting the shit. But then, ten minutes outside Pleasanton, Johnny's car started coughing and wheezing before it stopped dead.

"What's wrong?" I asked.

Johnny hesitated before saying it, but finally he had to.

"We're out of gas."

"You're one sorry son of a bitch," I said.

The story ended with the two of us on the side of the road, thumbs out.

* * *

You might say that the story of my recording career began at KBOP. I use the term "recording career" loosely. Though I loved being a deejay with a show of my own, I never gave up my ambition to write and record songs of my own—not for a minute.

Because I had this access to so many records, I was always inspired. I was spinning discs by Faron Young, Ray Price, Porter Wagoner, Marty Robbins—every country star in the nation. I also slipped in pop hits that I loved—Sinatra's "Young at Heart" or Nat King Cole's "Answer Me, My Love."

I had the additional good fortune of working at a radio station at the birth of rock and roll. I imagine I was among the first deejays in Texas to play "Rock around the Clock" by Bill Haley and the Comets, a record I loved.

But not everything was good. There were a lot of shit records being put out. Which got me to thinking: *Hell, I can do better.*

With that in mind, I used the equipment at KBOP to record a couple of songs—just me and my guitar. I sent them to a man who had a little label in Luling, Texas. Never did hear back.

Was I discouraged? Not on your life. I was just getting started. I was stubborn as hell, still certain this music thing was gonna work out.

"It's all gonna work out just fine," I told Johnny Bush after he heard me convince a lady who owned the Red Barn, a club in Leming, Texas, to hire our four-man band.

"But Willie," said Johnny, "we don't got no four-man band.

All we got is you and me. She wants a fiddler and steel player and we don't got either one."

"No worries," I said.

Come the day of the gig, we'd found a steel player, but no fiddler.

"No fiddler," said the owner, "no money. Folks come here to dance. And without a fiddler, they won't be dancing, which means they won't be drinking, which means you won't be seeing a red cent."

"We'll have a fiddler by tonight," I told the lady.

Outside, Johnny said, "You're crazy, Willie. You're making all sorts of promises you can't keep. How can you stand there and say it's all gonna work out?"

"'Cause it will."

And it did.

Later that afternoon, who should turn up but my dad, Ira Nelson. He had come to see his little granddaughter, Lana.

"Bring your fiddle, Dad?" I asked.

"Naturally."

"Feel like playing?"

"Always."

That night the music was hot enough to burn down the Red Barn.

7

POSITIVE THINKING

MY MARRIAGE TO MARTHA WAS unpredictable as a Texas twister.

Even though I adored little Lana and pledged to be a better husband and responsible dad, the nightlife kept calling. The nightlife meant playing any club that would have me. It meant driving long distances and staying out till three or four in the morning before heading over to KBOP for my early shift. It meant meeting some mighty pretty ladies who didn't require any wooing. They were more than willing.

It meant facing a fact that, as a young man, became more and more apparent to me:

A hard dick has no conscience.

Some might say that's low-consciousness thinking, but I do believe it's true. At the same time, my mind has always been open to high-consciousness thinking.

When I was scrambling around Texas in the 1950s, for instance, I happened to pick up a book by a pastor named

Norman Vincent Peale. The title intrigued me: *The Power of Positive Thinking.*

"Many people make life unnecessarily difficult for themselves by dissipating power and energy through fuming and fretting," wrote the minister before quoting Scripture, John 14:27: "Peace I leave with you, my peace I give unto you."

I soon saw that the book was about peace of mind—peace that can be realized by replacing a negative thought with a positive one.

"When you expect the best, you release a magnetic force in your mind," said Peale, "which by a law of attraction tends to bring the best to you."

I loved the pastor's attitudes and took them to heart.

A peaceful mind generates power.

A relaxed attitude receives peace.

To be in tune with the infinite is to embrace His positive energy.

Positive thoughts lead to positive actions.

And there's nothing more positive than love.

The message of the book never left my mind, even—and especially—during times when I might be thinking in a negative way. Just like that, I brought myself back to Peale and his message of inner peace. That attitude got me through a whole bunch of career roadblocks, not to mention domestic wars.

Martha and I brought our love wars to Fort Worth. We figured we might find some peace there—and work to boot—since the San Antonio/Pleasanton circuit had run its course.

I loved Doc Parker, I loved playing with Johnny Bush, but the gigs were drying up. Time to move on.

Fort Worth was calling principally because sister Bobbie was living there. She and Bud were divorced and entangled in a nasty dispute over the custody of their sons, Randy, Freddie, and Michael. Sister needed my moral support. My father was also in Fort Worth—another plus. The closer I got to family, the better.

When it came to country music, Fort Worth was Honky-Tonk Central. One joint after another—rough joints frequented by rough characters—lined the Jacksboro Highway: illegal gambling joints, dance joints, beer joints, buckets of blood. You could hear live music from one end of Fort Worth to the other. The stockyards and slaughterhouses gave the city a distinctive stink. The whorehouses ran night and day. Gangsters fought over territory with live ammunition. Fort Worth was "where the West begins"—the *Wild* West.

My kind of town.

After arriving, I landed a deejaying job in Denton. The 120-mile-round-trip commute was a killer.

I soon found something better at KCNC in Fort Worth. I had two shifts—early morning and early afternoon—and took this gig very seriously. In my eyes, Fort Worth was a big market and I wanted to be heard.

Though I stole some of the riffs from other on-the-air personalities, my sign-on had a certain flair. Sometimes I still say it in my sleep.

"This is your ol' cotton-pickin', snuff-dippin', tobacca-chewin', stump-jumpin', gravy-soppin', coffeepot-dodgin', dumplin'-eatin', frog-giggin' hillbilly from Hill County, Texas."

I thought I was hot shit.

When I wasn't thinking of myself, I was often thinking of sister Bobbie. Because I thought the world of her, it tore me up to see her dealing with these painful family problems. I also deeply respected how, faced with adversities that would overwhelm most people, she stayed true to music. Bobbie was resourceful. Musically, she could hold her own at any honky-tonk, but how many honky-tonk piano players could land a job demonstrating the Hammond organ? In addition to selling organs at music stores, Bobbie was playing in clubs, while on Sundays she commanded the organ at the very proper Highland Park Methodist Church in Dallas.

Fred Lockwood was never very proper. He and his brother Ace were musicians who worked the seedy clubs on Jacksboro Highway, Mansfield Highway, Hemphill Street, and White Settlement Road—the down-and-dirty joints where shootings and stabbings were every-night occurrences.

We were in one of those joints, sitting at the bar and nursing our whiskeys, when the Army-McCarthy hearings came on TV. It was a nasty business—Senator Joseph McCarthy accusing everyone and his mama of being a secret commie—so I downed my drink and ordered another.

"We'd probably get happier faster if we blew some tea," said Fred.

"Never tried it," I said.

"It's time you did."

Naturally I knew about pot. Musicians called it tea or weed or boo or reefer. They said it made the music sound better while making you horny. They said it put a nice filter on things.

But hell, I was a hick from Abbott. I'd seen *Reefer Madness,* and I was a little worried that a little pot might get me crazy. Wasn't I crazy enough? Besides, whiskey was working for me.

Or was it? Booze emboldened me. Brought out the fighter. And on more occasions than I wish to remember, the fighter picked on guys bigger than him. Because I had already started studying jujitsu and martial arts, there were times when I prevailed. I wish I could tell you that those times were frequent. But honesty requires that I admit that more often than not I got the shit kicked out of me. Booze did nothing to improve my dexterity or my judgment in provoking an opponent.

But booze would remain the main ingredient for years to come. I wasn't ready for reefer, at least not then.

"Take this little joint anyway," said Fred, handing me a skinny cigarette twisted at either end.

When I eventually did light it up, I hadn't been schooled on how to smoke it. So I inhaled and exhaled like I was puffing on a cigarette. I didn't get high. I didn't see the big deal.

Some time later Fred gave me another joint that we smoked together.

"No, you dumb son of a bitch," he said. "You don't treat it like no Lucky Strike. You hold in the fuckin' smoke. Watch."

I watched, I learned, I got high.

From time to time, I'd smoke a joint if someone handed it

to me. But I never bought penny matchbooks or lids like other musicians. Because I was a chain-smoker, I saw grass as merely another thing to smoke when the occasion arose. It'd take years before I'd understand its beneficial properties. In the meantime, I stuck to my main two habits: cigarettes and booze. I was too young and dumb to see the harm they were doing.

When it was time to go on the air, I was dead sober. I called my radio show *Western Express,* and I promoted it tirelessly.

Every afternoon when I came on the air, I'd spin a beautiful song called "Red Headed Stranger." It was the perfect tune to help parents put their kids down for a nap. Guitar Boogie Smith's version was a classic. When I played it, I'd give a shout-out to baby Lana at home.

"This one's for my little girl," I'd say.

When I got home that night, she'd want me to sing the song. When I did, she fell asleep in my arms.

The song was both simple and profound, a deep Western yarn of a cowboy from Blue Rock, Montana, who, mourning the loss of his love, has fallen into a murderous rage. The rage, though, is hidden inside. The song sounds innocent as a nursery rhyme. I loved the line that says, "He's wild in his sorrow, he's riding and hiding his pain."

I could see the redheaded stranger. I could feel his heavy heart. And yet singing this song, I could also feel how little kids, unaware of its tragic message, were mesmerized by the sweet melody, the easy rhythm, and the beautifully repeated patterns that warn us not to boss him or cross him, not to fight him or spite him.

I saw the song as an epic movie. And as a redhead, I naturally cast myself in the leading role. But that was just the idle fantasy of a twenty-two-year-old kid running around Fort Worth, figuring out ways to promote himself.

For instance, I'd do remotes from all over the city—Leonard's Department Store, car dealerships, any business that would have me. I was determined to get my name out there.

That was daytime. Come nighttime I circulated around the city's nightclubs, where, little by little, I gained a reputation as a guy who could sing and play.

Then came Sunday. On Sunday, look for me at the Metropolitan Baptist Church, where, in addition to attending services regularly, I taught a Sunday school class. That's where my dad and his wife were members. It was also where, as an adult, I was baptized, a ritual that deepened my faith.

At this point the Nelson brood—Ira's family, my family, and Bobbie's—was living in Arlington, halfway between Fort Worth and Dallas, where apartments were cheap.

I'd often run over to Dallas, a city whose cultural climate was very different from Fort Worth's. Dallas saw itself as highfalutin. But Dallas also had a vital country music scene. There were huge venues like the Longhorn Ballroom and the Sportatorium, home of the *Big D Jamboree*. The stage at the Sportatorium was a wrestling ring. On Friday night you might see a wrestling match with Gorgeous George or Killer

Kowalski. Come Saturday night, though, you'd get to see stars from *The Grand Ole Opry* or *Louisiana Hayride* like Webb Pierce or Roy Orbison.

I was dead set on getting into that wrestling ring. I wanted to play in front of six thousand folks so bad I could taste it. Meanwhile, I didn't mind playing in front of sixty people back in Fort Worth at Gray's Bar on Exchange Avenue, where I was hired by a Mexican band to sing lead and play guitar. Might sound funny, but the leader, a man named Momolita, had me singing jazz tunes like "Sweet Georgia Brown." Black musicians would come up and jam. It was a free-feeling mixture of different styles, all dipped in the blues.

I'd experienced some criticism of my singing style before—and would experience a lot more in the future—but these guys understood me completely. Like me, they didn't adhere to strict timing. The music we made was loose, unpredictable, and lovely. I felt secure up there on the bandstand, not only because of the easy-flowing, easygoing musical conversation with my peers, but because chicken wire had been rigged in front of the stage to protect us from the flying beer bottles and switchblades.

Great characters were popping up everywhere I looked.

Take Paul Buskirk, a brilliant banjo player. Paul had superb musical knowledge and became a mentor, encouraging my singing, playing, and writing. He was deep into Django. He understood that the bridge between country and jazz has traffic moving in both directions. His singer, Freddy Powers, also became a pal, another man infatuated with a variety of musical styles. The three of us would chew the fat and jam for hours.

"Don't think of music in terms of categories," Paul liked to say, "unless those categories are 'good' and 'bad.' The good musician can go from blues to country back to jazz and swing. He's not afraid of playing anything outside his comfort zone because his comfort zone keeps on widening—long as he's following his heart."

Paul and Freddy would come by KCNC, where they'd sit in with me every day at noon for thirty minutes. Oliver English was part of this same scene. He was another major musical mentor. Not only was his own guitar technique superb, but he had tastes that went far beyond my usual territory. Like Paul Buskirk, he was a devotee of Django, but he also loved Andrés Segovia, the great Spanish classical guitarist.

"Listen to the sound of Segovia playing Bach," said Oliver, "and you'll think you're hearing a whole orchestra."

I listened, I learned, I saw my world widening.

I saw Oliver bring his brother Paul English to the station one day.

I liked Paul from the get-go. In nothing flat, he laid out his life story. He'd been busted for some petty crimes and gone to jail in Waxahachie. He was running whores out of some Fort Worth jail. He talked about how he'd been on the *Fort Worth Press*'s "10 Most Unwanted" list five years in a row. He was a gun-toting, fun-loving outlaw with plenty of charm and no fears. But like his brother Oliver, was he also a musician?

"Get that cardboard box over there," said Oliver. "Give Paul some brushes and let him play drums."

Paul impressed us with pretty decent time.

Some time would pass before Paul and I hooked up again, but when we did, it would be forever.

I didn't see myself in Fort Worth forever. Fact is, I didn't see myself there for more than another month or so. The radio show was fun, but the club gigs weren't coming fast enough or paying enough.

Time to hit the highway.

As you've already seen, this was the early pattern of my life.

Go here, go there, stay for a short while, and then move out.

If you had asked, I couldn't have told you exactly why it was time to make that move. I could have kept hustling in Fort Worth. I could have gone back to San Antonio or even to Waco. I could have done anything. The fact that I said to Martha, "Let's try California," doesn't indicate that I had a plan. I didn't. I didn't have shit—no money, no blueprint for the future.

"Why California?" asked Martha.

"Why not?" I answered.

The answer was good enough for Martha, who understood my wanderlust because she had so much wanderlust of her own.

"Where in California?" she asked.

"Might as well start in San Diego."

"I hear they got good weather down there."

"Well, maybe San Diego's the spot," I said.

"It's got my vote."

"When do you wanna leave?"

"Yesterday."

"That means tomorrow."

"That means right now."

8

COASTIN'

THE BLUES ARE DEEP—A DEEP part of American music, a deep part of my own life.

I love the blues for showing me how my feelings, no matter how sad, can be turned into song.

But I can't say I loved the blues when they swept over me and nearly wiped me out.

The blues can be unrelenting—attacking in the morning, attacking at night, making you feel that nothing's ever gonna be right.

I got the blues in San Diego.

When I moved out there with Martha and little Lana, I couldn't find any work. Martha, bless her heart, supported us with another waitress gig. I felt guilty that I couldn't care for my own family.

I arrived with high expectations. After all, Charlie Williams, the deejay who'd been at KCNC in Fort Worth just before me, had been hired by a country music radio station in L.A. California liked Texas deejays.

But not me. No San Diego station was interested.

No matter. San Diego had a big navy base with lots of bars and dance clubs. One way or the other, San Diego was sure to accommodate me. I'd find a gig somewhere.

"If you wanna gig," said one club owner, "you gotta join the union."

"What union?"

"The musicians' union."

I'd never been in a union before in my life. But why not? I looked up the number and called.

"What does it take to join?" I asked, half expecting I'd have to prove that I could play.

"A hundred bucks."

"I don't have a hundred bucks."

"Well, buddy, that's your problem."

Night after night, my problem got worse.

I figured there had to be some beer joint owner who didn't give a shit about union membership, but I figured wrong. No work anywhere in San Diego.

The can't-find-no-work-nowhere blues are bad blues, the kind of blues that suck your soul dry.

The blues got me down. The blues got me scared. The blues got me out beating the bushes, going from dance club to beer joint to nightclub, anywhere they might need a picker or a singer.

No one needed shit.

No one needed me.

Despair took hold of me, grabbed my neck, cut off the circulation.

And one night, with ten bucks in my pocket, I cut out. Left Martha and the baby with the car and walked to the main highway, where I stuck out my thumb in the direction of L.A.

Just me, my guitar, and a small suitcase.

L.A. was sunny, but L.A. was dark. L.A. was the same ol' story as San Diego. Night after night, club after club, L.A. said no. We don't know you. We don't need you. We don't want you.

Only good thing in L.A. was two sweet women who took a liking to me. After singing them a couple of songs, they said they heard something sweet. They took me in and said they wanted to help.

They said they knew the music scene and would take me around.

Thank you, ladies.

They took me here and they took me there. I had a couple of short auditions where everyone smiled but no one said yes. Everyone said no.

This went on for a week.

L.A. is a fantasyland, but in L.A. I had to face reality. And reality couldn't be plainer: California was a fuckin' bust. I had to get out. Here I was, homeless, jobless, and too ashamed to go back to Martha and admit defeat.

Instead, I did what little boys do when they're scared and feeling lost:

I went to see my mother. Mom and her husband, Ken, had moved to Portland. Portland had a music scene and my mother had a house. I left my suitcase with the two ladies and gave them Myrle's address with instructions to send on my stuff in a few days.

I left the ladies that night and headed out to hitch to Oregon.

No rides.

I gave up about 4 a.m. and slipped into a ditch to catch some sleep. It was a cold night so I gathered up some newspaper and kindling and built a fire. The blues just about did me in—literally. The smoke just about asphyxiated me.

But there's something about human nature that says, "Get up and move on. Do what you got to do. Survive."

So I got out of the ditch and hitched over to the railroad yard, where I hopped a freight heading north.

The freight rolled through one night and then another, me clutching my guitar, hungry as hell but somehow certain that I had to be moving in the right direction.

I thought of Norman Vincent Peale and all his positive thoughts. I thought of how he said no situation is too negative to be turned around. I thought of Daddy Nelson and Mama Nelson and sister Bobbie and Martha and Lana and all the people who loved me. In that boxcar, for hours on end, I meditated on love. I prayed that love would see me through. And on a brisk winter morning, I was delivered.

I opened the boxcar door and the cold Oregon air smacked me in the face. I saw we were in Eugene, a hundred miles south of Portland.

With guitar in hand, I caught a ride.

"Going to Portland?" I asked.

"'Fraid not," said the truck driver, an older man, "but I'll drop you at the Greyhound station, where you can catch a bus."

I just nodded and said thanks.

The trucker looked me over and read my soul.

"You don't got no money for a bus ticket, do you, son?" he asked.

"Nope."

"Well, this is your lucky day. Don't know why I'm doing this, but something tells me you're on a worthwhile mission. So here's ten bucks for the bus."

I was moved to tears. "Why are you doing this?" I asked.

"Don't get mushy on me, boy. Just take the money and skedaddle."

With great gratitude, I made it to Portland, where I called Mom from a phone booth.

She didn't sound surprised to hear from me.

"We been waiting on you," was all she said.

Her husband, Ken, came to get me at the bus station. He was all smiles.

When we arrived at the house, the smiles got wider.

There was my mother, there was Martha with little Lana in her arms. All safe, all home.

"I figured you'd be making your way to your mama's home," said Martha. "So I called her and she kindly sent us plane tickets."

For once, there were no recriminations, no questioning of why I had disappeared in the middle of the night, no fighting. Just hugs and kisses.

"You're crazy as a loon, Willie Nelson," said Martha, "but I love you."

Heard someone say that just when you're sure things are coming apart, they're actually just coming together. That's the lesson I learned in Portland. Hang in there long enough and your change will come.

Beautiful things started happening in Portland. The most beautiful of all was the birth of Susie, our second daughter, on January 20, 1957. I thought it was gonna happen a couple of weeks earlier, when we took a little trip to Mount Saint Helens. By then Martha was eight-and-a-half months pregnant. We were walking around the grounds surrounding the mountain when we heard rumbling. Before we knew it, the volcano had blown its top. I couldn't help but wonder whether the eruption would coincide with Susie's birth. I saw a first aid station and was about to run for help when Martha said no, Susie wasn't quite ready.

When Susie did make her appearance, we welcomed her with open arms. She was gorgeous. Along with Lana, Susie became the love of our lives. At twenty-four, I was blessed with two miraculous daughters. More than ever, I needed to provide for them.

And I'm proud to say I did.

Martha's folks came up from Waco to help care for Susie and Lana while Martha found work—you guessed it—as a waitress. Then Myrle told me about a radio station in Vancouver, Washington, a smaller town some fifteen miles from

Portland. That's where I found work. Fact is, that's where I found myself. I rediscovered who I was.

In a matter of weeks, I went from being a vagrant in a boxcar to an on-the-air personality on KVAN, 910 on your dial, serving Portland/Vancouver.

"We're the station with the sense of humor," the promos said. "The station with the personalities."

Those personalities included deejays Shorty the Hired Hand and Cactus Ken. Add one new addition to the roster:

Wee Willie Nelson.

Yes, sir, I was back on the air, back with the name of my show in Texas—*Western Express*—and back with the same can-do positive attitude that said, "Friends and neighbors, this is a man who's got the music you love, a man you gotta like."

First they had me on in the afternoon. I was so well liked they moved me to a morning slot, where I competed with Arthur Godfrey, whose national radio show was one of the most popular in the history of radio. I actually held my own against Godfrey.

The folks at the station saw how I was catching on. They even took out a newspaper ad, touting my show. The ad features a photo of me, hair combed nice and straight, big grin on my face. Across from me is a drawing of a donkey holding a guitar. The jackass is looking at me and asking, "Who, him?"

The copy reads:

"Why, he's yer cotton-pickin', snuff-dippin', tobacca-chewin', stump-jumpin', gravy-soppin', coffee-pot-dodgin', dumplin-eatin', frog-giggin' hillbilly from Hill County, Texas...

"Willie Nelson!

"Just rode into town to take over his own show on KVAN. . . . See that pan-handled description up there? Them's his very own words! Willie's got wit, warmth and wow . . . !"

In Oregon, the roller-coaster ride from burnout to recharge was just beginning. The ride would last a lifetime. But at this point, in my mid-twenties, the fact that I could reinvent myself and find favor among the good folks of the great Northwest calmed my soul.

The year all this happened—1957—was a big one in the music biz.

As a deejay, I was in the driver's seat. I got to pick and choose the songs I loved most. Those included hits like Ferlin Husky's "Gone," Johnny Cash's "There You Go," and Ray Price's "My Shoes Keep Walking Back to You." But I also got to play Elvis, who had exploded on the scene a year earlier with "Hound Dog" and "Heartbreak Hotel."

I was an Elvis fan from the get-go. I heard he was essentially a country boy raised up in country music, but I also heard that, like me, he had absorbed a big dose of black blues. There was also a gospel strain in Elvis's voice. He wove all these strains together and came out rocking with an energy that lit up the world. From where I was sitting at KVAN in Vancouver, I saw he wasn't only dominating the pop charts; he had number one hits on country stations across the nation: "All Shook Up," "(Let Me Be Your) Teddy Bear," and "Jailhouse Rock." I never understood why certain Elvis songs charted on the country stations when others didn't. What makes "Teddy Bear" and "Jailhouse Rock" country? Who knows? And who cares? The truth is that no one knew how to categorize Elvis.

He busted through all the categories and turned the industry on its ear.

Outside the station, things were starting to work, too. I found music gigs all around the region. Tiny Dumont's Dance Hall, a pavilion much like the places I'd played back in West and Hillsboro, was filled with country-music-loving folks looking to unwind and cut a rug to western swing.

I swung out in other directions, too. Wearing a white Stetson cowboy hat and a fancy white-fringed black leather suit sewed by Martha, I jumped on the back of a palomino that I had bought from an engineer at the radio station and paraded down Main Street during every holiday ceremony.

Here comes Wee Willie Nelson from KVAN!

I attended civic events and car dealership promotions in Davy Crockett gear—raccoon-skin cap and all—since this was the era of the Fess Parker franchise of that celebrated folk hero.

Did I see myself as a folk hero? Hell, no. I was merely a self-promoting deejay looking to get my picture in the papers to boost my ratings.

You suggest it, I'd do it. I was the first, for instance, to sign up for a highly publicized stock car race where all the deejays in Oregon got behind the wheel and went for broke. A race was all I needed to fire up my competitive engines. Watching those other fuckers falling behind, it pleased me no end to finish first.

It pleased me even more to cut a record, my first, and hustle it on the air. I used the station's equipment to record two songs.

I wrote the first. I called it "No Place for Me" and, typical of my early stuff, it's about loneliness, man rejected by woman. "Your love is as cold as the north wind that blows," I wrote, "and the river that runs to the sea . . . but, baby, there's no place for me." The B side was "Lumberjack," a tale of the logger life written by my pal Leon Payne.

I got Starday, a little label in Houston run by Pappy Daily, to press up five hundred copies. They didn't see it as a seller so I wound up paying for every last disc. It was up to me to sell the song on the air. And I did. I told my listeners, "For the low, low price of a measly dollar, I'll send you a copy of Texas Willie Nelson's latest release—the song 'No Place for Me' that you already love. But that's not all. Call within the hour and I'll include, free of charge, a genuine autographed eight-by-ten glossy photo of yours truly. How can you resist? You can't. So don't even try. Do yourself a favor, friends. Pick up that phone and let me hear from you. Do it now!"

Though the single was hardly a national hit, I did manage to sell out the first pressing and a few thousand more.

I was on a roll, but I remained unsatisfied. My restless nature was stirring me. Oregon was cool, but the Oregon market was small. Oregon was just one small corner of a wider world I needed to explore.

That need was validated in an unexpected way.

I was doing my show at the station one day, taking the listeners from the Everly Brothers' "Bye Bye Love" to Webb Pierce's "Honky Tonk Song" to Jerry Lee Lewis's "Whole Lot of Shakin' Going On," when I heard someone say that Mae Axton had just arrived to say hello to the deejays. That news stopped me dead in my tracks.

Mrs. Axton worked for Colonel Parker, Elvis's manager, and was promoting a Hank Snow tour. Snow had hired Elvis to open for him; it was Hank Snow who had hooked up the Colonel and Elvis. Mae Axton was in the middle of this mix. She had cowritten "Heartbreak Hotel," Elvis's first number one hit. I'd been reading about her in *Billboard*. She was a nationally known figure who enjoyed a first-rate reputation as a woman who knew songs and songwriting. At the end of my set, I immediately sought her out.

I'd been working on a song I thought had possibilities. It came from a deep place: Mama and Daddy Nelson's home in Abbott and their abiding connection to the Good Book. The song was born out of my memory of hearing my sweet grandmother sing "Rock of Ages." I called it "Family Bible."

"Don't mean to bother you, Mrs. Axton, but I'm a great admirer of your work. And I'm a songwriter myself."

"What's your name, son?" she asked.

"Willie Nelson."

She was a well-spoken, well-dressed lady of confidence and composure. She had keen intelligent eyes and a straightforward but gentle demeanor.

"Weren't you just on the air?" she asked.

"Yes, ma'am. I was."

"You're from Texas, aren't you?"

"I am."

"I heard it in your voice. Well, I hope tomorrow you'll put in a good word for the Hank Snow show that's coming to town."

"It'll be my pleasure."

"Much appreciated. And when Hank's here I'll be sure and get him to come by the station."

"I'd be honored to meet him."

"Good meeting you, Willie."

"Before you go, Mrs. Axton, there is one thing I'd like you to hear."

"What's that?"

"A song I wrote and sang. I made a little demo version—just me and the guitar—that I'd like to play for you. Will take only a minute."

"I got a plane to catch, son."

"I'd be much obliged."

"All right. Go ahead and play it."

I switched on the tape recorder. The words said,

There's a family Bible on the table
Each page is torn and hard to read
But the family Bible on the table
Will ever be my key to memories
At the end of day when work was over
And when the evening meal was done
Dad would read to us from the family Bible
And we'd count our many blessings one by one
I can see us sittin' round the table
When from the family Bible Dad would read

I can hear my mother softly singing rock of ages
Rock of ages cleft for me

Now this old world of ours is full of trouble
This old world would also better be
If we'd find more Bibles on the tables
And mothers singing rock of ages cleft for me
I can see us sittin' round the table
When from the family Bible Dad would read
I can hear my mother softly singing rock of ages
Rock of ages rock of ages cleft for me

Mrs. Axton was moved. Her business manner melted. She looked at me like a mother. She asked me to sing a couple of other things. When I was through, in the softest voice imaginable she said, "Son, you have something."

"I do?"

"You have a precious gift. I wish I had more time to spend with you because there's more I can tell you. For now, just remember two things. The first is that you're looking at a lady who, if she had half your writing talent, would be the happiest gal on earth. And secondly, if you're to develop that talent, you can't keep hiding out here in the Northwest. You've got to move on, son."

"To where?"

"Maybe back to Texas. Texas is a big market, a good market. Texas is your home market. But as you know, the biggest market for a songwriter is Nashville. I believe that sooner or later you're gonna have to go on to Nashville."

Mrs. Axton's words haunted me.

Back to Texas.

On to Nashville.

It was as though she saw my future in front of her. Because she was so clear in her pronouncement, I had to believe her. Besides, she was a well-respected figure on the national music scene. She went so far as to give me her unlisted number. She did more than encourage me. She actually said, "I could always raise a couple of hundred dollars to help you."

I saw the conviction in her eyes. I felt her sincerity. Just based on the words of this wonderful woman, I knew what I had to do. For all my local success, I had to leave Oregon.

That evening I didn't make my usual late-night rounds. I stayed home. I helped Martha put Lana and Susie to sleep before wandering out to the backyard alone.

The sky over Oregon isn't as big as the sky over Texas, but it's plenty big.

On a clear night like this you could reach up and touch the stars.

I wanted to touch a star. No doubt about it, I wanted to be a star. I wanted to glow. I wanted to shine.

I searched the vast sky for Sputnik, the Russian satellite that had just been launched. I wanted to see it circling the earth. I wanted to hitch a ride on the back of Sputnik and take a spin around the planet. I wanted to explore, to fly free, to move into dimensions I could only dream of.

I'd been writing songs since I was a kid. But the songs I'd been writing recently felt different. These songs felt serious. Mrs. Axton saw that seriousness.

"Songwriting," she had said, "is serious business. And there's no reason, son, why you can't take that business by storm."

Serious business, serious songs.

Was I ready to take a spin around the planet?

Was I ready to wholly commit myself and my life to my songs?

The answer was in the stars, but the stars weren't talking. The stars were just winking and blinking and setting my restless soul on fire.

PART TWO

SONGS FALLING FROM THE SKY

Back to the Future

In the early nineties, the press I was reading couldn't have been worse.

Texas Monthly, the state magazine that had once celebrated my music, ran an article titled "Poor Willie," followed by "The IRS nailed him for millions, only to find that Willie Nelson had already given it all away."

I didn't bother to read it. I didn't need to know how much I had given away to family and friends. If I had it, I gave it. And if I gave away too much, that was a helluva lot better than not giving away enough.

Looking back at the events preceding this financial burnout,

I began to understand that the seeds to what was now being called my implosion were sowed in the seventies.

I look back at the seventies as the start of the cocaine blizzard that blew across the music business—and the rest of the country—creating havoc in its wake. I was one of the lucky ones. I tried coke and instinctively mistrusted the energy it generated. Others said the energy was positive; I found it poisonous. The drug boosted the ego to ungodly proportions. I use the word "ungodly" purposely because when most folks are jacked up on coke they get to believing that they're God. With cocaine, there's no room for a higher power. You become your own higher power. You're under the illusion that you're all-knowing, all-powerful, and invulnerable. In short, you become a raging asshole.

Early on, I restricted the use of coke in my band. I put out the word: "If you're wired, you're fired." And that was it.

At the same time, I stuck to a judge-not-and-be-not-judged policy when it came to the wider world. My good buddy Waylon Jennings loved coke. I didn't say anything. Let him love it. Waylon was a strong man with a strong will, a brilliant artist, and one of the best friends I've ever had.

It was through Waylon that I met a man named Neil Reshen, a street tough New York manager who, with Waylon as his client, took Nashville by storm. Because his other big client was Miles Davis, Neil already had a reputation as "the man who could manage the unmanageable."

These were the days when Waylon was still in the clutches of the RCA Nashville establishment that demanded he sing certain songs a certain way. Neil put a stop to that. He backed down the establishment. Through Neil, Waylon was able to win back his artistic freedom. Neil also decimated the low royalty–low advance structure that typified Nashville. He renegotiated Waylon's contract in a way that revolutionized the industry.

I was impressed.

"Talk to Neil, hoss," said Waylon. "He can do for you what he did for me. You need a mad-dog manager like Neil Reshen. This man has no fear."

Being something of a scoundrel myself, I've been attracted to scoundrels my whole life. Starting with Zeke Varnon, I've liked tracking the unsavory ways of unsavory characters. I have a high tolerance for miscreants. I get a kick out of watching a clever manipulator work the angles.

Neil was a super-clever manipulator. And starting in the early seventies, he began working for me.

Because I had already taken a stance as an antiestablishment artist, I thought, what the hell, I'll hire me an antiestablishment manager.

I knew who he was. I knew his bulldog energy was put into a frenzied overdrive by all the coke he consumed. I knew he wasn't a straight shooter. He'd do whatever he needed to do to get his artist what he thought his artist deserved.

Well, I was willing to be that artist. I was willing to put up with his blow-snorting ways... as long as he served my purpose, protected my artistic integrity, and made sure my financial house was in order.

"Count on me for all that, Willie," said Neil, "and more. Count on me to take a bullet for you."

"I've never been comfortable with a manager," I told him, "because I've never wanted to be slowed down or contained."

"I'll never get in your way," he said. "Matter of fact, I'm gonna make life easier for you. I'm gonna take the pressure of all those nagging money details off your mind. I'm setting it up so all you gotta focus on is music, music, music."

"And my taxes?"

"Hell, Willie, that's the easiest part. I'm a tax expert. I've got one of the best tax minds of anyone in the country."

In the early nineties—when the shit hit the fan—I clearly remembered that conversation from the early seventies.

I also remembered that it was in the late seventies when I learned that Neil had filed tax extensions for me for the past four years—and never paid the taxes.

I remembered getting hit with a tax bill for millions of dollars and being told by Neil that my tax records had gone missing.

I remembered thinking, "Oh shit, the rottweiler I bought to protect me has ripped into my own ass."

The thought crossed my mind:

If I don't get hold of this tax thing, it could more than bite me. It could take me all the way down.

9

BACK TO COW TOWN

BEFORE I HEEDED THE ADVICE of Mae Axton—whose son Hoyt, by the way, would gain big stardom in the sixties—I gave KVAN, the Vancouver radio station, one last chance.

"All it'll take to keep me," I told the manager, "is another hundred dollars a week."

The man just smiled a little smile, chuckled a little chuckle, and said, "Be careful that door doesn't knock you on your ass on the way out."

I could have bitten the bullet and gone to Nashville right then and there. In my gut, though, I was hesitant. Mrs. Axton had suggested going home to Texas and, at least for now, that seemed a safer move. I wasn't ready to swim with those Nashville sharks.

We headed back to Fort Worth, where my dad and his wife, Lorraine, said we could move in with them. Good thing, since Martha was pregnant with our third child.

Before we arrived, though, we stopped in Springfield, Missouri, for a while and stayed with Billy Walker, a pal from my Waco days who'd gone from being a deejay to a recording artist. Billy was a rising star.

"Stay long as you like, Willie," he said. "We got lots of room for you, Martha, and the babies."

As usual, Martha got a job as a waitress. I tried to get on *Ozark Jubilee,* a country music radio show where Billy was working. I auditioned but didn't make it. Didn't take it personally. In my heart, I knew I was better than they thought I was. But better or not, I still needed money. So I got a job washing dishes.

One night Billy and I got to talking. That's when I played him some new tunes. Billy was a generous listener. He said that he admired my songwriting and encouraged me to pursue the craft. I told him about the encouragement I had gotten from Mae Axton and mentioned the idea of skipping Texas and moving straight to Nashville.

"You could do that," said Billy, "but I'm sensing that it might be a bit too soon."

Billy accurately sensed my hesitancy. I challenged us both when I asked, "Why do you say that? Why don't you think I'm ready for Nashville?"

"I'd turn that around and ask, 'Is Nashville ready for me?' Listen to the songs coming outta Nashville, Willie, and you sure don't hear anything close to what you're writing. There's a formula to those tunes. Musically, Nashville is a cookie-cutter town, and you're not a cookie-cutter writer. Your songs are strong, but they're strange. They come from the dark corners of your mind. I don't think Nashville is too interested in those dark corners."

Fort Worth had its dark corners, but I saw the city in a positive light. Not long ago, I'd been a radio personality there. I had musician friends all over town. And I was always welcome in the home of my father, whose steady job as a Ford mechanic had given him stability. I needed to borrow from his stability. I needed to put my nose to the grindstone.

In terms of steady income, music continued to be an unreliable mistress. I loved her with all my heart, but the sweet thing just couldn't pay my bills. At the tender age of twenty-five, I was still struggling financially.

Sister Bobbie had remarried. Her husband, Paul Tracy, owned a gas station where I could pick up a little money pumping gas and changing oil. But I needed something better. So I went back to selling encyclopedias, where the potential was greater.

This time I hooked up with Encyclopedia Americana, a high-class brand of books that had a canned sales technique. They called it negative sales because you began with a negative. As a positive thinker, that should have tipped me off as being wrong. But I was hungry and willing to do whatever it took to earn commissions.

I was given a list of customers in Fort Worth who had just gotten their first phone. This meant young couples with children. The plan was to make six appointments a day and turn half of those meetings into sales.

The opening negative was, "I'm not a salesman. I'm not trying to sell you anything. I just want to ask a few questions about your future and the future of your family."

This was a lie. But I was a salesman desperate to close a deal. I'd drive to the home and park my borrowed pickup truck down the street in order not to make a bad impression.

When the door opened, I offered my best smile. My approach was low-key. I called on my easygoing charm to chat up the woman or the man or the couple. I talked about the beauty of knowledge and education. The more knowledge, the more education, the more prosperity. Self-education was the easiest way to improve our lot. And for merely the daily cost of a pack of Camels, I was offering a whole new world to these newly married couples. I was offering them a gift.

My sincerity came through, and my concern for their well-being and my down-to-earth honesty. First day out I sold three sets at $400 a pop. I felt great, but I also felt like shit.

As I looked around their bare apartments and sparsely furnished little homes, I saw that the last thing these couples needed was a multivolume set of encyclopedias. They needed food and furniture. They needed medical insurance. They didn't need me selling them a bill of goods.

My conscience got to me, and in short order I quit the job. I couldn't feel good selling a product that people really didn't need. That's when I turned to a more practical product. Vacuum cleaners. No question about it, everyone does need a good machine to tackle dirt.

Kirby vacuum cleaners were the best machines of that era. The problem, though, was that they were costly. To justify that cost I had to demonstrate their power. I did that by talking customers into letting me overturn their mattresses to reveal the accumulation of dirt that the Kirby and Kirby alone could suck up in nothing flat. People were amazed at how much dirt had accumulated under the mattress. They were equally amazed at how quickly the Kirby made that dirt disappear. I sold a boatload of Kirbys. And while I felt less guilty selling vacuum cleaners than encyclopedias, the net effect was the same: I was using the power of my personality to get people to buy an expensive product that, at the end of the day, I'd never buy for myself.

I felt like I was exploiting my natural ability to communicate with people. There had to be a higher purpose.

I considered that higher purpose during my Sunday school classes at the Metropolitan Baptist Church. Those discussions provided an opportunity for me to look inward. Because of my openness in exploring spiritual issues, I became a popular teacher. That same openness, though, did not please the preacher who led the church.

"In those lessons you've been giving," he said, "you've talked about the spiritual feeling you get while playing your music at nightclubs."

"That's right," I said.

"And you're still playing those nightclubs?"

"Every chance I get."

"Then I don't see how you can keep teaching Sunday school."

"Not sure I understand, preacher," I said.

"Those two worlds are incompatible. You can't be singing for drunkards on Saturday night and then speaking to God's people on Sunday morning."

"Aren't those drunkards God's people as well?"

"That's not the point. The point is that this church cannot harbor hypocrites."

The truth is that I didn't feel hypocritical in the least. I also didn't feel compelled to defend myself. If anything, I saw the church—supposedly open to all sinners—as hypocritical. At the same time, why argue with the preacher? The best thing was simply to get up and leave.

I missed the services and the fellowship, but I took my dismissal from the Metropolitan Baptist as an opportunity to delve deeper into the mystery of the Holy Spirit. More than ever, I sought to learn about the Lord.

I haunted the Fort Worth Public Library, where I checked out a pile of books on religion. I read about Judaism and Buddhism, but my focus was on the faith in which I'd been raised—the moral lessons of Jesus. I soon learned that there were hundreds of respected scholars who did not take the King James version of the Bible as literal truth. One book, *The Aquarian Gospel of Jesus the Christ,* impacted me as greatly as did *The Power of Positive Thinking.* It took a positive approach to the question of Jesus's whereabouts between, say, the ages of twelve and thirty. *The Aquarian* postulates that the Lord went to India, Tibet, Egypt, and other centers of mystical learning outside Palestine. It was there that he fell in love with a woman but overcame carnal desire in order to demonstrate divine love to all mankind. It was where he discovered—and embraced—the notion of reincarnation.

From the first moment I considered the concept, reincarnation made sense. The old paradigm was just too cruel, just too unchristian, to be believed: If you die in your sin, you spend eternity in hell. How could the compassionate God of mercy ever set up such a system? On the other hand, I was drawn to the idea that you keep coming back till you get it right. Reincarnation seemed merciful and completely Christlike. Jesus got it right the first time around because he was, after all, God incarnate, perfect man. But the rest of us would need several lifetimes to shed our sins and learn the lessons necessary to heal our troubled souls.

Enlightenment was a long process. The goal was beautiful: to achieve a chilled-out state of endless calm and undisturbed grace. I sought that goal.

As my life struggles continued, I found increasing comfort in my relationship to spirit and pure love.

Further proof of miraculous love came with the birth of our third child and first son, Willie Hugh Nelson Jr., born May 21, 1958. We called him Billy. He warmed my heart and had me redouble my commitment to my family.

That commitment had me back out on the Jacksboro Highway, playing whatever beer joints would give me a few bucks. I had the music club territory mapped out—from Waco to Dallas to Fort Worth. And at the better venues, I saw the big-name stars and couldn't help but believe that the songs I was writing were more than suitable for their styles. But how do I get to them?

I listened to all the great sidemen—fiddler Johnny Gimble with Bob Wills, and pedal steel players Jimmy Day with Ray Price and Buddy Emmons with Ernest Tubb. I found some work as a sideman myself. I sat in with whoever would have me. But compared to Gimble, Day, and Emmons, my chops were limited. Leaders weren't begging me to join their bands.

I'd say it was back to the grind, but the grind had never stopped.

If selling encyclopedias and vacuum cleaners led to a dead end, why, I'd find work at a grain warehouse on the north side of the city. When I fell asleep on the job—I'd been up the night before playing music till 3 a.m.—I didn't let my dismissal get me down and got myself hired by a carpet removal service. But that didn't last long either. In between rolling up nasty old shag carpets, I took out too much time writing down the song lyrics floating through my mind. The boss saw that I was distracted and let me go.

I tried to hang on. I found a spot in the band at the Cowtown Hoedown. This was a Saturday night country music show put on at the Majestic Theater, an old downtown movie palace gone to seed. I played guitar in the support band. One week Webb Pierce was the headliner, the next week Bob Luman or Johnny Horton. I was in the background, which was fine with me. The background was a great place for learning, for seeing how the stars—whether Roy Orbison or Faron Young—commanded the stage. The show was broadcast on the radio. And though our salary, ten bucks a show, wasn't much, I was close to the spotlight.

Through the Hoedown, I also got close to the show's producer, Uncle Hank Craig, who worked with two radio stations: KCLE in Cleburne and XEG in Mexico. Like Doc Parker, Uncle Hank was an older man who took an interest in me. He was all heart while, at the same time, all business.

"You got musical talent," he said, "but you also got hustling talent. I say let's put that hustle talent to work."

Uncle Hank's hustle was simple: he had me record a long commercial for XEG, the station operating out of Mexico, that urged aspiring songwriters to send me their half-finished songs and, for the low, low price of just ten dollars, I'd finish the song for them, record it, and send them a disc.

They could have the beginnings of a melody without words, or a few words without melody. Didn't matter. All it took was ten bucks and I'd do the rest. I'd cut the record with professional musicians in just a matter of days.

The response was good. I completed and cut several dozen songs. It was a fun idea, but truthfully, in the culture of XEG, a station that recruited promoters like Uncle Hank, this songwriting ploy was mild. They had ministers hawking baskets of baby chicks, bottles of holy water—hell, they'd sell autographed pictures of Jesus if they could.

It was Uncle Hank who mentioned Pappy Daily, the man down in Houston whose Starday label had previously rejected my songs and charged me to press up copies of my "No Place for Me."

"I don't think Pappy has a high regard for me," I told Uncle Hank.

"Pappy has a high regard for anything that sells. Once I get him to thinking that your songs are going to be big sellers, Pappy will be kissing your ass."

Uncle Hank hooked me up with Pappy, who did, in fact, pay me this time for the recordings of two songs in a Fort Worth studio. I cut my "Man with the Blues" and "The Storm Has Just Begun." The titles tell you all you need to know about my mood.

The 45 single didn't create any excitement, but Uncle Hank was arguing that I had to create that excitement on my own. The songs weren't going to go out and do it by themselves.

"You're an exciting personality, Willie," he insisted, "but you gotta get your ass out there on the big stage. You gotta get unstuck."

Uncle Hank's words hit home. Stuck in the backwaters of Fort Worth, I was ready for any kind of change.

"If you really, truly want to change your circumstances, Willie," said Uncle Hank, "get the hell outta Fort Worth. Fort Worth is for shitkickers. If you want big money, get to a big city. And Houston's the biggest fuckin' city in Texas."

10

DARK NIGHT OF THE SOUL

SEEMED RIGHT. Seemed reasonable. Seemed like the sane thing to do.

I'd done all I could back home in Hill County. I'd played every hole-in-the-wall in and out of Waco. I'd done San Antone, I'd done Dallas, I'd done Fort Worth two goddamn times.

When it came to big places in Texas, Houston was all that was left.

Houston was one vast urban sprawl that went on forever. Houston was all about sticky stinking humidity, chemical plants, and oil refineries, a ring of faceless suburbs.

Houston gave me another bad case of the blues.

I found a little apartment for us in Pasadena, one of those lonely-looking industrial suburbs in the shadow of the ship channel, lined with factories spewing out petrochemical toxins into the stale night air.

From there I went out on my own, going from club to club, wandering up and down the Gulf Freeway, looking for a break. But nothing broke. Nothing was happening. Drinking gave me little consolation. A little consolation was better than none at all.

By then I had already accumulated a large inventory of songs written in the margins of my days and the loneliness of my nights. But in Houston those nights got lonelier. With a wife and three kids at home, I needed money—and I needed it now. Yet this new locale was not yielding immediate results. I was still up against some slow-moving shit. It was during these long dark nights of the soul—driving here, driving there, stopping anywhere and everywhere a wandering minstrel might find work—that I reached even deeper down and found solace in words and melodies that expressed the anguish gnawing at my insides.

When songs fall from the sky—even the polluted midnight sky of Houston—all I can do is catch them before they land. They are mysterious gifts. I know they are born out of experience and genuine grief. I know they are born of uncertainty and fear. I implicitly trust their sentiments. I trust their sincerity. The deepest songs expose vulnerability. They strip me bare and leave me amazed.

Where the hell did they come from?

Did I really write these songs, or am I just a channel chosen by the Holy Spirit to express these feelings?

I really didn't know. I don't remember creating the words.

High school hero

My grandmother meant
the world to me.

In the air force

Doing my best in a Nashville studio

New deejay in town

My first wife, Martha, a good woman with a great spirit

My children with Martha—Lana, Billy, and Susie

Beautiful family portrait of Lana, Billy, Martha, and Susie

Shirley and me, in perfect harmony

Sweet memories of Connie, Amy, and Paula

Willie Dons Tux, Ac[illegible]
As Son's Best Man

The customarily casual Willie Nelson donned a tuxedo last night to be Best Man at his son's wedding.

Nelson's only son, 25-year-old Billy, married Janet E. Caldwell of Joelton at 7:30 yesterday evening at First Baptist Church on Broadway, and just about the entire Nelson clan was in town to celebrate.

Billy H. Nelson is the youngest of the three children born to Willie Nelson and his first wife, Martha Matthews. His oldest sister is Lana, the author of *The Willie Nelson Family Album* and the script writer of the popular *Pancho and Lefty* music video that [illegible] father and Merle Hag[illegible] Billy's

Wedding day for my son Billy. I was proud to be best man.

Sister Bobbie,
the real musician
in the family

Leon Russell, one
of the greatest
entertainers of
our time

Waylon Jennings, Hank Williams Jr., Johnny Cash, and Kris Kristofferson

Annie, love of my life

On the beach in Paia, Hawaii, with Micah, Annie, and Luke

My musical mainstays—from left, Paul English, the late Bee Spears, and Mickey Raphael

Mickey Raphael, a hero of the harmonica and a forever friend *(Danny Clinch)*

The family and crew. I couldn't make it without them.

A crazy crowd—from left, Poodie Locke, my stage manager (in a woman's wig); Owen Wilson, Bo Franks, my daughter Paula; and just below her, Jessica Simpson, Dan Rather, Woody Harrelson; and, on top, director Jay Chandrasekhar

The words just came. I can't remember creating the melodies. The melodies were already there. The songs arrived prepackaged. There was a distinct beginning, middle, and end. In my head, I heard a groove that would drive the rhythm. In my head, I heard the accompanying instruments.

Without trying, I heard everything.

And I heard myself ruminating about the nightlife.

It ain't no good life, but it's my life. I see life as just another scene in this ol' world of broken dreams. Oh, the nightlife, it ain't no good life, but, Lord, it's my life.

Listen to the blues that they're playing. And listen to what the blues are saying. They're saying that nightlife ain't no good life, but it's my life.

While I made those endless loops around the Houston highways, that song grew out of the soil of my soul. It happened because I was living it.

The Night Life.

A few hours or a few days later—I can't remember which—here comes more thoughts, more feelings.

Well, hello there.

I imagine a man, someone like me, who runs into an old girlfriend.

My, it's been a long, long time. How you doing? Me? Well, I guess I'm doing fine. Been so long now, but seems that it was only yesterday.

Gee, ain't it funny how time slips away.

The words of the song seep out of the darkness. They fall from my imagination like tears from my eyes.

How's your new love? Hope he's doin' fine. Heard you told

him you'd love him till the end of time. That's the same thing you told me, seems like just the other day.

Ain't it funny, baby, how time slips away.

On another night—or the same night—I imagine that the rest of the world is asleep. The rest of the world is comprised of normal people with normal jobs. This gal works as a secretary. This guy is an accountant. They go about their nine-to-five lives. They earn their money, they buy their groceries, they raise their children.

They're not crazy.

But what about me?

Why am I crazy?

Crazy, for feeling so lonely, crazy, for feeling so blue.

Why am I imagining a man like me facing the loss of his deepest love?

I know you'd love me as long as you wanted, then someday leave me for somebody new.

Why do I let myself worry, wondering what in the world did I do?

I can't get this man off my mind. His blues are my blues. He's crazy, and so am I.

Crazy, for thinking that my love could hold you.

Crazy for crying, crazy for trying, I'm crazy for loving you.

Is it crazy to think that this song, fallen from the sky, has a haunted beauty that could last forever?

Or is that just my ego speaking?

I hum the melody again. I see how each note is perfectly married to a lyric. Is that marriage of my making? It feels like it is. It feels like it isn't. Putting it together was too easy. I can hardly take credit. Yet who else is around? Nobody but me, driving along the highways of Houston, songs filling up all the space in my head, songs crowding my heart.

A song that says, *Mr. Record Man, I'm looking for a song I heard today. There was someone blue singing 'bout someone who went away. Just like me his heart was yearning for a love that used to be. It's a lonely song about a lonely man like me.*

Am I inventing this character or am I merely writing about myself? How is it possible to step out of myself while, at the same time, delving deeper?

I was driving down the highway with the radio turned on—and a man that I heard singing sounded so blue and all alone.

Who is doing the singing? Who is doing the listening?

As I listen to this lonely song I wonder, could it be—could there be another lonely man like me?

And how could this man lose his loneliness? What's a lonely man to do?

Well, I gotta get drunk and I sure do dread it, 'cause I know just what I'm gonna do—I'll start to spend my money calling everybody honey, and wind up singing the blues.

And I do just that. I live the life I'm singing about in my song.

I gotta get drunk, I can't stay sober. There's a lot of good people in town that'd like to see me holler, see me spend my dollar, and I wouldn't think of letting them down.

I know I'm running into a dead end. Know I'm acting the fool, but that don't stop me.

There's a lot of doctors tell me that I'd better start slowing it down. But there's more old drunks than there are old doctors. So I guess we better have another round.

I'll spend my whole paycheck on some old wreck and, brother, I can name you a few. Well, I gotta get drunk and I sure do dread it 'cause I know just what I'm gonna do.

After the drinking is over, I realize what has to happen next. I realize the next song is one that says, *Turn off the lights, the party's over. They say that, 'All good things must end.' Let's call it a night, the party's over, and tomorrow starts the same thing.*

But the party has hardly been fun. Look at me, I'm almost crying. That don't keep her love from dying. Misery...'cause for me the party's over.

Within an astoundingly short period of time—a week or two—I'd written a suite of songs that reflected my real-life situation. I knew these songs were damn good, but at the same time, I didn't know what to do with them.

In spite of cutting those two tunes back in Fort Worth, I hadn't been able to get through to Pappy Daily here in Houston. All I could do was keep hustling on my own.

There was hardly any method to my hustle. Every time I spotted a decent-size barroom, I'd pull over, walk in with my guitar, and ask for the owner in the hopes of getting hired. Invariably my hopes were dashed.

My hopes were high when I stopped at the Esquire Ballroom

and heard a country band in the middle of rehearsal. Sounded good.

"I'm Willie Nelson," I told the leader.

"Larry Butler. What can I do you for, Willie?"

"Looking for work."

"You a singer?"

"And a picker."

"Afraid we don't need either one."

Feeling a little desperate, I said, "Well, I also write. Fact is, just wrote me a buncha new songs."

"If you're willing to sing 'em, I'm willing to listen."

I sang 'em all—"Night Life," "Funny How Time Slips Away," "Crazy," "Mr. Record Man," "I Gotta Get Drunk," "The Party's Over."

Larry Butler looked stunned.

"What do you think?"

"I think they're great. Very goddamn great."

"Good. 'Cause I'll sell 'em to you. I'll take ten bucks a song."

"You mean I give you ten dollars and I have the right to put my name as the composer of those songs and do whatever the hell I want with them."

"That's right."

"That's insane. You can't do that. Those are hit songs you've written. They could be worth thousands of dollars. You just can't give 'em away."

"I'm not. I'm selling 'em to you."

"Well, I'm not buying. I couldn't do that to you."

"Why? You'd be doing me a favor."

"You'd be cheating yourself, Willie."

"Hell, I can always write more songs. That's not a problem."

"Let's do this. Let me just loan you fifty bucks. You can pay me back by playing in my band. Meanwhile, hold on to those songs."

Whoa. Suddenly I had a musical home in Houston—the Esquire Ballroom—and enough money to keep the family in food and diapers. That single meeting turned things around.

I also had new confidence to go back to Pappy Daily, but Pappy still didn't see me as much of a writer or an artist. When I played him my stuff, he was lukewarm. Because Pappy had launched the career of George Jones by releasing George's big hit "Why Baby Why," I had to respect him. But when it came to scrutinizing my talent, I sure as hell didn't have to believe him.

I was more inclined to believe Paul Buskirk, my old pal who had also relocated to Houston. Paul was a first-rate musician. His opinion mattered. Hearing the same songs I'd played for Pappy, Paul didn't hesitate to say, "Pappy's got his head up his ass. These songs need to be recorded."

"By who?"

"Let me worry about that, Willie."

Paul put his money where his mouth was. Right then and there, he bought two of my tunes—"Family Bible" for fifty dollars and "Night Life" for a hundred and fifty dollars. Before I knew it, he took singer Claude Gray into the studio to cut "Family Bible" with "The Party's Over" on the flip side and convinced Pappy to release it on D Records. It took a while but the single started climbing to the top of the country charts. My name wasn't anywhere on the record, but I was still thrilled. I'd proven I could write a hit record.

Paul had great faith in me. He'd begun a thriving side business—Paul Buskirk School of Guitar—and wanted me to teach there.

"Teach?" I said. "Hell, I need to be taught. I need to go there and take lessons."

"You're better than you think you are, Willie," Paul assured me. "It's a beginner's course. Just stay a chapter ahead of the students and you'll be all right."

"As long as you walk me through that chapter."

Paul did just that. He took the weekend to teach me what had to be taught. Because he was such a fluent musician himself, able to play beautifully in any style, he was a fluent teacher. He gave his lessons a flow that I, in turn, was able to impart to my students. It was another one of those unexpected blessings. And, like at my Sunday school lessons back at the Metropolitan Baptist Church in Fort Worth, I found myself learning far more than I taught.

In Houston, I also learned that my days as an early morning deejay were numbered. I'd found a job at a little station that gave me the 5 a.m. to 10 a.m. shift. But my late nights at the Esquire Ballroom took their toll, and after showing up late more than once, I was unceremoniously canned.

But thank God for Paul Buskirk. Paul always had a plan.

"I'm taking you to Gold Star Studios," he said, "and we're cutting 'Night Life.'"

"With Claude Gray singing?" I asked.

"Hell, no. With *you* singing, Willie. That song came out of your heart. No one can sing it like you."

That was music to my ears.

Gold Star was the best studio in Houston. George Jones had recorded there. It was also where the Big Bopper had cut his big hit "Chantilly Lace." Gold Star was home to the great bluesman Lightnin' Hopkins.

The session was relaxed, mainly because Paul was in charge. He wrote the arrangement, picked the musicians, and, along with me, played lead guitar. As far as producing my vocals, he had little to say beyond, "It's your story, Willie. Sing it the way you feel it."

At the end of the day, we were sure we had a hit.

"When Pappy Daily hears it, he'll love it," said Paul.

"I hate it," said Pappy Daily when we played it for him the next day. "That ain't no country song. It's a blues song, something for Lightnin' Hopkins. No country station is ever gonna play it."

"You're wrong," said Paul.

"Wrong or right," said Pappy, "I got Willie under contract—and I sure as hell ain't releasing this."

Not to be discouraged, Paul put the song out on another label, Rx, using the name "Paul Buskirk and the Little Men featuring Hugh Nelson."

Don't think we pressed up more than a few hundred copies. Didn't get the distribution we had hoped for. A few deejays, like Uncle Hank at XEG in Mexico, gave it a spin, but it soon disappeared.

"It's a goddamn good song," Paul kept insisting. "One day it'll find an audience. One day it'll become a standard."

In 1960, I had no way of knowing that Paul was prophetic. All I knew was that even after having fucked around Houston—playing the Esquire and deejaying and working with D Records—I was still broke as the Ten Commandments.

I loved my wife, Martha. I loved my beautiful babies, Lana, Susie, and Willie Jr. I wanted to do right by them. I wanted to do right by myself. I wanted to get out of the financial doldrums. I wanted to make a living singing and picking and writing. And I didn't want to bullshit myself. I wanted to accept the cold reality of who I was and what I could do.

What was that reality?

As a singer, I had a style, but not everyone liked that style. I liked my style, but I knew my style was quirky. Besides, I didn't have a big booming voice like Johnny Bush. In traditional terms, I couldn't consider myself a great singer.

Nor was I a great guitarist like Paul Buskirk. I could make my way around the guitar. I could accompany myself and sculpt solos that made sense. My playing had feeling and expressed my soul. But my playing was limited.

When I looked at my writing, though, I saw something I genuinely liked and admired. These recent songs I had written compared favorably with anything I heard on the radio. The fact that one—"Family Bible"—had sold nationwide confirmed my confidence.

I was a good writer, and there was no reason I couldn't compete in the arena where the best writers worked.

That was Nashville, Tennessee.

Ever since I'd met Mae Axton, Nashville had been on my mind. I'd postponed going there because... well, I was scared. Scared of not making it there, of not measuring up.

The fear wasn't entirely gone, but in 1960, at about the time I turned twenty-seven, in the battle between fear and faith, faith finally took the lead.

11

THE STORE

NASHVILLE LIKED TO BILL ITSELF as Music City. I just saw it as the Store. The Store is where you shop. If you're a music producer, you shop for songs at the Store. I needed to get the Store to stock my merchandise. I thought my merchandise was good, so that should have been a simple task.

It wasn't.

Nashville was a struggle. There were good moments, but it was an uphill battle. I did get my merchandise in the Store, but that wasn't enough to get me over. With all the music coming out of Nashville—all the great musicians and legendary producers—you'd think I'd be a natural fit. I never was. For that I don't blame Nashville. I blame my own peculiar nature.

Knowing it might take a while to get going, I took Martha and the kids to Waco to stay with her folks before heading out to Tennessee in my broken-down 1950 Buick.

Soon as I hit Nashville and turned the corner on Music Row, where the big record companies had their offices and studios, the Buick laid down and died. That should have told me something.

I didn't know what to do or where to go, and I only had enough money for one night at a fleabag hotel. So you can guess where I stayed. Next morning I was sitting in a coffee shop when who should walk in but Billy Walker, my pal from Texas.

"Willie! Good to see you, buddy. What are you doing in town?"

"Same as everyone else. Selling songs."

"Sold any yet?"

I laughed. "Just got here."

"Well, lemme see if I can help you."

Billy's words nearly brought tears to my eyes. Like Paul Buskirk, Billy turned out to be one of those guardian angels disguised as a musician.

He had gone from *Ozark Jubilee* to Nashville, where he'd been hired by *The Grand Ole Opry.*

"They don't pay shit," he said. "But the *Opry* connects you with everyone in town. Through the *Opry* I got me a deejay job at WSM doing a noontime show. There's work here, and with your talent you'll find something soon."

What I did find was a loyal and loving friend in Billy Walker. He and his wife let me stay in their home for three months. Billy personally took me to all the studios and introduced me to all the producers. Some took the time to listen to my songs; others didn't. I couldn't thank Billy enough. Either way, though, no one bought a goddamn thing.

"I can see by how you present yourself that you can sell," said Billy. "If the songs aren't selling, maybe there's other stuff you can sell."

"I've sold vacuum cleaners, I've sold sewing machines, I've sold encyclopedias," I said.

"If you sold that stuff in Texas, no reason why you can't sell 'em in Nashville. I know some people."

Those people were looking for encyclopedia salesmen.

So there I was again, out on the streets, going house to house, sticking my foot in doors before they closed on me, barely avoiding physical attacks by angry dogs and verbal attacks by angry housewives who didn't want to hear my pitch. My pitch wasn't all that great because my heart wasn't into selling encyclopedias. My heart was into selling these songs that were still pouring outta me.

My heart was warmed by the arrival of Martha and the kids. But the warmth didn't last for long. All we could afford was a nasty little trailer at Dunn's Trailer Court that sat between a used car lot and a cemetery. Rent was twenty-five dollars a week. My salesman's commissions weren't nearly that much. It was Martha who saved the day, Martha who got a waitress job at the Hitching Post. The owner was so impressed that he soon made her manager. That gave her the flexibility to find a second job, waiting tables at the Wagon Wheel. Without a doubt it was Martha who kept us afloat.

I was grateful for this hardworking woman, but I was also humiliated. My family's living conditions had never been worse. I was unemployed and, for all the ambition and courage it had taken to move to Nashville, I still had nothing to show for it.

It was small comfort that other Nashville writers had started out in this same trailer park. Hank Cochran had lived there, and so had Roger Miller, who would later immortalize the dump in his song "King of the Road."

Hank and Roger were two of the tunesmiths I met hanging out at Tootsie's Orchid Lounge. Tootsie's was across the alley from the Ryman Auditorium, home of the Grand Ole Opry, the high church of country music. Tootsie knew everyone, including all the stars from the Opry. But Tootsie had a heart for the everyday folks like me who had come to Nashville with a pocketful of dreams. She was our mother hen—patient, kind, and always encouraging. Wasn't easy mothering a herd of pickers and writers who were inclined to drown their sorrows in booze.

The more I drank, the further I fell into the depths of despair and jealousy. Even though I might go off with a willing woman, I couldn't stand the idea of Martha being with another man. I lived with a double standard: it was okay for me to cheat, but not Martha, who was hauling in good tips at the Hitching Post, right across the street from the Orchid Lounge. To her credit, Martha didn't put up with my hypocrisy. If she wanted to drink, she drank. If she fancied another man, that was her business. Our fights were brutal. One time she bit my index finger to the bone. I worried about what that would do to my picking. Took weeks for me to regain my guitar chops. Martha knew how to hurt me, and vice versa. After a knock-down, drag-out battle, she'd run out and leave me with the kids for a couple of days, or I'd do the same to her. This went on for years.

I tried to hold on to those good affirmations of positive thinking. But given enough hard drinking, even the most faithful can fall. And when a cold front hit Nashville that winter, I sat at the bar at Tootsie's and gazed out the window, watching the drifting snow, feeling as low as low can be. My soul was frozen over. The warm sunshine of hope was a million miles away.

I didn't know how long I could go on in Nashville. I still hadn't found a way to get my songs in the Store. And even though I had found good pals like Roger and Hank and deejays Grant Turner and Ralph Emery, I felt like I was sliding down a slippery slope.

You can bet I'd been downing big quantities of whiskey and wine and beer. I was no longer in my right mind. I was in my who-gives-a-fuck mind. I was out of my mind. I got up from the barstool and walked out into the cold. I didn't have a heavy coat, just a denim jacket, but the freezing temperature didn't bother me. The chilling wind didn't bother me. The snowfall didn't bother me. Nothing fuckin' bothered me.

The city was still. Hardly any traffic. No one on the street except me. A weird peace came over me as I walked off the sidewalk into the middle of the street, where—don't ask me why—I decided to lie down and rest.

Right then and there, I lay on my back, eyes wide open, watching the snowflakes fall on my head.

I considered the possibility that a car might well roll over me. I guess I must have been okay with that possibility because, for at least ten minutes, I didn't move.

Maybe I knew that, given the stormy conditions, traffic was so light that I would survive.

Or maybe I didn't know that.

Maybe I was looking for an out.

Or maybe I was just taking a break. Or a chance.

It's tough to know exactly what I was up to. I was drunk, and, as a rule, drunks do crazy shit.

Under the craziness, though, there had to be a design. Or a dare.

I can't tell you that I was trying to commit suicide, because I wasn't. In those days, I usually packed a pistol. In my young and stupid macho mind, I thought that's what real men did. If I were really interested in ending it all, I could have shot myself in the head. But that thought did not cross my mind.

Instead, it was just a matter of reclining in the middle of the street on a snowy night in Nashville.

I might have written a song about it, but I didn't. After I lay there awhile, I simply got up, shook off the snow, and strolled back into Tootsie's.

No one had seen what I had done.

"Hey, Willie," said one of the regulars. "What the hell were you doing out there in the cold?"

"Just needed a bit of fresh air," I said.

"Looks like you can use a drink. Can I buy you one?"

"Sure thing," I said. "Much obliged."

The world took a turn, as it always will, and a week later I was back at Tootsie's. In the wake of the storm that I'd weathered, I'd found a certain calm. I brought along my guitar and welcomed what songwriters called a pulling. That's when we trot out our songs and play 'em for each other. The mood was a mix of friendly competition and brotherly support. You might have to endure a few cutting remarks, but if your song was good, you'd be encouraged. It was hard for your song not to sound good when you were jamming with Jimmy Day and Buddy Emmons, the great steel guitarists who were regulars at Tootsie's.

The songwriters included gifted guys like Hank Cochran, Harlan Howard, Mel Tillis, and Roger Miller. I felt lucky to be in their company.

Hank Cochran, who was actually selling songs when I wasn't, treated me like I was already a winner.

"You'll make money at this, Willie," he told me at one of the pullings. "You're too good not to."

"Appreciate the kind words, Hank," I said, "but I'm feeling like I'm going nowhere fast."

"That's 'cause you're going to the wrong places. You need to come with me."

"And where might you be going?" I asked.

"Goodlettsville."

"What's there?"

"Pamper Music."

"And what's that?"

"Music publishing firm where I'm the top writer and top song plugger. The head honcho, Hal Smith, has an ear. His business partner is Ray Price. Hal's gonna like your stuff. I guaran-goddamn-tee it."

Few days later Hank drove me out to Goodlettsville, twenty miles outside Nashville, to play my songs for Smith. I trotted out my best stuff—"Night Life," "Crazy," "Funny How Time Slips Away."

"Sounds good," was all Smith said. "Let me get back to you."

Hank drove us back to the trailer park.

"What do you think?" I asked.

"I'm thinking only positive thoughts, Willie. I'm thinking that Hal's too smart not to offer you a writer's deal."

Wasn't twenty-four hours later that Hank came back to the trailer park to tell me the news himself.

"You're hired," he said. "How does fifty bucks a week sound?"

Sounded great. My first job as a professional songwriter. It would take me years to learn that it was Hank Cochran, not Hal Smith, who really gave me the break. When Hal had told Hank that he couldn't afford another staff writer, Hank had said, "Instead of giving me that fifty dollar a week raise you offered last week, apply it to Willie's salary."

Hank turned out to be another guardian angel. This was especially beautiful because it was unexpected. I didn't expect generosity like that from a killer competitor like Hank. His song-plugging exploits were legendary.

For example, if Burl Ives was coming to Nashville to listen to the latest compositions by the city's leading tunesmiths, Hank would position himself to be last in line. After six or seven writers would display their wares, Hank would barrage Burl with his full catalog.

"If you don't like this one," he'd say, "I got another one even better."

Hank would keep going until Burl agreed to cut at least one of his songs. Getting last licks usually assured him of a sale. Or if Burl was reluctant to commit that evening, he'd find Hank waiting for him in the hotel coffee shop the next morning with a new set of songs.

Hank was always selling—cornering artists backstage at concerts, showing up at their homes uninvited, popping up at radio stations where the artists were promoting their concerts. The man was unrelenting.

Yet the man could not have been kinder and more helpful in pushing me into the position of full-time songwriter. Part of his motive was pure generosity, but another was that he saw in me a worthy songwriting partner.

"Together," he said, "we can make ourselves some real money."

The fifty bucks a week salary meant I could move the family out to a decent place in Goodlettsville, close to the Pamper Music offices. This was a whole new world for me—actually going to a nine-to-five where my only job was to write songs. It felt strange. That's 'cause I'd always written on the fly, while driving the car in the middle of the night, while walking the dog in the middle of the morning, while sitting by the side of a creek and daydreaming about nothing in particular. These songs came when they came.

"No pressure," Hank assured me when I met him at the publishing company on Two Mile Pike. "We'll just hang out in the writers' room and see what happens."

The offices were modest. Before we got started, Hank would spend an hour or two calling around town to see who needed material.

At the start of the sixties, the two most powerful men in Nashville music were Owen Bradley, a piano player and head producer at Decca, and Chet Atkins, a world-class guitarist and head producer at RCA. Between the two of them, they had sculpted the Nashville sound. The idea was simple: to sweeten up country music with strings and background singers and make it more palatable to the masses. Atkins and Bradley, both whizzes in the studio, had a mandate from their bosses to make sure their music crossed over from a narrow country market to the broad mainstream. Big productions were in. Songs like Marty Robbins's "El Paso" and Ferlin Husky's "Wings of a Dove" were topping the charts—not to mention Elvis's "Are You Lonesome Tonight?"

"Don't worry 'bout what other writers are writing," said Hank. "We don't need to copy no one. We got our style. In our own way, we got something to say."

But what *did* I have to say?

I'd never asked myself that question before. As a writer, I'd never been self-conscious. Starting out as a kid writing poems, I never worried about when the words would make an appearance. Now, though, as Hank showed me the bare-bones writers' room—a converted garage with no phone, two desks, two chairs, and an old portable tape recorder—I realized this was creativity on demand. This was something different.

First few days found me a little uneasy. I had my guitar, a pencil, and a blank notebook. Hank might throw out an idea, hoping it would spark something in me. When that didn't work, he might tell me a joke, or I might tell him one, hoping that joking would lead to some kind of song. It didn't.

Hank didn't seem concerned. And one afternoon, after we had just sat around throwing the bull, he said, "I'm going to the office to make a few calls. You work on something by yourself."

Work on what? My mind was blank. All I could do was look around and say, "Hello, walls."

That was probably a stupid way to start a song, but what the hell? It was better than nothing.

"Hello, walls," I kept singing to myself. "How'd things go for you today?"

But where was the story? I needed a story. What was I going to say to the walls?

"Don't you miss her since she up and walked away?"

That was it. That's all I needed. I was up and running.

"I'll bet you dread to spend another lonely night with me. But lonely walls, I'll keep you company."

Well, hell: if I could talk to the walls, I could sure as shit talk to the window.

"Hello, window. I see you're still here. Aren't you lonely since our darling disappeared? Is that a teardrop in the corner of your pane? Now don't you try to tell me that it's rain."

And if I addressed the walls and the window, what about the ceiling?

"Hello, ceiling. I'm gonna stare at you awhile. You know I can't sleep so won't you bear with me awhile?"

Basically, that was it. Sitting in that garage room, all I had to do was deal with what was in front of me—the walls, window, and ceiling. I just had to look around and suddenly the song was there.

By the time Hank came back from his phone call, I'd found a little harmony to carry the lyrics.

"Come up with anything?" he asked.

"Came up with something pretty silly," I said, "but maybe it's worth a listen."

Hank listened to me singing it and said, "It's worth a fuckin' fortune. Willie, my friend, you just wrote a hit."

12

HELLO, HITS

In 1961, Faron Young's record of "Hello Walls" went to number one on the country charts and sold two million copies. That's when my world turned upside down.

Before the record came out, I was still barely getting by. When Faron heard the song, he said, "This thing's gonna make us both a bunch of money. Lemme loan you five hundred bucks to tide you over."

Few months later my first royalty check was $3,000. I couldn't believe it. Like a bat outta hell, I took off for Tootsie's, where Faron was holding down the fort, doing some heavy drinking with his cronies. I ran up, kissed him on the mouth, and tried to put five crisp hundred-dollar bills in his hand. He wouldn't take it.

"Hell, Willie," said Faron. "I don't need your money. I hear you bought some calves. When one of 'em gets good and fat, I'll take one."

Few weeks later we were back at Tootsie's when Faron

saw me and said, "How's my fat calf coming, Willie? Must be at least four, five hundred pounds by now." I laughed, offered him the $500 again, but he still refused to take it.

Years passed. I was playing a rodeo in Austin when they auctioned off a bull. My son Billy bought it but didn't have the cash, so I wound up paying the $15,000. I loaded it in a trailer and sent it to Faron's office in Nashville. He went out to the driveway and found a registered two-thousand-pound prize Seminole bull with a note that said, "Here's that calf I owe you." Faron took the bull out to pasture, where he and his partner Jimmy C. Newman, a star of the Grand Ole Opry, used it for breeding for years.

Tootsie's was the launching pad for all kinds of grand connections. One night I spotted Charlie Dick. He was Patsy Cline's husband and manager. I had with me a copy of "Night Life" that I'd cut with Paul Buskirk in Houston. I put it on the jukebox, cranked up the volume, and asked Charlie if he wouldn't mind listening.

"I like it," said Charlie. "It's not right for Patsy. But what else you got?"

I had a rough demo of "Crazy."

"Would you consider a song called 'Crazy'?"

"Hell, I'd consider anything. Long as it's a hit."

I put on "Crazy."

Charlie listened carefully. Couldn't tell by the serious expression on his face whether he loved it or hated it.

"I love it," he said. "Let's go."

"Where we going?"

"To the house. Gonna play it for Patsy. Come on."

"It's one a.m., Charlie. Patsy's probably asleep."

"Well, we'll wake her up. She has to hear this song."

When we got to the house, I didn't want to go in. I'd never met Patsy Cline and didn't want to disturb her. I waited out in the car.

But Patsy, who was a sweetheart, wouldn't have it. After Charlie woke her up and said he had a hit song she had to hear—and that the songwriter was waiting in the car—she came out to get me.

The three of us—me, Charlie, and Patsy—listened to it on the phonograph in their den.

"Glad you woke me up," Patsy told Charlie. "Glad you wrote this song," Patsy told me. "I'm recording it."

I wasn't at the session, but from what I heard, it almost didn't happen. Patsy was so taken with the way I'd sung the song that she tried to follow my phrasing. No one should try to follow my phrasing. My phrasing is peculiar to me. I'll lay back on the beat or jump ahead. I'm always doing something funny with time because, to me, time is a flexible thing. I believe in taking my time. When it comes to singing a song, I've got all the time in the world.

Patsy's producer, the great Owen Bradley at Decca, was losing patience with her.

"Screw Willie Nelson and his screwy sense of meter," Owen was said to say. "Forget how Willie sings it. You sing it your way."

"But it's his song," Patsy protested.

"Okay, but now it's time to make it *your* song."

Patsy did just that. Her version of "Crazy" became one of the best-selling country songs of all time. Of all the versions of my songs covered by other artists, it's my favorite. She understood the lyrics on the deepest possible level. She sang it with delicacy, soul, and perfect diction. She didn't overdo it or underdo it. Patsy did the song proud. She did me proud. I'm forever grateful for what I consider a perfect rendition.

I kept hearing about the originality of "Crazy." Industry people were saying that they'd never heard a song like it. The truth is that, while the lyrics are highly unusual, I actually borrowed the first few notes of the song from Floyd Tillman's "I Gotta Have My Baby Back." It wasn't intentional. Must have been unconscious. When I compared the two tunes, though, it was obvious. I didn't worry about it, though, 'cause I knew Floyd didn't care. Good songwriters realize that a little borrowing now and then is part of the process. As time went on, I was flattered when other writers borrowed from me. Far as I'm concerned, all the notes are free.

After "Crazy" hit, so did Billy Walker's version of "Funny How Time Slips Away." I was also thrilled when Ray Price—co-owner of Pamper Music and my publishing boss—thought so highly of "Night Life" that he recorded it himself. To my ears, Ray Price has the most comforting voice in country music. Like Patsy, he has unerring taste. There's never too much emotion or too little. Ray Price gets it right every time.

So just like that, in the course of a year, I had four songs on the top-twenty country chart. To make matters sweeter, two of those songs—"Hello Walls" and "Crazy"—also crossed over to the pop charts.

In short, I was in the money. It felt great to be able to move the family into a nicer house and not worry about putting food on the table. Felt even greater to have the certain knowledge that my songs were selling like hotcakes.

If I were a normal person, I'd have settled down and simply written more songs, since all the producers were knocking at my door. A normal person would start saving his money. A normal person would realize that, given the fickle nature of the music business, his hot streak could turn cold any second.

But being far from normal, I did something that took everyone by surprise. I went to work in Ray Price's band, the same Ray Price who co-owned Pamper Music and had sung the hell outta "Night Life."

Ray called me and said, "My bass player, Donny Young, up and quit on me. Can you play bass, Willie?"

Donny Young—who'd later rename himself Johnny Paycheck—had been one of the anchors of Ray's band.

I laughed and said, "Can't everyone play bass, Ray?"

I got the job, but the truth was that I'd never played bass before in my life.

Because Ray had been in Hank Williams's band—and took over the band when Hank died in 1953—I felt like part of history. Hank Williams's Drifting Cowboys had become Ray's Cherokee Cowboys. It was the same band that, at one time or another, featured Buddy Emmons, Darrell McCall, Jimmy Day, and Roger Miller. So when Ray hired me at twenty-five dollars a day, I was thrilled.

I took my royalty money, bought Ray's 1959 midnight-black Caddie, and gave it to Martha, hoping that'd make her happy. I was happy to inherit Donny Young's bass and his pink jacket covered with rhinestones.

On the way from Nashville to our first gig in Winchester, Virginia—Patsy Cline's hometown—Jimmy Day taught me to play the instrument. He showed me that the top four strings on a bass are the same as on a guitar. He also went over Ray's songs, which were mostly simple three-chord structures. Jimmy got me through. Years later, when I asked Ray if he had known I couldn't play bass when he hired me, all he said was, "Yup."

I loved being a Cherokee Cowboy onstage, backing up Ray, who, like Bob Wills, was the ultimate pro, playing one crowd-pleaser after another.

For my part, I pleased my fellow Cherokee Cowboys by going hog wild with my songwriting money. Heavy drinking had a lot to do with it. So did my I-don't-give-a-fuck attitude. When we checked into a hotel, I'd get the penthouse or presidential suite and have the boys up for an all-night party. I did that for weeks on end until my royalty money ran out.

"I think you might want to be a little more prudent with your earnings," Ray said to me.

"I'm not sure what that word means."

"Well, son," he said, "you better find out."

I'll tell you just what a great friend Ray turned out to be. When it was time to record in the studio, he didn't need me. He hired the best bass players in Nashville. But he had me come along anyway so I could get some union pay. He gave me a guitar with no amp, which meant no one heard me. I'd play into an ashtray and pretend it was a mic.

Good as everything was going with Ray, that's how bad things were going with Martha. She and I had been washed up for longer than I'd been ready to admit. One of the worst moments happened at Tootsie's. We'd both been doing some heavy drinking that led to heavy accusations about our past behaviors. Can't remember the exact details, but it wouldn't be far off to say that Martha had found out about some two-timing on my part and wanted the world to know about it. She was screaming, I was screaming for her to stop screaming, and when she finally did stop screaming, she started into throwing whiskey glasses at me. I ducked, but my pal Hank Cochran didn't. Shattered glass cut his face. I took him to the hospital, where, still plastered, I wouldn't let the doctor on duty treat him. I insisted that no respectable doctor would be working the graveyard shift at the county hospital.

"Shut the fuck up, Willie," said Hank, "and let this man sew me up before I bleed to death."

The death of my marriage to Martha finally came in 1962. We'd been together ten turbulent years. Even when I knew we couldn't make it any longer, I gave the woman all the credit in the world for putting up with my sorry ass. Martha was a firebrand, an indomitable spirit, a beautiful woman who, in spite of my shenanigans, stood tall and proud. But all her good qualities didn't keep me from falling for another beautiful woman. This lady had the further advantage of being a singer. She heard me so deeply and harmonized with me so closely that I just knew we were meant to be together. First we made music together and then we made love. The only complication, of course, was that we were still married to other people.

Shirley Collie, wife to my deejay friend Bif Collie, was well-known in the country field as a fine lead and harmony singer. She was also a great yodeler. She'd played on *The Philip Morris Country Music Show* with Red Foley and had performed with Grady Martin, the great guitarist.

I had run into Shirley and Bif on the road. That was in the late fifties. Then our relationship was renewed in 1961, when Hank Cochran tried to get her to sing a few of my songs. That happened at a session at Radio Recorders, a studio in L.A. where I was cutting my first sides as an artist for Liberty Records.

Hank had convinced Liberty's A&R man for country music, Joe Allison, that I was the next big thing. Liberty was a strong label with an interest in a wide variety of styles. Everyone from Jan and Dean to Julie London to Vikki Carr to the Chipmunks was on Liberty. And Bob Wills was on Liberty. That's all I really needed to know. When they offered me a contract as a country artist, I jumped at the chance.

Allison knew that there wasn't any way I was gonna change my singing style—and that was fine by him. He understood me. He just wanted me to sing my own songs in my own way.

It was while I was cutting "Mr. Record Man," the song I had written during my dark days in Houston, that Hank Cochran brought over Shirley and Bif. "Mr. Record Man" was my first single for Liberty. It didn't set any sales records, but it got me decent airplay.

Meanwhile, I was still on the road with Ray Price and the Cherokee Cowboys, and from time to time, Shirley and Bif would come to the gigs. No doubt Shirley and I were impressed with each other. She was a pretty-as-a-picture redhead who could not only sing like an angel but wrote beautifully and even played a mean bass.

We got involved both romantically and musically at about the same time. Joe Allison thought it would be a good idea for us to record some duets. They gave us an excuse—and an occasion—to spend lots of time in each other's company. Our voices fit together perfectly. So did our bodies.

Hank Cochran wrote a song, the first we cut, called "Willingly." It told our story. The song said that we both knew it was wrong—"to someone else we both belonged." Yet willingly we fell in love. Shirley sang, "Willingly, I fell, although I knew." And I sang, "Sweetheart, I knew the same as you." But that "knew" made no difference. We were willing to take the risk.

The B side was a song of mine, another duet with Shirley: "Chain of Love," a pretty good description of what was going on in our messed-up marriages.

"When the chain of love is broken," we sang in close harmony, "its pieces scattered all around, in the hasty search for reason, sometimes a link cannot be found."

As if I were speaking to Martha, and Shirley were addressing Bif, we sang, "I say you're wrong to say it's my fault, you saw it coming all along. We've lost a link of understanding. Our chain of love cannot last long."

It didn't last long.

Martha did what any self-respecting woman would do. She headed out to Vegas in Ray Price's big black Cadillac and got a divorce.

"This chain of love we've pieced together," Shirley and I kept singing, "with the links of understanding gone. The link of patience must work overtime—our chain of love cannot last long."

I wanted to be understanding. I wanted to be patient.

But more than anything, I wanted to be with Shirley. I wanted to move in a different direction.

I had never met another singer who could follow my strange phrasing so closely. If it worked in music, I was also sure it would work in life.

"I believe we're meant to be together," I told Shirley.

"I believe it, too," she said.

"You gotta understand that I'm a country boy from Abbott, Texas."

"And I'm a country girl from Chillicothe, Missouri."

"I like this singing and picking just fine," I said, "but one day soon I might retire to a farm and leave it all behind. What do you say about that?"

"I say I'll be right by your side."

13

THE OFFENDERS

In 1963, I turned thirty. I had me a new wife, had me three great kids, had me a fiery former wife, and had me a lucrative career as a songwriter and a half-assed career as a recording artist. I was feeling feisty. I was doing what I wanted to do, and no one could tell me to do otherwise.

For a short while, Shirley traveled with me and the Cherokee Cowboys. But seeing how she and I made beautiful music together, we decided to go out on our own. Jimmy Day, a poet of the steel guitar, left Ray Price to join us. I informally referred to our little trio as the Offenders because we weren't in the least concerned about offending anyone with the music we played.

Our shows would start off with Shirley. She'd sing songs like "Penny for Your Thoughts" and then yodel her heart out on "Bet My Heart I Love You." I'd come out and sing whatever songs I'd been working on. Didn't matter to me whether the audience knew 'em or not. I was hell-bent on trying out new material. Of course this went against what I'd learned from Bob Wills and Ray Price. Their mantra was always, "Play the familiar. Play what folks wanna hear."

Well, I was going through one of my rebellious periods. I had this royalty money from my songs. I had a recording contract. And even though my first album on Liberty—*...And Then I Wrote*—was far from a sensational seller, I had all the confidence in the world. Shirley and I recorded more duets, songs like "You Dream about Me (and I'll Dream about You)" and "Is This My Destiny" that reflected our newfound love. Our harmony was so close there wasn't the slightest spec of daylight between her voice and mine.

During our shows I'd break into songs like "Columbus Stockade Blues," a jazzy up-tempo number too fast for the dancers. I'd experiment on songs like "Second Fiddle" and my own "Half a Man."

Granted, "Half a Man" was one of my stranger songs. It's about a guy who considers what it would be like, in the name of lost love, to start losing body parts.

"If I only had one arm to hold her, better yet I had none at all," I wrote, "'cause then I wouldn't have two arms that ache for you.

"If I only had one ear to listen to the lies that she told me, then I'd more closely resemble the half a man that she made of me."

I take it even further, imagining what it would be like to have only one eye, and then only one leg to stand on, and then a heart that turns to ashes. All this in pursuit of painting a portrait of "Half a Man."

This wasn't exactly a song that made you want to dance. But the Offenders wasn't a group looking to please the public. Instead, I was looking to experiment. I had these two wonderful elements—Jimmy Day's brilliant steel guitar and Shirley's fabulous voice—to weave together with my own picking and singing. When I sang straight country like Hank Williams's "There'll Be No Teardrops Tonight" or tried-and-true pop standards like "Am I Blue," Jimmy and Shirley added the kind of sensitive accompaniment that made me smile.

When it came to my own compositions, I was also trying for sensitivity. For example, I wrote something I called "Home Motel." It was another study in despair about a guy who finds himself in "a crumbling last resort," where "the rooms are all shambled, things are scattered on the floor," a place to "hang a neon sign with letters big and blue—'Home Motel on Lost Love Avenue.' "

It was a thrill to play the song live. Jimmy Day had his steel guitar weeping just enough, Shirley added just a touch of harmony, and I got to sing my blues the way the blues should be sung: no frills.

Yet when I brought the song into the Liberty studios, the producers felt compelled to put on the frills.

"Aren't you worried you're burying the soul of the song?" I asked.

"More worried about the song not selling," was the usual answer.

That meant putting on sweet strings or a chorus of light-sounding singers. The idea was to sculpt an acceptable sound—something easy to digest.

I didn't argue. In those days, big productions like Johnny Cash's "Ring of Fire" were huge hits. I loved Johnny and, even though his song was heavily augmented by horns and harmony voices, I could hear his soul. So if it worked for Johnny, maybe it'd work for me. I went along with the program.

"These arrangements take your songs to a higher level," the producers argued.

I was skeptical of that kind of thinking. I didn't really think I had to be brought up to a higher level. I was perfectly fine where I was. At the same time, I had this thing inside me called ambition.

Being a best-selling writer was fine, but I wanted more. I wanted to be a best-selling artist. The producers claimed to know the public taste. If that were the case, fine. I let them fool with my music and adapt it to that taste. The problem, though, was that even with all those augmentations, my stuff for Liberty still didn't sell.

I took my frustrations to the boxing ring. I found a fight instructor, put on the gloves, and discovered that, as a pugilist, I could hold my own. Disciplined training did me a world of good. I needed a healthy outlet for my aggressions. After mixing it up with a strong opponent, I often saw that my mind began to clear. After a vigorous fight, I was able to address some of the big questions that had been haunting me. The biggest question was also the simplest:

What did I really want to do with my life?

"I want to get off the road," I told Shirley. "I want to settle down somewhere peaceful."

"I'm all for it, sweetheart," she said.

"Let's find us a nice piece of land. Let's get back to the land."

Shirley smiled and gave me all the support I needed.

I had great love for the land. It'd been too long since I felt the connection with the natural world. And since I had enough money, why not look for a spread to call my own? Why not grow vegetables and raise animals and return to the simple pleasures of watching golden sunsets in the evening and radiant sunrises in the morning?

Before that happened, I stayed on the road with Shirley and Jimmy Day. Along the way I picked up Johnny Bush, the great singer, who made some gigs with us. For a while we settled in Fort Worth, still home to my dad and sister Bobbie. That's where I rekindled my friendship with Paul English, who'd developed his drumming skills. I'd go out on small tours now and then, bringing along whatever musicians were available. In addition to me and Shirley, I might be lucky enough to get Paul Buskirk on guitar or Ray Odom on fiddle.

I had something of a circuit going. I could count on certain clubs in Texas, California, and Arizona. I even started a booking agency—Willie Nelson Talent—with my new producer at Liberty Records, Tommy Allsup. The idea was to build up a roster of artists, book them, and pocket a nice commission. Ever since, as a kid, I'd booked Bob Wills back in Hill County, I'd entertained notions of myself as a promoter. Sometimes my promotions had paid off, but more often than not they hadn't. Willie Nelson Talent, as an ongoing enterprise, didn't last long.

Neither did our stay in Fort Worth. I kept running out to

L.A., where Liberty kept churning out my singles and albums. The critical praise was strong, but the public's reception remained lukewarm. It was my live performances, whether at the Longhorn Ballroom in Dallas or the Golden Nugget in Vegas, that helped me cultivate a small but loyal following. I also encountered some supersharp hustler/promoters, like Geno McCoslin in Texas—guys I could always count on to find me good-paying gigs.

Any way you looked at it, it was a hustle. I realized that everyone's gotta hustle to make ends meet, but there were also times in my life when hustling became a hassle.

Such a time was the winter of 1963.

Enough touring.

Enough recording.

Enough hustling.

Shirley agreed that we'd be happier settling down in the country. So when I found seventeen acres of prime land just north of Goodlettsville some thirty miles east of Nashville, I gave it serious consideration. The town was called Ridgetop and it was up toward the Kentucky/Tennessee border on Greer Road. I'd be close enough to Music City to keep my toe in the business, but far enough away to maintain a healthy distance.

In addition to a nice expanse of land, the place included a big single-story ranch house. It was set on a hill with groves of cedar, pine, and weeping willow trees. Underfoot, that fertile Tennessee red clay soil was good for growing all sorts of crops. One long walk around the property convinced me to claim it for my own.

"I'm gonna buy it," I told Shirley.

"You won't be sorry."

I wasn't—at least not for a while.

Not long after we signed the papers, I was at an airport headed to Dallas when the news came on the radio. It was November 22, and President Kennedy, our hope for the future, had been shot down in cold blood.

It was the end of an era, a time for grieving and deep reflection.

14

FARM LIFE

I FOUND THAT LIFE ON THE land afforded me just the sort of reflection I needed. I loved observing Mother Nature up close and personal. And I especially loved her creatures. The pigs were among my favorites. They're fascinating, funny, and smart. Man, I could watch pigs play around all day long. And for a while I did just that.

Johnny Bush, a country boy himself, helped me with my hog-raising enterprise. We bought us seventeen weaner pigs. Paid a quarter a pound. Happened during a harsh winter when we had to build the pigpen in the cold snow. But being amateurs, we built the lower plank too high. Next thing we knew, the pigs were escaping out under the bottom of the pen. So there we were—me and Johnny running all over hell and back rounding up the pigs. We got 'em all, lowered that bottom plank, and put in a feeder with a trough of water next to it. That was another stupid mistake.

I should have put the water far from the feeder. That way

the damn pigs would get some exercise. Instead, they got so fuckin' fat that a few actually ruptured themselves. Making matters worse, when I finally took them to market, the price per pound had fallen to seventeen cents. I had to eat $5,000.

Though I did work on my farm, I wasn't the one who was running Ridgetop. I hired a whiskey-drinking horse trader named Mr. Hughes and put him in charge. When it came to buying cattle and horses, he was an old hand. His wife, Ruby, who, at two hundred pounds, was twice his size, could cook up a storm.

I couldn't have been more pleased when Martha sent Lana, Susie, and Billy to live with us. Martha was in the process of ending another marriage and thought the kids might find more stability with me. Shirley accepted her role as mom but before too long relinquished it. Martha married a third time, and she and her husband, Mickey Scott, found a place not more than a mile away from us.

And that wasn't all.

I was happy when my father, Ira, and his wife, Lorraine, moved onto the farm along with my stepbrothers Doyle and Charles, who had families of their own. There was room for everyone.

And naturally I was overjoyed when Sister decided to join us. By then Bobbie had divorced her second husband and married her third. Bobbie brought along her sons, Randy, Freddie, and Michael. She found work playing piano at a local supper club. Bless her heart, Bobbie always found a way to take care of herself and her boys.

I was glad to see so many people living with and around us on

Greer Road, where the mailbox read, "Willie and Shirley and Many Others." I loved being surrounded by a big ol' extended family. Gave me a sense of security. There was more than enough love to go around. And somehow old adversaries—like me and Martha—managed to stay clear of each other. Sometimes there were clashes, but mostly smooth sailing.

Maybe I'm fooling myself. Maybe with so many different personalities and diverse people leading intertwining lives there was more dysfunction than I care to recall. For my part, though, I was happy to have this brood all around me. Felt like being a member of a special fun-loving tribe.

Got me even more land. With my song royalties mounting up, I bought another couple hundred acres and another assortment of high-priced hogs, sows, chickens, geese, and ducks. Because I love horses, I had three Tennessee Walkers, two palominos, two ponies for my children, and Preacher, my own quarter horse. An experienced cowboy taught me calf roping. Didn't win any rodeo prizes, but whenever I managed to rope and tie a calf, one of my partners would yell out, "That's one in a row!"

Just like my pigs, I wasn't getting enough exercise. Devouring all that wholesome food fresh off the farm, I put on thirty pounds. So I found me a serious kung fu master. I loved learning his moves. Loved those spinning side kicks, double chops, and lightning-fast takedowns. Within a few months, I had whipped myself back into shape.

Mr. Hughes would watch me break a thick wooden board in half with my bare hands.

"What's the point?" he'd ask.

"If I'm attacked by a board, I'll know what to do."

As if I didn't have enough going on, my friends liked making the trek up to Greer Road. Hank Cochran, Roger Miller, Mel Tillis—they'd drop by and we'd have guitar pulling sessions around the fireplace, trying out songs. Once a month or so I might drive into Nashville to let a producer hear some of my new tunes, but mainly I stayed on the farm.

I say mainly because from time to time, I still went on the road with my band. No matter what phase of life, I'm always ready to hit the road. Can only stay home for so long.

Well, that caused big trouble with Shirley. She wanted to come along. She still wanted to sing and play bass, but her domestic duties were so great I didn't see how that was possible. She stayed behind, and I gave her great credit for toeing the line. But I was a fool not to realize how her resentment—not to mention my out of town shenanigans—would eventually crush our relationship.

Shirley put up with a lot. When one of my mentors, Ray Price, asked me if he could let one of his roosters stay at our farm for a short while, I was happy to say sure.

"He just needs a little room to run," said Ray. "He's cooped up here."

Before I knew it, Ray's rooster had killed one of Shirley's laying hens. Shirley loved those hens—she had named each one—and was understandably upset.

"Better come get your rooster, Ray," I told him over the phone.

"I'll be there tomorrow," he promised.

But tomorrow came and went and the damn rooster killed another one of Shirley's hens.

Another call to Ray, another promise, and then another no-show.

After the death of a third hen, Shirley grabbed a shotgun. Because I was a better shot, I decided to do it for her. That night Ray's rooster made a delicious dinner.

When he learned what had happened, Ray hit the roof. He called me everything in the book. "I'll never sing another one of your goddamn songs," he swore. "I'll never let you near my band."

"Well, you should have fetched your rooster like you promised."

"That was a prize rooster."

"Hell, Ray, there ain't one fightin' rooster in all of Tennessee worth one good laying hen."

Took years for Ray to forgive me, but he did.

On the music business side of my life, it took only three or four years before Liberty Records gave up on me. Actually, they gave up on more than me. By 1964, they'd gotten out of the country music business altogether. I'd cut two LPs for the label: *...And Then I Wrote* and *Here's Willie Nelson*. Each had a picture of me on the cover—clean-shaven, smiling, and looking straight as your local insurance salesman—and each included a gang of good songs. But neither established me as an artist, like Buck Owens or George Jones, with a mass-market following.

Figured if I was a free agent, it made sense to see if the biggest producer in Nashville, Chet Atkins, was interested in signing me to RCA. Turned out he was. I liked Chet. I had great respect for his hit-making history and, of course, his own masterful musicianship. I had the feeling, though, that like so many others on Music Row, Chet saw me as an outsider writing outsider songs and singing in an outsider style. For all practical purposes, Chet was the ultimate Nashville insider.

At this juncture, I felt a little more comfortable with Fred Foster, another producer with a strong track record. Fred was the one who'd produced Roy Orbison, an artist who, like me, wasn't easy to categorize. I had heard how Fred let Roy be Roy. He promised to do the same for me at Monument Records.

Fred seemed willing to follow me off the beaten track. A good example was one of the first songs I recorded for him, a tune I called "I Never Cared for You." You'd have to call it an anti-love song. Don't know what I was going through when I wrote this stark poetry.

The sun is filled with ice and gives no warmth at all
And the sky was never blue
The stars are raindrops searching for a place to fall
And I never cared for you
I know you won't believe these things I tell you
I know you won't believe

Your heart has been forewarned
All men will lie to you
And your mind cannot conceive
Now all depends on what I say to you
And on your doubting me
So I've prepared these statements far from true
Pay heed—and disbelieve

Not exactly radio-friendly lyrics, but these were the sentiments lurking in the dark corners of my mind. The truth is that these thoughts probably didn't correspond to my personal life. The thoughts came out of my poetic life. In that life I could imagine all kinds of crazy shit—men who use bleak metaphors to lie to women and then warn the women to disbelieve the lies. Some men, maybe most men, find it tough to speak sincerely. We hide behind stories. And this story, set to the tune of a forlorn cowboy ballad, was plenty sad.

On the other hand, it was original. Fred Foster liked it enough to put it out as a single.

"Well, it ain't Roger Miller's 'Dang Me' or 'Chug-a-Lug,'" chuckled Fred, referring to two of the biggest hits of 1964. "But maybe that's good. Maybe it's so different folks will stop and listen."

Some folks did, but most didn't. The single wasn't a hit, but the song did find an audience, especially in my home state, where I could always work, no matter how strange-sounding my material.

But not every song fell on only one state's ears. Couple of months before Christmas I was walking around, just looking over my land, when my mind went back to someone I hadn't thought about for years: a man without legs who sold pencils and what he called "pretty paper" in front of Leonard's Department Store in Fort Worth. By "pretty paper" he meant wrapping paper. He had a way of crying out those words—"Pretty paper! Pretty paper!"—that broke my heart.

I can't tell you why in October of 1964 I had this sudden and vivid memory. But it was so powerful that I picked up my guitar and set the story to music. I cast it as a Christmas scene, thinking that would heighten the drama.

Crowded streets, busy feet hustle by him
Downtown shoppers, Christmas is nigh
There he sits all alone on the sidewalk
Hoping that you won't pass him by
Should you stop... better not... much too busy
You're in a hurry—my, my how time does fly
In the distance the ringing of laughter
And in the midst of the laughter he cries
"Pretty paper, pretty ribbons of blue
Wrap your presents to your darling from you
Pretty pencils to write 'I love you'"

I brought the song over to Fred Foster, thinking that it might be perfect for Christmas.

"I think it's perfect for Roy Orbison," said Fred.

Well, that certainly was an idea. Roy was a much bigger recording artist than me. As a songwriter, I've always wanted my tunes covered by big stars. At the same time, I saw myself singing the song.

While I was thinking, Fred was planning. "Roy's in London right now," he said, "but I'll play it for him over the phone. If he likes it, I'll book a studio over there and we'll rush it out in time for the holiday season."

I could have argued, but I didn't. A Roy Orbison cover would be a solid score. So I let Fred send the song, and the next thing I knew "Pretty Paper" was cut, released, and racing up the charts—all in time for Christmas.

Ironically, the release of Roy's version coincided with the end of my contract as a Monument artist. While Fred had successfully placed one of my songs with Roy, he hadn't been able to score any significant sales for my own records. That's when I moved to RCA. Figured it only made sense to let Chet Atkins take a shot at me, uniqueness be damned. If Chet couldn't do it, no one in Nashville could.

It was during this same holiday season that I made my first appearance on *The Grand Ole Opry*. I'd been waiting awhile to get the invitation, and when it came I was grateful. It wasn't a matter of money—the *Opry* paid very little; it was the exposure and prestige of playing on that same Ryman Auditorium stage as Roy Acuff, Minnie Pearl, Porter Wagoner, and Hank Snow.

As excited as I was, the *Opry* had some definite drawbacks. For one, I couldn't play with my own band. I was simply part of the ensemble. That limited the kind of material I could do. And because the *Opry* required me to do at least twenty-six shows a year, that meant twenty-six weekends when I couldn't be on the road making much better money playing my regular Texas venues.

After a year I quit the *Opry* but stayed on TV, thanks to Ernest Tubb. Tubb was the ultimate Nashville hustler—and I mean that as a compliment. He recorded, toured, and owned a record store in downtown Nashville. Not only was he on the *Opry,* but he had his own live show that followed the *Opry* every Saturday night. *The Ernest Tubb Show* was something else entirely, different from the sparkled-and-spangled look of the *Opry.* Ernest dressed more like Perry Como or Andy Williams than Ray Price or Hank Snow. He liked sweaters. I appeared on the show dozens of times from the mid-sixties on. My usual outfit was a plain turtleneck and black slacks. Nothing fancy. But it was more than the casual clothes that made me comfortable. It was Ernest's great backup band and his backup singers, the Johnson Sisters, that made it so easy. They never cramped my style. In fact, they followed me beautifully.

At RCA, I tried to follow Chet Atkins as best I could. I went along with his suggestion that we call my first album for the label *Country Willie: His Own Songs.* I also went along with his idea that I rerecord some of my songs that had been hits for other artists: "Hello Walls," "Night Life," "Funny How Time Slips Away." I added some new ones like "My Own Peculiar Way" and "One Day at a Time." On all of them, though, Chet added the requisite sweeteners—heavy string sections and heavenly choirs that were supposedly making my music more palatable. It didn't work.

"It's a cumulative process," Chet told me. "Be patient,

Willie, and you'll get that mainstream audience you've been looking for."

I was patient. I went along with the same process on my second RCA record, *Country Favorites: Willie Nelson Style.* This time it was all covers, no originals, including "San Antonio Rose," the calling card of my idol, Bob Wills. I still found the production heavy-handed and wondered why Chet was so adamant about putting the word "country" in the title.

"If we're going for that mainstream audience, doesn't 'country' restrict me?" I couldn't help but ask.

"One step at a time," Chet answered. "We solidify your country base, and then we expand out from there."

"Whatever you say," I said, but remained unconvinced.

15

WAYLON

IT WAS IN THIS SAME period of the mid-sixties that I happened to be working the Riverside Ballroom in Phoenix. Everyone was talking about a performer playing JD's, a huge nightclub close to Arizona State. I had a distinct memory of JD's. It was a good-time party scene, where, a few years earlier, an irate man had whacked me over the head with a car jack, claiming I'd been humping his wife. I hadn't been. I didn't even know the lady in question. But having seen her flirting with me when I was onstage, the husband assumed the worst. I needed quite a few stitches to sew up my skull. My head ached for weeks. Ironically, other men could have accused me and been right. In this case, when the guy was completely wrong, I got hammered anyway.

So JD's, a rough and rowdy dance hall and drinking hole, was where this new artist was making a name for himself. College kids loved him.

"Is he a country singer?" I asked.

"Kinda yes and kinda no," I was told. "He's part country, part rock and roll. He's got something of your attitude, Willie, even though he ain't nothing like you at all."

That explanation intrigued me to where I drove out to JD's to see what the fuss was all about.

Didn't take more than one song to convince me: this son of a bitch was going places.

"I feel like we're kindred spirits, hoss," was the first thing Waylon Jennings said to me when we met backstage at JD's. He was a big-boned man, an assertive man, with rugged looks, bright eyes, and an outsized personality. He was a force of nature.

"Why do you call us kin?" I asked.

"We're both ornery. We don't fit in. Fact is, we don't wanna fit in. We got a different idea of how to do things. And I suspect that's 'cause we came up the same way—the Texas way."

Waylon Jennings was right. He was younger than me by four years but had a similar background. He'd grown up in Lubbock and started out as a disc jockey. Like all of us, he idolized Bob Wills and cut his teeth on western swing. But he also loved folk music and rock and roll and wasn't about to be put in a box.

"The man who got me started was Buddy Holly," Waylon told me. "We both grew up in Lubbock. Buddy saw my talent before anyone. He recorded me and even put me in his band. Even with all those hits he had—'That'll Be the Day,' 'Peggy Sue,' 'Everyday'—he kept telling me I could be a hit maker, too. Buddy was a beautiful man.

"I was out there on the last tour with him in the winter of 1959. We had a gig at the Surf Ballroom in Clear Lake, Iowa. Tommy Allsup was also in the band."

"I know Tommy," I said. "He was one of my producers at Liberty."

"It was me, Tommy, Buddy, Ritchie Valens, and the Big Bopper," Waylon went on. "From Clear Lake we were due in Moorhead, Minnesota, the next night. It was more than four hundred miles, so Buddy decided to charter a plane and fly. The weather was bad. The snow was coming down hard, but Buddy couldn't see sitting on no bus for eight or nine hours. The problem, though, was that the plane only held three passengers plus the pilot. Two of us would have to take the goddamn bus.

" 'Hey Waylon,' the Big Bopper said. 'I think I'm coming down with the flu or something. You mind if I ride on the plane?'

"I thought about it for a second. Flying was a helluva lot easier, but how could I make the Bopper, who had to weigh at least 250, squeeze into one of those little bus seats?

" 'Sure thing, hoss,' I said. 'You go on the plane with Buddy.'

"Meanwhile, Ritchie Valens and Tommy Allsup flipped a coin for the third seat. After the gig, Buddy was hungry and asked me if I'd get him a couple of hot dogs. When I brought him his food, he said, 'Heard you ain't flying with me tonight. Heard you chickened out.'

" 'I ain't scared of no plane,' I said. 'I was just being a good citizen. The Big Bopper is coming down with something.'

" 'Well, I hope that damn bus freezes up on you,' said Buddy.

"And then I said the words that will haunt me till the day I die. I said, 'I hope that li'l ol' plane crashes.'

"The bus pulled into Moorhead at ten the next morning. It was bright and sunny. I'd slept all the way. When we got to the hotel, the tour manager came out and said he needed to tell me something. I knew by his voice and the look in his eyes that it was something I didn't wanna hear. So I just said, 'No. I don't want to talk to you. Talk to Tommy.' Tommy Allsup was the first to hear. He came and told me. 'They're gone,' was all he said. 'The plane went down in a blizzard, and they're all gone.'

"Well, Willie, it was like I had caused it. My fuckin' words had caused the plane to crash. I know that's crazy, but that's how my fucked-up mind was thinking. On any given night, I still do think that way. If I drink enough whiskey, sometimes I can chase the thought away. But thoughts of that tour always come back.

"After the crash, we were promised money to attend Buddy's funeral. But the money never came, and I never got to tell my friend good-bye. The boy was a genius. You know how old he was when he died?"

"Real young," I said.

"Twenty-two."

"A terrible loss."

"He was just getting started. I guarantee you, Willie, he would have been bigger than Elvis."

"Well, you're here, and you got yourself a great gig here in Phoenix," I said, wanting to change the subject, kinda surprised but honored he was trusting me with all this. "They're breaking down the doors to hear you."

"Maybe so, but tell you what, Willie. I'm about to get outta here."

"What's the problem?"

"Too fuckin' confining. Can't stay in one place for too long."

"Sounds like me. Where you headed?"

"Nashville."

"What are you gonna do there?"

"Cut me some hit records. Sell me some hit songs. What do you think, hoss?"

"I think you're gonna do what you're gonna do, Waylon. But if you're asking my advice..."

"I am."

"Well, sir, after having been in Nashville for some time, I don't see it as your town. Nashville will wanna mold you, and you don't need no molding. Nashville will wanna clean you up, and you don't need no cleaning."

"So what do I need?"

"You need to stay away from Nashville."

"I hear you, Willie."

Maybe Waylon did hear me, but the next thing I knew he'd packed up, left Phoenix, moved to Nashville, and, like me, was signed by Chet Atkins to RCA.

While Waylon was recording, I went back on the road. In 1966, producer Crash Stewart and I put together a Texas tour that included Hank Cochran, Johnny Bush, and my own band. By then Paul English had moved to my farm and become my permanent drummer—wild, street-smart Paul who always had my back and got me out of more scraps than I care to recall.

Crash wanted to add a new artist to the bill: Charley Pride.

"He's not only a good country singer," said Crash. "He's a novelty."

"Why's that?" I asked.

"He's black."

That worried me only because the tour was going into deep South Texas and roughneck Louisiana. I envisioned riots.

"Before you decide," said Crash, "listen to his single."

I listened and liked it. It was a song called "The Snakes Crawl at Night." Charley had a singing style all his own.

"Book him," I told Crash. "Paul and I will deal with the consequences."

Charley turned out to be a great guy—smart, congenial, and humble. Some country fans were taken aback when they saw a black man singing in my show, but the minute he opened his mouth they shut theirs. They heard that Charley could sing.

Then came the night I was off work and went to hear Johnny Bush at the Longhorn Ballroom in Dallas. That big barn of a nightclub was owned by Dewey Groom, who had a strict segregation policy when it came to artists and their audience. To use Dewey's unfortunate expression, he'd call Tuesday night "nigger night." That meant B.B. King or Bobby Blue Bland or Jimmy Reed was headlining and the crowd would be all black. Country music nights, like the one with Johnny Bush, were all white.

On this particular white night I got silly drunk and decided to take to the stage. My buddy Johnny didn't mind.

"What are you gonna sing for us, Willie?" asked Johnny.

"I'm not gonna sing a lick," I said, "but I am gonna ask a friend of mine to come up here and entertain you."

I had Paul go get Charley, who was waiting outside, and bring him to the stage.

I could hear all sorts of groans and moans and nasty catcalls. The loudest protest came from Dewey himself.

But I just held up my hand and said, "Wait till you hear him." And then, even surprising myself, I kissed Charley Pride full on his mouth.

Then silence.

Then Charley breaking into his beautiful "The Snakes Crawl at Night."

Then rapt listening.

And, when he was through, thunderous applause.

"You see?" I said to Dewey. "God didn't strike no one dead. The world is still turning. Along with everyone else, you just fell in love with Charley Pride."

Dewey was a good sport. He came back to the motel with all of us, where we had an all-night guitar pulling session. Everyone got plastered. When morning came, I looked over and saw that Dewey and Charley had both passed out on the same bed. Due to my own inebriation, I lacked the presence of mind to snap a photo. But I did manage a smile and offered up a prayer. I thanked the Lord for strange bedfellows.

* * *

Shirley and I still shared a bed when I was home, but those times became more and more infrequent. The more tense our marriage, the more I stayed away from Ridgetop. I also had the excuse—and it was a good one—that in order to keep this farming enterprise going, I needed to make money. If I had wanted to, I could have put Shirley in my road show. But the plain truth is that I didn't want to. And if from time to time she got fed up with me and threw me through a screen door, I couldn't blame her. I had shut her out of my inner circle.

By 1967 or so, that circle included Johnny Bush on drums, Jimmy Day on steel, and David Zettner on bass. When David was drafted, he suggested his buddy Bee Spears, only nineteen. Bee was from San Antonio. Didn't have great chops at first, but Jimmy Day schooled him in a hurry, and just like that, Bee held down that bottom bass part just fine.

We had different names on different tours. Sometimes we were the Offenders. Sometimes we were the Record Men. Other times we went out as just the Willie Nelson Show. At one point we went out with a Lincoln Continental pulling a trailer. Then there was a big ol' Mercury Marquis station wagon.

We played clubs in New York and California, but Texas was always our money state, even though the money was hardly huge. For all my songwriting success, my RCA albums languished on the shelves. I was far from what you'd call a superstar. I wasn't playing concert halls or arenas. I was still playing joints.

On the road, I didn't dress like a country singer. I'd given up all the fancy frilly Nudie costumes long ago. A Nehru suit was as dressed up as I got. I told the boys in the band to wear whatever they liked.

"I like that black cape for you," I told Paul one afternoon as we window-shopped in Hollywood.

"It'll make me look like the devil."

"With that face hair, you already look like the devil. Why else are those gals chasing after you?"

I went in and bought it for Paul. He wore it onstage for the next fifty years.

Back in Nashville, Chet Atkins was still racking his brain, trying to find ways to get my records to sell. He came up with a concept, *Texas in My Soul,* that had me singing songs about my home state. Not a bad idea. Sang stuff like "Streets of Laredo" and Cindy Walker's "The Hill Country Theme." But when I tried to use my road band in the studio, Chet said no. Same thing happened on the next album—*Good Times*—where my lead vocals were drowned in a pool of overly sweet string arrangements and syrupy backgrounds by the Anita Kerr Singers. If you can believe it, the bizarre cover was a photo of me on the golf course instructing a cute young lady on how to putt. The album sank.

Once again, I was stuck in a rut. The music I played on the road, the music I'd cultivated with my band, had vitality. It was live music played for live people. I knew how to entertain a crowd for two, three, even four hours at a stretch. I knew how to keep them happy, keep them dancing—slow dancing, fast dancing—and touch them where they lived. They lived in the now. If I wanted to get fancy, I could call it the eternal now.

Onstage, I knew how to ignite and sustain that now. Onstage, I had my own band that, with David Zettner back from the armed forces, was better than ever. Onstage, I was in charge. But in the studio, I wasn't in charge and consequently the now escaped me.

I had great respect for Chet Atkins's musicianship and accomplishments as a guitarist and producer, but in working with Chet the now eluded us. Because Chet was convinced I could be a superstar, it was hard to walk away from his operation. I had stars in my eyes. Always had, and probably always will. I wanted more. I wanted the most and the biggest and the best. Chet saw my ambition and, rather than temper it, he excited it with a promising prospect: that his way of producing would get me what I sought. Yet his way of producing, for all its technical wonders, fenced me in. I knew it, but, blinded by ambition, I accepted his formula.

I should have known better, but the truth is that it took me a long time—all of the sixties, in fact—to finally see the light.

I remember being moved by Ray Charles's foray into country music. His huge hits like "I Can't Stop Loving You" and "You Don't Know Me" didn't top just the country charts, but the pop charts as well. Before this, Ray was seen as strictly a rhythm and blues artist. His label was afraid that by leaving the R & B field he'd alienate his core fans. Well, Ray didn't listen to his label. He sang country songs because he loved country songs. And he sang them in his own bluesy way.

Didn't try to be anything he wasn't. Music fans felt his heart in those songs, and they responded by buying millions of his records. He broke a mold.

I'd seen how Bob Dylan had broken a couple of molds, too. First he was a folkie not inclined to electrify his guitar. When he did plug in and pulled in elements of rock and roll, the folkies might have been pissed, but a bigger audience was there to cheer him. By the end of the sixties, he went even further with *Nashville Skyline,* where he embraced country music and did a duet with Johnny Cash on "Girl from the North Country."

Artists like Ray Charles and Bob Dylan had a strong sense of where they wanted to go artistically. Their inner confidence was greater than the outside influence of record moguls or best-selling producers. They resisted the pressure to conform to conventional wisdom. I saw that. I respected that. But I wasn't there yet. I was still caught up in a system—the Nashville music assembly line—where conformity was mandatory, and where it seemed to come with string sections and choirs of angels.

On the farm, I was my own man, cultivating my own land. On the road, I followed my fancy, even when it led to some questionable places. But in the studio, I gave my power away.

The power of a man to make decisions is a helluva thing. Sometimes ambition will cloud those decisions, but ultimately our independence is always there. It's an independent decision to go this way or that, to toe the line or rebel, to stay home and repair our relationships or wander off and form new ones.

I'm a wanderer. I'm a rebel. I've always been that way. That was my nature. Maybe I didn't have the consciousness to see how some of my choices would cause havoc. Maybe I didn't want that consciousness. Maybe I was just happy to be moving from here to there, making music, making friends, treating today like there might not be no tomorrow.

Problems?

Complications?

Consequences?

I'd deal with all those things when I had to.

But not tonight.

Not now.

16

NOW

WHAT THE HELL IS THIS?" Shirley asked me, her face red as a fire engine. She was holding a letter in her right hand. Her hand was shaking.

"Not sure," I said, looking up from the morning paper. I'd been reading about Spiro Agnew, vice president under Nixon, who'd been saying all kinds of dumb shit about hippies and protesters. The country was fed up with a purposeless war. At home, the culture wars were brewing. I was pissed at politicians like Agnew who did their best to widen that war. Now here was my wife, going to war with me.

We were up on Greer Road. We were nearing Thanksgiving, and I was looking forward to the traditional family meal.

"I want to know what this is," Shirley demanded. "I need a goddamn explanation—and I need it now."

"I can't see what you're holding," I said.

With her hand shaking even more, she handed the letter to me.

I glanced at the top of it and saw it was an invoice from a hospital in Houston. No big deal.

"It's just a bill," I said. "I needed to go to a hospital in Houston for something minor."

"It's not a bill for you," said Shirley. "You're not reading it. Read what the bill says, Willie. Read it out loud."

I looked down a little further and saw why Shirley was shaking with rage. The bill listed charges incurred for the birth of a baby girl, Paula Carlene, born October 27, 1969, to Mrs. Connie Nelson.

"Read it out loud!" Shirley screamed.

"I don't need to read it. I know what it is."

"Well, what in tarnation is it? Who is this Connie? Whose baby is this? What the goddamn hell is going on?"

It was simple: I was caught.

Connie Koepke, a beautiful young woman in her early twenties, had been my girlfriend for several years out there on the road. I'd met her in her hometown of Houston. She got pregnant by me. When it was time to have the baby, I made sure to be there and register her at the hospital. When they asked me where to send the bill, for some insane reason—maybe because deep down I wanted to be caught—I listed my address on Greer Road.

Now, in plain terms, I told Shirley the truth.

"How could you?" she asked.

"Hell, woman," I said, "we really haven't been together for years."

I didn't go into details. I didn't have to. I didn't have to remind Shirley that we'd both been down in the dumps with heavy drinking and pill popping—not to mention the crazy shit I'd done, running around the country, staying away from home for months at a time.

Our home life had been a mess. My road life, especially when I was with Connie in Texas, had been peaceful and calm. No fighting, no fussing, just lots of easy talk and good loving.

Even after this revelation, Shirley and I tried to make it work, but by then it was unworkable. I could understand why she was disgusted with me. I could see why one day she just packed up and left. It was damn near ten years later before I saw Shirley again. It happened when she showed up at one of my shows. She sang with me that night. She sang pretty as a nightingale. She still had her incredible yodel. And as if to prove that love wasn't ever the issue, we got along just fine.

Back in the winter of '69, when Shirley moved out, Connie and baby Paula moved in with me, Lana, Susie, and Billy. Except for one or two incidents, you could say we were one big happy family. One of those incidents was no small matter. It came to be known as the Great Shoot-Out.

Had to do with me being an overly protective dad. Turned out that Lana—like my mother and Susie, Billy, and Lana's own mother, Martha—got married when she was sixteen. Just after Connie and Paula came to join us in Tennessee, Lana came over to our house with a black eye and bloody nose. Her husband, Steve, had beaten her up. I walked her back to her place. Steve was there. I bitch-slapped him a couple of times. He whined and ran. As he drove off, I shot out one of the tires on his car. I went out back to the barn and was feeding my horse when a car came roaring by. Shots rang out and a bullet missed my head by about a foot. A little later the cops came by, wanting to know what happened. I told them and they left. Thankfully no one was hurt, but for a while it looked like the Beverly Hillbillies had come to Tennessee.

In the midst of this madness, I still managed to make music. In fact, music was the refuge from the madness. The more intense my personal life became, the more I concentrated on making sounds that soothed my soul. The actual sound itself was important to me. I paid careful attention to the instruments I played. Early on, I'd used Fender Telecasters and Stratocasters with their small necks and piercing electric sound. I switched over to a big Baldwin hooked up to an aluminum amp. When the neck broke, I traded it in for a Martin made of rosewood, an acoustic model with the richest, most soulful tone I'd ever heard. I had my man Shot Jackson, a guitar genius in Nashville, customize the Martin by integrating the guts and pickup from the Baldwin. It worked. I had the sound I'd been looking for. I heard it as a human sound, a sound close to my own voice. Didn't take long for me to pick a hole in it. That's 'cause classical guitars aren't meant to be picked. But that hole, along with the aluminum amp—aged by just the right amount of beer that'd been spilled inside—seemed to deepen its soulful tone. I named my guitar Trigger, thinking of the closeness between Roy Rogers and his beloved horse.

Hearing my new sound, producers at RCA had a new idea for me: they thought I'd be a natural as a folk artist. Following Bob Dylan's Nashville album, the trend was to repackage country music with elements of folk.

"Hell, hoss, they got me singing that stuff," said Waylon Jennings when I ran into him at the studio. "Now they got me recording 'MacArthur Park' and 'Norwegian Wood.' Now they're calling me 'country folk.' Before that they were calling me 'country rock and roll.' Truth be told, these fuckers don't know their elbows from their assholes."

Well, I did sing Joni Mitchell's "Both Sides Now" and "Everybody's Talkin'" from *Midnight Cowboy* and James Taylor's "Fire and Rain," not because I wanted to reinvent myself in the folk medium, but only because I really liked the songs. I was happy to do "Sunday Mornin' Comin' Down" by Kris Kristofferson, a brilliant writer who'd been everything from a janitor to a Rhodes scholar to an army helicopter pilot.

Also sang Merle Haggard's "Today I Started Loving You Again." Another great writer and singer, Merle had come out of the Buck Owens music scene in Bakersfield, California. I met him when he was playing bass with Wynn Stewart at the Nashville Nevada Club in Las Vegas. Then I invited him up to Ridgetop, where we played poker. Merle was another one of those rugged individualists who, like me, was trying to make sense of all the nonsense in the music business. We became buddies for life.

My own songs remained reflective of my own life. Folk be damned—given my domestic complications, it's no wonder I rerecorded "I Gotta Get Drunk."

"Bloody Mary Morning" was another boozy song about this boozy period of my life. Its origins might be found in those days on the road when I was still living a double life between Shirley and Connie. Like most songwriters, I changed around the facts to suit the rhythm and rhymes of the song.

It's a Bloody Mary morning, baby,
Baby left me without warning sometime in the night
So I'm flying down to Houston
With forgetting her the nature of my flight
As we taxi down the runway with the smog and haze
Reminding me of how I feel
Just a country boy who's learning
That the pitfalls of the city are extremely real
All the nightlife and parties
Temptation and deceit the order of the day
Well, it's a Bloody Mary morning
And I'm leaving baby somewhere in L.A.

The song had me running fast. The song had me looking for a way to deal with a hangover. I was hungover from too much liquor and too much running. It all made sense in a song, even though I still lacked the good sense to give up booze. I was a lousy drunk, a foolish drunk, a fighting drunk, a drunk who did himself much damage. But I was still caught up in the culture of drinking. That's what country singers did, right? That's what pickers did. That was the life.

The country music lifestyle was a heavy thing. I had come up in that lifestyle. It was all about Hank Williams singing the loneliest blues any white man had ever sung. The sadness was born out of many things: poverty, heartbreak, the endless grind on the farm and on the road. As a boy, I felt that sadness and wrote about it before I was old enough to fully understand it. When I did understand it, when I felt the full power of the blues, I also learned to drown my sorrows in a sea of booze. That only made me sadder. It also may have helped me write some sad songs, like "Bloody Mary Morning," that I'm still singing today. I regret none of this. At the same time, in the last half of the sixties I began witnessing another lifestyle that made more sense to me.

At first I witnessed from afar. My kids Lana and Susie, as well as my bandmate David Zettner, had come back from the Atlanta Pop Festival all excited. They talked about seeing Janis Joplin and Joe Cocker and Creedence Clearwater Revival and Delaney and Bonnie and Blood, Sweat and Tears and Led Zeppelin and the Staple Singers. They said over 150,000 came for the Fourth of July weekend. They said it was peaceful. Everyone was mellow. Everyone was stoned—peacefully stoned. Everyone shared the music and shared the pot.

"It was your kind of scene, Daddy," Lana said to me. "If you had played your music, everyone would have loved it."

It got me wondering.

I knew a lot of the music, just by listening to it on the radio, and I liked what I heard. Most of it came out of the blues. I heard Led Zeppelin as a blues band. Janis Joplin sure as hell was singing the blues. Same went for Delaney and Bonnie. Their Oklahoman piano player, Leon Russell, had written a bluesy hit, "Delta Lady," that Joe Cocker sang the shit out of.

Turned out that Leon had been a sideman on one of my first Liberty records. In those days, he dressed normal like the rest of us and did his best to blend in. Now, with hair down to his shoulders and carny-type clothes, he definitely stood out.

Leon was part of what everyone was calling the hippie movement, a generation of kids opposed to the Vietnam War and the uptight, hypocritical establishment. Kids who saw beauty in love, not violence. I liked that they put flowers in their hair and wore bright tie-dyed blouses and bell-bottomed pants. I liked that they had courage to look and act any damn way they pleased. And naturally I liked their notion of free love.

That was the summer of Woodstock, another big revelation for me. The Hippie Nation was growing by leaps and bounds, a nation that held American roots music close to its heart.

Wasn't long after that I caught Leon Russell on his Mad Dogs and Englishmen tour. He knocked me out. I told Connie, "This man is one of the greatest entertainers I've ever seen." I understood how his image—with his crazy stovepipe hat and dark aviator glasses—added to his mysterious allure. Beyond the mystery, though, I heard that his musical roots and mine were the same: Hank Williams, Bob Wills, country black blues. To me it felt as familiar as an old pair of jeans.

The new world represented by the Grateful Dead or the Jefferson Airplane was new only in appearance. That appearance appealed to me because it was bold and creative and said to the world, "To hell with what you think. I'll dress any way I please." The music might have had a new configuration, but hell, I could trace it back to Lightnin' Hopkins, who I had heard back in Houston in the fifties. The music was as old as time.

It thrilled me to watch the sixties settle in, even as everything else was feeling pretty settled in. In time, the domestic situation at the farm calmed down. Connie and Paula melded in with the rest of the brood. Periodically I went back out on the road. I also went back to writing with my old partner Hank Cochran, a man who thoroughly understood my many moods.

One December night, Hank and I wrote seven songs. The last one we put together was the saddest.

What can you do to me now?
That you haven't done to me already
You broke my pride and made me cry out loud
What can you do to me now?
I'm seeing things that I never thought I'd see
You've opened up the eyes inside of me
How long have you been doing this to me?
I'm seeing sides of me that I can't believe
Someway, somehow, I'll make a man of me
I will build me back the way I used to be
Much stronger now, the second time around
'Cause what can you do to me now?

Even though the title—"What Can You Do to Me Now?"—seemed to invite trouble, the story was really about getting strong in the face of adversity. Like almost all my songs, I didn't write the lyrics to reflect my literal real-life situation. Because I'm the composer, there are always elements of me in the story. But the woman I was addressing wasn't Martha or Shirley or Connie. She was a make-believe character in a drama in which a man faces the difficulty—the impossibility—of straightening out his romantic relationship. That man is not me. But when I'm singing the song, the man has to be me. I've written the script; I've customized the part, the main role, for myself. I've got to make you believe that this story is real. And when I'm performing, you can bet your boots it is. I'm crying real tears.

I suppose I could have been crying over the fact that my RCA records still weren't selling, but I wasn't. The label was still giving me money to go in and record. Chet Atkins was still trying to package my music and expand my market. Even though his vision and mine were different, I couldn't get mad at a man who believed so deeply in my talent—especially when that man happened to be one of the best guitarists in the world.

Who was I to complain? I had my family up on Greer Road. I had a wonderful new woman and, in addition to my three other great kids, my baby daughter, Paula. I was surrounded by friends like Waylon. I had all my close musician buddies, like Paul English and Bee Spears and David Zettner, living right close by. Writing partners like Hank Cochran were always stopping by. My poker partners would show up three, maybe four times a week.

Like my newly recorded song said, "What can you do to me now?"

Well, sir, the world had an answer to that question.

Happened on December 23, 1970, the day after I wrote that prophetic song. I was at the King of the Road club in Nashville, having a ball at Lucky Moeller's annual Christmas party.

"Phone call for you, Willie," said the bartender.

I went behind the bar to take the call. The party noise was so loud I could hardly hear. It sounded like Randy, one of sister Bobbie's sons. He sounded all worked up.

"That you, Randy? Speak up, son, 'cause I can barely hear you."

He was practically yelling, but his words were slurred together and I couldn't quite make out the meaning.

"What is it, Randy? What are you trying to say?"

"Uncle Willie, you gotta get up here. You gotta come right now."

"Why? What's the big hurry?"

"Your house is on fire. Everything's burning down."

Just like that, a million thoughts crossed my mind. I tried to focus on the most important things.

"Is everyone out safely—the kids, Connie, everyone?"

"No one's in there. Everyone ran out in time."

"Good. Is the garage on fire?"

"Not yet, but the flames are close."

"Take my old car and park it in the garage."

"Are you kidding, Uncle Willie?"

"I'm dead serious, son. Insurance is gonna pay for all this. Might as well pay for a new car."

Didn't take me more than twenty-five minutes to race up to the house. When I arrived, the fire was in full force, the fire department doing their best to contain it. The family was huddled together, amazed and frightened at what was happening. Before I had time to comfort anyone, I ran into the house. The firemen protested, but I couldn't be stopped.

Somehow I managed to make it back to my bedroom, where, dancing between the flames, I grabbed two guitar cases. One contained Trigger and the other two pounds of primo Colombian pot.

Back outside, I put down the cases and put my arm around Connie, who was holding Paula.

"It's going to be all right, baby," I said.

"It's all gone, Willie," said Connie. "It's all gone up in smoke."

"All that's gone is material stuff," I said. "Our spirit ain't gone. Our spirit's stronger than ever."

PART THREE

TEARDROPS AND FLOWERS

Back to the Future

At the start of the nineties, with my back to the wall, with the world saying that my finances and career were in the toilet, I had to do what I've always done during hard times: rely on my faith.

My faith was in the fact that I could look for light rather than darkness. I could look for mercy and compassion rather than bitterness or rage.

"Faith is a beautiful thing," said my manager, Mark Rothbaum, a man who dealt with hard practicalities and saved my ass more than once. "You wouldn't be who you are without it, but we're going to need more than faith to get you solvent, Willie. We're going to need a plan."

"Don't wanna hear another word about bankruptcy," I told Mark. "I'm not about to burn my creditors. That's not how I was raised."

"I know that, Willie, and I respect that. My plan isn't bankruptcy. My plan is a lot more radical than that."

"What is it?"

"Take on the IRS."

"How are we going to do that?"

"Aggressively and creatively. Creativity is your strong suit. Now you just have to apply it to fighting the feds."

Some of my other advisers nixed the idea.

"Too risky," said one.

"You'll be digging yourself into a deeper hole," said another. "The IRS will eat you alive."

I took an afternoon to reflect. It was one of those beautiful Texas days in early spring. I walked around my little Western town called Luck, which had been created for the movie I had made, *Red Headed Stranger.* When the movie was over, the town—that included an old saloon where I now play poker and dominoes—remained. I called the saloon World Headquarters. Beyond the town, some thirty miles outside Austin, I owned seven hundred acres of land, prime Texas hill country, where the Pedernales River empties into Lake Travis. On this land were two other prized possessions: the Pedernales nine-hole golf course and the Pedernales state-of-the-art recording studio.

This afternoon I just wanted to walk the land. Just wanted

to breathe in the fresh air, look at the ducks and geese, the rabbits and the deer that roamed free.

I was in my late fifties and had worked a lifetime—had put in a million miles on the road, had written and recorded hundreds of songs—to get to this point.

"You're going to lose it all," one naysayer insisted. "And now if you're foolish enough to go after the IRS, you'll really fuck yourself. Not only will they grab every last piece of your property, but you'll be turning every last concert ticket and record sale over to them."

I walked up the big hill to where I'd built a log cabin on bare land into a livable home. On the outside, it was still a log cabin, but on the inside I had all the modern conveniences.

Standing in front of the house, I had a spectacular view of some of the most beautiful land on God's green planet.

I took in that view.

I loved everything: the hills, the trees, the wildflowers, the birds, the bees, the bugs, the clouds, the sky.

I sat down on a chair on the porch and took a deep breath.

I could feel myself growing tense. I had a decision to make.

I lit a joint and held in the smoke a good long while before exhaling. It never failed. The good weed melted my tension.

I reflected on the last thing the naysayer had said: "This could be the most important decision you'll ever make, Willie. Throw caution to the wind and you'll wind up on your broken ass."

I went inside, picked up the phone, and called my manager, Mark, whom I trusted implicitly.

"Been thinking about your crazy idea of going after the IRS," I said.

"And have you made up your mind?"

"Yup."

"So what do you say?"

"I say let's do it."

17

TIME

WHEN A FIRE BURNS UP all your worldly possessions, you can't help but be philosophical.

The fire happened in 1970, when I was thirty-seven years old. I had a beautiful woman, four beautiful children, two beautiful former wives, and a semisuccessful career. Monetary success had come initially through songwriting, but after that, only modest success as a performer and recording artist. I still had to play dives to scrape by. And although I was signed to RCA, a big-time label, my royalties didn't amount to much. The insurance money was enough for me to rebuild Ridgetop—but that would take time.

In the meantime, I figured the most comforting place to go would be home. That meant Texas. Crash Stewart, who'd been helping me hustle up gigs, found a dude ranch some fifty miles outside San Antonio that was shut down for winter. He talked to the owners, who were willing to let me and my crew hunker down. The little town was Bandera, and the countryside, with its rolling hills and flowing creeks and rivulets, suited me just fine. This was where I got my first taste of golf, a sport that, like smoking pot, was a habit that I enjoyed cultivating.

The house where the ranch foreman had once lived was perfect for Connie, Paula, and me. Everyone else in my traveling tribe—my other kids, assorted relatives and bandmates with their families—was comfortable in guest cabins scattered over the property.

It was in that valley during the winter of 1971 that I allowed myself some deep reflection. I dipped back into scriptures, the foundation of my faith, but supplemented that reading with the work of Khalil Gibran. His spiritual meditations called *The Prophet* touched my heart.

When he wrote, "Let there be spaces in your togetherness, and let the winds of the heavens dance between you. Love one another but make not a bond of love," his words made sense. He understood that we can make music as a family, but that each of us must stand alone—"even as the strings of a lute are alone though they quiver with the same music."

I was with all the wonderful people in my life, but I also stood apart from them. As both a musician and a man, I had to follow my own individual path. Edgar Cayce was another writer/mystic/healer who helped me find that path. Before he passed on in 1945, he left a series of books. With the Power of Your Mind he showed how thoughts are linked to the infinite. He explained how he achieved cosmic consciousness through relaxed contemplation. In fact, they called him "the sleeping prophet" because, at will, he could lie down, close his eyes, place his hands on his stomach, fall into a deep sleep, and still answer the most probing question with brilliant insight.

I was also influenced by a highly nonconformist Episcopal priest in Dallas, Father A. A. Taliaferro, who liked to say, "Everything is great and wonderful. It always was great and wonderful. It will always be great and wonderful. So if we say something is not great and wonderful it's because that's the way we think." Like Norman Vincent Peale and Edgar Cayce, Father Taliaferro convinced me that, even in most dire circumstances, I could keep negative thoughts from clouding my vision.

Power over my own thoughts—that's a helluva concept. It means that you don't ever have to fall into the trap so many people can't seem to avoid: victimhood. That's the worst feeling in the world 'cause it means that there ain't shit you can do about your current situation.

I'd had my share of low moments, but I was learning that there's always something you can do. You can train your mind to look up, not down and not back.

When spring came to Bandera, I found myself looking up at the blue Texas sky and the bluebonnets and bluebells running riot over all the land. I didn't look back at the Nashville fire as a disaster and I didn't look down at my stalled record sales at RCA as a failure.

I looked up and simply began asking questions. Rather than keep those questions to myself, I put them into songs. The songs became my own particular prayers, my own personal reflections. I strung those prayers and reflections together in a loose-fitting suite. Music critics were throwing around the term "concept album"—like the Beatles' *Sgt. Pepper's Lonely Hearts Club Band* or Marvin Gaye's *What's Going On*. I suppose you could say that this new notion of mine came together as a concept album. Rather than try to write a bunch of hit singles, I simply followed the natural path taken by my mind.

My mind was overwhelmed by one question, which is where the record begins:

"You do know why you're here?"

"Yes," I answered. "There's great confusion on earth. Perfect man has visited earth already, and his voice was heard. The voice of imperfect man must now be manifest. And I have been selected as the most likely candidate."

"Yes," said the voice on high, "the time is April and therefore you, a Taurus, must go. To be born under the same sign twice adds strength, and this strength, combined with wisdom and love, is the key."

When they heard this album—that I eventually called *Yesterday's Wine*—some people said I thought I was Jesus. Now that's a fucked-up interpretation. Jesus was "perfect man." I was the "imperfect man." I was everyman trying to figure out my place in the universe. I was the man singing...

Explain to me, Lord, why I'm here... I don't know
The setting for the stage is still not clear
Where's the show? Where's the show?
...Before I begin this elaborate journey
Portraying earth's typical man

Last minute instructions would surely be welcome
Please, Lord, let me hold your hand

I needed to remind myself that, although I've strayed from the straight and narrow, I never strayed from my core beliefs. In "In God's Eyes," the next song in the sequence, I made that very point.

In God's eyes we're like sheep in a meadow
Now and then a lamb goes astray
But open arms should await its returning
In God's eyes he sees it this way

Before I moved forward as "typical man," I decided to go back to my beginnings: the home of Mama and Daddy Nelson in Abbott. That was the setting of a song I had written years earlier and decided to record again, "Family Bible," where the Good Book is the focus of my childhood faith. There could be no *Yesterday's Wine* without "Family Bible."

The questions raised by the Bible—questions that had been entertained by deep thinkers like Khalil Gibran and Edgar Cayce—had no easy answers. I imagined a blind boy in a school yard, listening to the other children play. Again, the questioning began...

Dear Lord above, why must this be
When these words came down to me
After all, you're just a man
And it's for you to understand

"It's Not for Me to Understand" became one of the key songs and led to even more pleadings on my part.

These are difficult times
Lord, please give me a sign...

The sign came in the form of lyrics. I didn't feel that I wrote them. More accurately, I have to say that I felt like I channeled them.

Remember the good times
They're smaller in number and easier to recall
Don't spend too much time on the bad times
Their staggering number will be heavy as lead on your mind
Don't waste a moment unhappy
Invaluable moments gone with the leakage of time
As we leave on our separate journey
Moving west with the sun to a place very deep in our minds

I couldn't write a suite of songs, no matter how spiritual, without reference to romance. I looked on "Summer of Roses" and "December Day" as love poems. In the first song, love was fleeting, tragically brief; in the second, love was remembered "as my memories race back to love's eager beginning... reluctant to play with the thoughts of the ending...the ending that won't go away...and this looks like a December day."

The theme song itself—"Yesterday's Wine"—was set in a bar, a hangout of mine, where I encountered a nameless stranger who gave "the appearance of one widely traveled." Rather than tell a story, it was time to listen to *your* story. It was enough for me to simply say, "I'm yesterday's wine, aging with time."

If I were to tell a story, there was none better than the adventures of "Me and Paul," a song that described the road that my drummer and best friend, Paul English, and I had been riding together.

It's been rough and rocky traveling
But I'm finally standing upright on the ground
After taking several readings
I'm surprised to find my mind's still fairly sound
I guess Nashville was the roughest
But I know I've said the same about them all
We received our education
In the cities of our nation
Me and Paul...

Almost busted in Laredo
But for reasons that I'd rather not disclose
But if you're stayin' in a motel there and leave
Just don't leave nothin' in your clothes
And at the airport in Milwaukee
They refused to let us board the plane at all
They said we looked suspicious
But I believe they like to pick on me and Paul

On a package show in Buffalo
With us and Kitty Wells and Charley Pride
The show was long and we're just sitting there
And we'd come to play and not just for the ride
Well, we drank a lot of whiskey
So I don't know if we went on that night at all
But I don't think they even missed us
I guess Buffalo ain't geared for me and Paul

Once I recovered from the road, I was back asking the questions, back in this dialogue with the spirit, wondering why I was here. My mind couldn't help but race ahead to the end of the story. That's why I wrote a song that envisioned my own demise, a song called "Goin' Home" that pictured my own funeral.

The closer I get to my home, Lord
The more I wanna be there
There'll be a gathering of loved ones and friends…
A mixture of teardrops and flowers
Crying and talking for hours
'Bout how wild that I was
And if I'd listened to them, I wouldn't be there
…Lord, thanks for the ride
I got a feeling inside that I know you
And if you see your way, you're welcome to stay
'Cause I'm gonna need you

I was pleased to end that suite with my need for faith. That need would never change. I was pleased to have mixed all my questions and doubts with my faith. The songs, in fact, were open expressions of how I tried to cling to faith in the face of the challenges of life on the road. They all connected, with each other and with me. I thought *Yesterday's Wine* was my most honest album to date.

"It's your fuckin' worst album to date," said one high-placed Nashville record exec at the label. Had to love the honesty.

"You don't like the songs?"

"I don't know what the hell the songs are about, Willie—and neither will your fans."

I didn't reply. I didn't feel like my songs needed explanations or defenses. They were what they were.

"This is some far-out shit that maybe the hippies high on dope can understand, but the average music lover is gonna think you've lost your cotton-pickin' mind. What the hell were you thinking, Willie?"

At this point I was tempted to say something, to show how the songs fit together in one cohesive story, but I stuck to my guns and stayed silent.

"Well, if you can't explain your goddamn music to me, how the hell do you expect me to explain it to my sales force?"

"I don't expect you to explain shit," I said. "These are my songs. I like 'em. I'm proud of 'em. And that's it."

When the record came out and bombed, I was still proud of those songs. One of them—"Me and Paul"—eventually became a classic. For the past five decades, I've been performing it during practically every one of my shows. Unlike that suit back in Nashville, the fans don't seem to have any problems understanding what I'm singing about.

Nashville and I had been trying damn hard but we hadn't really seen eye to eye for most of the sixties. I felt like I had shown goodwill and decent patience. I'd given the Music City establishment a fair chance. After *Yesterday's Wine,* I cut other records for RCA, but the story was always the same. The sales were slow and the producers lukewarm about my output. My career was stalled.

So even when the house on Greer Road was rebuilt and ready to reoccupy, I had my misgivings. I did move back to Tennessee, but this time my attitude had changed. This time around, Nashville didn't sit well with me. I'd sensed something happening back in Texas that felt right.

I tried explaining the feeling to my pal Paul but couldn't put it into words.

"You already explained yourself," said Paul.

"How's that?"

"You said it feels right. Well, if it feels right, just fuckin' do it. You know damn well that the rest of us are gonna follow you."

"I got no plan," I admitted.

"That's what makes it fun."

"And I really don't know what I'm doing."

"Hell, Willie," he said, "you never have."

18

REBOOT

I MARRIED CONNIE IN THE SPRING of '71.

I divorced Shirley in the winter of '72.

I know that's ass-backwards, but those are the facts.

Here's another fact:

In 1972, Johnny Bush called me with part of a song he'd written with Paul Stroud.

I took the song the way it was but adapted it to my style, which was more blues than rock.

"Whiskey River" turned out to be a big hit for Johnny as both a writer and artist, and I've been opening shows with it ever since.

At roughly the same time I adopted "Whiskey River" as part of my repertoire, I threw whiskey out of my life. Any fool could see that booze was bad for me. Booze made me say shit I shouldn't say and fight guys I shouldn't fight. Booze made me headstrong, violent, and dumb as dirt. Booze jacked up my ego and drowned out my humanity. On top of that, I still had a two-to-three-pack-a-day cigarette habit. The combination plate of liquor and tobacco was slowly killing me.

In the culture-shifting late sixties and early seventies, I was doing some shifting of my own. I had smoked pot for some time—as evident by the stash I rescued during the Greer Road fire—but I treated weed as a supplement rather than a mainstay. As I moved closer to the Woodstock Nation, as I bore witness to their music-loving, life-loving, peace-loving ways, I saw the key role played by pot. Pot was a communal experience. Unlike cigarettes, you didn't smoke a joint alone. You shared it. You passed it around. Pot was a plant, a natural substance whose positive uses, I would soon learn, were varied. Hemp, a form of cannabis, had been grown for centuries. As an agricultural product, hemp was lauded by many experts. Growing it, for instance, requires only water. The pioneers used hemp in the canvas of their covered wagons. Thomas Jefferson used hemp paper to draft the Declaration of Independence. The first Levi's were made from hemp.

I wasn't yet ready to make any formal declaration of my own—the penalties for smoking pot back then were still brutal—but I did see a world of difference between the two highs: booze and weed. Liquor emboldened me when I needed to be less bold. Weed took the edge off foolish boldness and made me mellow. Liquor agitated me. Weed calmed me. Liquor sped me up. Weed slowed me down. Liquor made me reckless. Weed made me careful. And when it came to two of life's greatest pleasures—making music and making love—liquor made me sloppy while marijuana made those experiences rapturous. The good herb was the best aphrodisiac I'd ever encountered.

In short, I fell in love with this lovely leafy plant. As time went on, as I quit tobacco and booze entirely, my love grew. As the years went by, as the growers of the crop learned to cultivate an increasingly satisfying product, my appreciation increased. Just as I've always loved robust coffee beans and the strong buzz produced by the brew, I felt the same way about cannabis. It pushed me in the right direction. It pushed me in a positive direction. It kept my head in my music. It kept my head filled with poetry.

Pot was plentiful at the Dripping Springs Reunion, a three-day outdoor festival on a ranch west of Austin in March of 1972. Some called it country music's answer to Woodstock. The first night had more traditional artists like Earl Scruggs, Buck Owens, and the Light Crust Doughboys. The second night had big stars like Tex Ritter, Roy Acuff, and Hank Snow. The final night had artists like Kris Kristofferson, Waylon, Merle Haggard, and me. We were seen as the outsiders. Personally, I didn't see it that way; I saw it as one big continuum.

What I mainly saw was some ten thousand fans who loved music enough to drive out to this dusty, deserted ranch to hear a bunch of pickers. And it wasn't your typical country music crowd. A good number of longhairs showed up as well. At a time when the old and new generations were supposedly at each other's throats, there were no incidents at Dripping Springs. Music was the bond. The promoters said they lost a ton of money, but I saw beyond this particular weekend. I saw the possibility of these huge gatherings on an annual basis. They were beautiful communal events, and Texas seemed the right place to stage them.

When I decided to move back to Texas, I had Houston in mind. But Dripping Springs changed my attitude. Dripping Springs was linked to the music-loving fans of Austin. Austin had the great state university. Austin had the most progressive politics of anyplace in the state. Austin had the most kicked-back vibe of any urban area in Texas. Austin was also a friendly home to the hippies. Austin was deep Texas, but Austin was also *different* Texas. Austin had natural beauty: Barton Springs, Lake Travis, hidden lagoons, and the nearby hill country. Back then Austin was still small—no more than 250,000 citizens. Austin had a live-and-let-live attitude about lifestyles. Austin had funky ol' houses and coffee shops where you might hear bluesmen like Mance Lipscomb picking up a storm. Austin had San Francisco–styled venues like the Armadillo World Headquarters, a big ol' armory converted to a funky show palace, where you could hear Ravi Shankar one night and Frank Zappa the next. Austin had Marcia Ball's Freda and the Firedogs; Michael Martin Murphey, the Cosmic Cowboy; and Jerry Jeff Walker, a former folk singer from New York who set a musical tone that appealed to rednecks and hippies alike. It was Jerry Jeff who wrote the heartbreaking "Mr. Bojangles."

Austin also had my close buddy Darrell Royal, coach of the national champions the University of Texas Longhorns football team, and America's biggest music fan.

"You gonna be loved anywhere you live, Willie," Coach

told me, "but you'll be more loved in Austin than anywhere. Whether you know it or not, Austin is your city."

Above all, Austin had my sister, Bobbie. As always, Bobbie was my heart and the strongest link to my past. She had come back from Tennessee to Texas, where she had played piano for shopping center openings, in hotel lounges, at country clubs, and for diners at El Chico, the area's biggest chain of Mexican restaurants. Bobbie had moved down to Austin with her boys and, in usual fashion, earned a living through her resourceful musical skills.

"Come to Austin," Bobbie was saying to me. "Things are changing around here. Things are opening up. I do believe that you'll take over in no time."

"If I did come down, what would you think about playing with my band, sis?"

"I wouldn't be thinking, Willie. I'd be crying with joy."

Before I moved there, I started out slow in Austin, just playing a few benefits for antiwar candidates and progressive politicians like Sissy Farenthold, who was running for governor. Didn't matter to me that they didn't have much chance of winning. I admired their progressive politics and was happy to help anyone committed to stopping our tragically misguided meddling in Vietnam.

On the same bill were Greezy Wheels, the Conqueroo, and other psychedelic-styled bands. Wasn't sure how our music would be received. So when the reception was positive—lots of flowers thrown onstage—I felt even better about Austin.

I also played west of town in the Soap Creek Saloon with my friend Doug Sahm, a killer musician who walked a perfect tightrope between hard-core San Antone Mex-Tex country and the Age of Aquarius rock. Doug was comfortable with all the generations.

"Hell, Willie," said Doug, "so are you. You just don't know it yet."

Wasn't until late summer of '72 that I played the 'Dillo.

Before the show I still wasn't sure whether we were the right match for this venue. The Soap Creek Saloon was one thing, but the Armadillo World Headquarters was something else entirely. Would I be ushered through the pearly gates of Hippie Heaven or laughed off as some weird country music act? For the first time I'd be facing the Woodstock Nation full on. The Grateful Dead played the 'Dillo, as did the Flying Burrito Brothers and Dr. John, the Night Tripper. What the hell was I doing here?

I was doing what I always do. I was singing my songs. I sang "Crazy" and "Night Life" and "Hello Walls" and "Funny How Time Slips Away." Without talking in between numbers, I sang my usual fast-moving set and saw, much to my delight, that the kids went for it in a big way.

We sure didn't have a flashy presentation. Except for Paul English and his black velvet cape, we dressed plain. So it couldn't have been our stage presence that got them. It was the music. I saw these kids react to the music in the same way kids reacted to Bob Wills in the dance halls of my youth. They got high on our music. They let the music take them away—far, far away from a world of anger and strife.

I liked this new world. It fit me to a T. I never did like putting on stage costumes, never did like trim haircuts, never did like worrying about whether I was satisfying the requirements of a showman.

It felt good to let my hair grow. Felt good to get onstage wearing the same jeans I'd been wearing all damn day. Felt good to tie a red bandanna around my forehead to keep the sweat from getting in my eyes. Felt good to no longer give a flying fuck about making a proper appearance.

I liked being improper.

Don't get me wrong. As a performer always interested in making a living, I understood the upside of changing my image. I knew I was appealing to a big new tribe of music fans. And I also knew that I'd be more acceptable if I didn't dress like an uptight leftover from the early sixties. At the same time, while I was conscious of the fact that I was changing my look to change with the times, that change felt completely natural. It was organic. As I look at it, I was turning exactly into the person I was.

In 1972, I was a man on the move. And that move was to Austin. Our first apartment was on Riverside Drive, right in the middle of town, with a view of Town Lake. I was a proud father of a son and three daughters and one on the way. Connie was pregnant with our beautiful Amy.

Following my natural bent, I soon moved everyone out to

West Lake Hills. More room to roam around and commune with nature.

Wasn't settled in for long when I heard from Waylon.

"What the hell you doing in Austin, Willie?" he wanted to know. "There ain't nothing down there but those crazy-ass hippies. You ain't turning into no hippie, are you?"

"Come down and see for yourself," I urged. I wanted him to see it, to feel what I was feeling.

"If I do, I ain't putting no flowers in my hair."

"Fine. You can put the flowers up your ass. Just get here."

The night Waylon was booked at the 'Dillo, I turned up for moral support. The flower children were out in force for the opening act, Commander Cody.

From the side of the stage, Waylon looked out there and complained. "Those fuckin' weirdos are gonna hate me," he said.

"Why do you say that?" I asked.

"'Cause I hate them."

"Hell, Waylon, you don't hate no one. Just get out there and play."

He did, and the hippies loved him so much the fucker had to play a half-dozen encores.

"You may be right, Willie," Waylon said after the show.

"Right about what?" I asked.

"Austin. This town ain't half bad."

19

GAME CHANGERS

EVERYONE IN NASHVILLE HATES HIM," said Waylon.

"And that's a reason for me to hire him?" I asked.

"That's right, hoss. That's the best reason of all. These motherfuckers at the label have us buffaloed. My old candy-ass managers were too scared of the system to challenge it. But this new guy isn't. This new guy is from New York, and he's a fuckin' bulldog."

"What'd you say his name is?"

"Neil Reshen. He's checking I'm getting all my royalties and he's also demanding that they change up the royalty rates that haven't changed since Thomas fuckin' Edison invented electricity. That could mean millions for me—and you."

"Who are his clients besides you?"

"Only one other: Miles Davis. I don't know what you know about Miles..."

"I know his music. I love it."

"Well, I don't really know his records. But I do know Miles don't mess around. He's all business. He's about the only jazz musician out there getting rich—and that's 'cause he's got Neil Reshen taking on the label bosses."

I decided to meet Neil and make up my mind.

Waylon was right. He was the opposite of the laid-back country boys who ran the conservative world of Nashville music. Neil was a pistol, a loaded gun aimed at anyone who stood in the way of his client and his client's money. He was fast-talking and fast-moving. Along with Waylon, he liked getting blasted on cocaine. When he did, though, that seemed to increase his concentration on the business of making more money.

I didn't like cocaine, but I wasn't about to judge anyone who did—especially someone like Neil. When he talked about tripling or quadrupling my income, I couldn't help but take a liking to the guy.

I hired him and gave him a free hand to overhaul my business and manage my career. Bad move.

At roughly the same time, one of my best moves was to hook up with another hard-charging New Yorker. This was Jerry Wexler of Atlantic Records, the label that had made Ray Charles and Aretha Franklin.

I happened to be at a party at my buddy Harlan Howard's home in Nashville during the week of the Country Music Association Awards. Me and some of the boys were taking turns playing our new songs. This went on till the wee small hours of the morning. When it was my time, I can't remember exactly what I played, but you can bet it wasn't fully formed. It was probably one of my weird reveries about a man trying to figure out the meaning of life.

"I know what you're all about," said Jerry Wexler, after I was introduced to him by Doug Sahm. "You're about artistic integrity. Man, I love what you just did. Sounds like a continuation of *Yesterday's Wine,* one of my favorite records."

This sounded like a man I needed to sit down and talk to. So I did. Turned out Wexler, for all his R & B background, was a stone-cold country music scholar. He knew all about Bob Wills, Lefty Frizzell, and Adolph Hofner. He said he'd been following me for years. Even better, Atlantic was opening a Nashville office and he wanted me as his first signing.

"Nashville hasn't been the happiest recording experience for me," I explained.

"I'm hip," said Wexler. "Our office will be in Nashville for sales purposes, but I want you to come up to New York to record. Change will do you good."

"I've never cut a record there."

"All the more reason to do it. I also feel strongly that you should use your own band. Tell you why. When we first signed Ray Charles in the fifties, we provided the studio musicians for him. But Ray never really found himself until he started using his own cats, his own songs, and his own concept.

"Ray taught me something I'll never forget. As a producer, sometimes the best thing I can do is get out of the way. Record for Atlantic, Willie, and I'll guarantee you: I'll get out of your way."

"I got some pretty strange concepts."

"Stranger the better."

"What I got in mind is a gospel album."

"Love gospel!" Wexler said excitedly. "My favorite Aretha record is *Amazing Grace*. We cut it in a Baptist church. I'd been after her to do a gospel record for years. I felt that she needed to connect with her roots."

"I've been feeling that same need."

"Then do it, Willie."

"You're not worried that it's not commercial?"

"Fuck commerce. You're going for art. You're going for truth. And when the art is truthful, sales will follow. You don't need restrictions, Willie. You've had enough of those. What you really need is artistic freedom, and I'm here to give it to you."

I'd never heard a record man talk this way. On the spot, I decided that Wexler was my man. Fortunately, our talk coincided with the end of my contract with RCA. I told Neil Reshen to cut a deal with Jerry Wexler, and just like that, I was on my way to New York City to make some music.

Naturally I was taking Bobbie with me. For years I had wanted her in my band. But life circumstances had kept that from happening. Now that we were both in Austin, and now that I had a producer who gave me free rein, I wanted Bobbie on my records. We had never recorded together before.

Bee Spears, Paul English, Jimmy Day, and Doug Sahm flew to New York with me and Bobbie on a cold day in February 1973. At the Atlantic studios, Wexler was true to his word. He let me run the sessions. I had Wexler's help, and the help of Arif Mardin, a fine producer and arranger. They inspired me, and the songs came pouring out.

The gospel album came to be known as *The Troublemaker,* named for a song that portrayed Jesus as the ultimate hippie: a longhair peacenik rebel scorned in his own time for an agenda of radical love. Most of the other numbers came straight out of the hymnal of the Abbott United Methodist Church—"Uncloudy Day," "In the Garden," "Sweet Bye and Bye," "Precious Memories," "Will the Circle Be Unbroken."

Bobbie anchored me—in memories and faith—in a way that no one else could. With Sister on the sessions and Wexler cheering me on from the booth, in two days' time we cut a dozen songs. For the first time in God knows how long, I was recording outside Nashville. Unlike the producers there, Jerry and Arif weren't interested in sweeteners—no angelic choirs, no overwrought strings. They wanted it raw, right, and real.

"Why don't you stay around and cut some more tunes?" suggested Jerry. "Now that you've praised the Lord, isn't it time to give the devil his due?"

"What do you mean, Jerry?"

"Put together a record of your worldly stuff."

"You want something new?"

"Something old, something new, something borrowed, something blue. I'll give you as much studio time as you want. Do whatever strikes your fancy."

Went back to the hotel and gave it some thought. Wexler kept saying that I didn't need a producer to tell me what to do. He said that I had a vision.

"Just give that vision an expression," he urged. "The studio is your domain. You shape your sound any way you please. That's what all the great artists do."

I liked the words, but I also felt the pressure. I needed at least two or three new songs to justify Wexler's faith in me. I needed to come up with something quick.

That night at the hotel I was in the bathroom, worrying about whether I could produce some great new song, when I noticed a dispenser for sanitary napkin bags next to the toilet. I took one out, got a pencil out of my pocket, and started scribbling whatever nonsense came to mind. The words came tumbling out.

Shotgun Willie sits around in his underwear
Shotgun Willie sits around in his underwear
Bitin' on a bullet and pullin' out all of his hair
Shotgun Willie's got all of his family there

Well, you can't make a record if you ain't got nothing
to say
You can't make a record if you ain't got nothing to say
You can't play music if you don't know nothing to play

John T. Floore was working with the Ku Klux Klan
The six-foot-five John T. was a helluva man
Made a lot of money selling sheets on the family plan

Wasn't much more than a variation on a twelve-bar blues. I figured the words wouldn't make much sense to anyone except me. Started out with me remembering that crazy day at the farm when I grabbed my shotgun and took aim at my daughter Lana's husband. The second verse was just me stalling for time till I could figure out something for the third verse. And the third verse was me remembering John T. Floore, owner of a honky-tonk dance hall outside San Antone, who, in his misspent youth, had supplied the Klan with sheets.

When I sang the song for Wexler, I was certain he'd think I was nuts.

"I think you're brilliant!" Jerry enthused. "Let's cut it. Lay down another bunch of songs and we'll call the record *Shotgun Willie*."

Wexler's attitude really pumped me up. I cranked out songs, one after another. The atmosphere was right. Whereas Nashville had always been uptight about musicians smoking dope in the studio, Atlantic didn't give a shit. Wexler got high with us. Wexler never bugged me to put on sweeteners to stimulate sales. I felt free to tap into my imagination, no holds barred. I felt free to go against the grain in tunes like "Sad Songs and Waltzes," a story about why this particular song would never sell.

I'm writing a song all about you
A true song as real as my tears
But you've no need to fear it
'Cause no one will hear it
Sad songs and waltzes aren't selling this year

I'll tell about how you cheated
I'd like to get even with you 'cause you're leaving
But sad songs and waltzes aren't selling this year
It's a good thing that I'm not a star
You don't know how lucky you are
Though my record may say it
No one will play it
Sad songs and waltzes aren't selling this year

I added a few songs close to my heart—"Local Memory," "Slow Down Old World," "Devil in a Sleepin' Bag"—and asked Wexler what he thought of my including a couple of Bob Wills covers.

"Do it, man!" said Jerry. "It's your roots! It's your heart!"

So we cut Wills's "Stay All Night" and "Bubbles in My Beer."

I decided to cover two songs that were on the opposite ends of the emotional Richter scale: Johnny Bush's rowdy "Whiskey River" and Leon Russell's rhapsodic "A Song for You."

In Nashville, I'd caught hell for my idiosyncratic singing. For years I heard producers tell me that my phrasing was off.

"Your phrasing reminds me of Ray Charles and Sinatra," said Wexler. "Like you, they're great proponents of rubato—elongating one note, cutting off another, swinging with an elastic sense of time only the jazz artists understand."

What others called a deficit, Wexler was calling an asset.

When I was through cutting *Shotgun Willie,* we had an album that would have never been allowed to be made in Nashville. But a New York–based label like Atlantic and a

New York R & B producer like Wexler couldn't have been happier. They put out *Shotgun Willie* before *The Troublemaker* and—wouldn't you know it—the thing sold like hotcakes. FM radio, all the rage back then, ate it up.

Much as I liked recording in New York, I was glad to be back in Texas, where Coach Darrell Royal had been telling me about Mickey Raphael, a harmonica man he'd heard play behind B. W. Stevenson and Jerry Jeff Walker. Coach loved to host jam sessions in his hotel rooms. I was at one of those sessions after a football game at the Cotton Bowl in Dallas when he introduced me to Mickey, who played the living hell out of the harp. He had a full cry, a blues cry, a big sound, and beautiful sensitivity.

The following week, I invited Mickey to come along and sit in with my band at an East Texas benefit I was playing. Along with Bee, Bobbie, and Paul, he fit in just fine. For the next few months, anytime we played Texas, Mickey joined us onstage.

At one point I asked Paul, "How much we paying him?"

"Nothing."

"Great. Double his salary," I joked.

But I knew that Mickey was no joke. And I began to see how, rather than as an occasional sit-in, he could become a permanent part of my family—a loose term that I started using to describe my band. As a depiction of people coming together to make music, I like the term "family" more than "band." It's a warmer word that suggests genuine care and love.

Mickey's welcome arrival in the family coincided with the departure of Jimmy Day, my man on steel guitar. The vocals–steel guitar conversation I had been used to with Jimmy became a vocals-harmonica conversation with Mickey.

Waylon had set the pattern by using Donny Brooks as his harmonica alter ego. Donny was a master. In fact, he was Mickey's mentor. Donny shadowed Waylon's voice in a way that raised the emotional stakes. The Waylon/Donny combination made me realize the potential of a Willie/Mickey hookup. Just as Jimmy Day's steel guitar had once wept behind me, I could now hear Mickey shaping those same kinds of crying notes.

As I turned forty, it was full steam ahead.

Had me a new manager who promised more prosperity ahead.

Had me a new label executive who helped me see how I could form my own musical future.

Had me a new harp player who deepened my sound.

Had Sister back on piano.

And I also had an idea born a year earlier at the Dripping Springs Reunion.

Why not promote a big ol' outdoor event of my own?

I'd invite all my friends from all walks of music. But I wouldn't call it an "event" or a "reunion." I'd call it a picnic.

20

HAPPY FOURTH, 1973

THE NIGHT BEFORE, LEON RUSSELL and I hadn't gone to sleep. We'd been joking and smoking and wondering how this great enterprise—the first ever Willie Nelson Fourth of July Picnic—was going to come off.

Leon was a major influence. I'd gone to Tulsa and seen how he had built his homegrown kingdom. He had a recording studio, his own label, and his own elaborate road show. If Jerry Wexler had given me the confidence to be in control of my recordings, Leon showed me how to be in control of everything else—my musical universe. Leon understood the high drama of rock and roll. He put all those theatrics in all his performances. And though he was one of the musical leaders of the Woodstock Nation, his roots in country and blues were always apparent. When I first talked to him about a Woodstock-styled picnic on the Fourth of July in Texas, he said, "You bring the rednecks, Willie, and I'll bring the hippies."

Both Leon and I were convinced that those two worlds

weren't that far apart. If anything could bring 'em together, it was music. At least that was our theory.

This picnic was testing that theory. And maybe the reason we'd been up all night at that seven-thousand-acre ranch at Dripping Springs was because we were nervous that the theory might prove a bust. We'd advertised the hell out of the event. We had big-name acts on both sides of the generational divide. For the traditionalists, there was Loretta Lynn, Ernest Tubb, Charlie Rich, and Larry Gatlin. For the nontraditionalists, there was Waylon, Kris Kristofferson, Rita Coolidge, Asleep at the Wheel, and Doug Sahm. There was something for everyone.

But when the light broke on that Wednesday morning of the Fourth of July, we were feeling jittery. To calm down, Leon and I went onstage, turned on the sound, and started playing gospel hymns as the sun rose over the great expanse of empty land set out before us. Felt good to praise the Lord in song, but what if we wound up singing to ourselves? What if, for all our efforts, we were courting a disaster? What if no one showed?

We had stopped playing, and it must have been around 9 or 10 a.m. when we saw a few stragglers wandering into the pasture. They looked like lost pilgrims. For an hour or so, there couldn't have been more than a dozen people. But then, slowly but surely, the number increased. And by noon there was a steady flow of fans—individuals, couples, families, and finally what looked like whole tribes of music lovers. They kept coming and coming. What had begun as a smattering of curious souls wound up being a throng of enthusiasts, all ages, all appearances, all ready for the time of their lives.

We might have been more than a little unorganized, but we pulled it off. The music was great. The crowd was happy. Buzzed on beer or high on weed or tripping on acid, the different cultures got along great. No name-calling, no pushing and shoving, no cracked skulls. I have to say that, given the potential for disaster, I felt relieved. In my name, a peaceful Fourth of July picnic had unfolded under sunny skies.

Financially, it was a wash. The two main promoters were my manager, Neil Reshen, and Geno McCoslin, that wild and crazy hustler from Dallas who'd been booking me for years. Neither one of these gents would ever be accused of being overly honest. They were both selling tickets on the roads leading into the picnic and pocketing the proceeds. I didn't mind. I figured most managers and agents steal. I had an attitude that said it was okay, as long as they didn't steal too much.

The picnic was exciting, but nowhere near as exciting as the gift that arrived immediately afterward. On July 6, Connie gave birth to our second daughter (and my fourth): sweet Amy Lee. Another precious blessing.

Around the same time *Shotgun Willie* hit the airwaves, Waylon came out with *Honky Tonk Heroes,* featuring a gang of kick-ass numbers written by Billy Joe Shaver, a friend and fellow Texan who had performed at the picnic. The songs had a strong rock-and-roll feeling. Along with Kris Kristofferson and Merle Haggard, Waylon and I were being put in another category outside the box of straight-ahead country. The labels were many, from "progressive country" to "outlaw country" to "renegade rock." Critics struggled to find the right words, and for my money, they never did. I would have preferred no label at all.

Because I was playing bigger venues and enjoying better record sales, I was able to buy a forty-acre ranch outside Austin. Connie wanted more privacy for the family and the place wasn't giving me enough space. I wanted to get back to the land.

I wasn't there long before Wexler called with an idea.

I had told him about another concept album I was considering. It was all about a couple's divorce. Side one would be told from the woman's point of view, side two from the man's. It was all about the pain, uncertainty, and fear that accompany a failed relationship. There'd be no happy ending.

"You have any of the songs?" asked Jerry.

"All of them."

When I sang them, Wexler was in tears.

"Let's cut it," he said, "but let's do it in Muscle Shoals."

"Why Muscle Shoals?" I asked.

"You've written a blues story, Willie, and Muscle Shoals has the funkiest rhythm section in all creation."

Muscle Shoals was where a slew of rhythm and blues smashes had been recorded, hits by Aretha Franklin and Wilson Pickett. When music execs told Wexler that Muscle Shoals was too

R & B for Willie, Wexler shot back, "Willie is too R & B for Nashville."

The song cycle that comprised the concept album *Phases and Stages* was all new except for one song. "Bloody Mary Morning" was a spillover from the sixties, but the sentiment fit the story. Playing with the Muscle Shoals rhythm section, I was able to sharpen the edges. Wexler was right. That studio brought out the blues in me, big-time.

This second time around, the single "Bloody Mary Morning" caught on. For all its strangeness, the album itself was an even bigger seller than *Shotgun Willie.*

I'd poured my heart into songs like "It's Not Supposed to Be That Way."

When you go out to play this evening
Play with fireflies till they're gone
And then you rush to meet your lover
And play with real fire till the dawn
It's not supposed to be that way
You're supposed to know that I love you
But it don't matter anyway
If I can't be there to console you

The subject was grief, grief, and more grief. In "I Still Can't Believe You're Gone" I wrote,

This is the first day since you left me
And I've tried to put my thoughts in a song

But all I can hear myself singing is…
I still can't believe you're gone

Some people presumed I was writing about myself. I wasn't. The song was about the untimely death of Carlene English, the wonderful woman who was my pal Paul's beloved wife.

The overall theme was not a reflection of my own life. At that point Connie and I were cool. I was simply making up a story. Sure, I'd gone through breakups and heartaches of my own. What human soul hasn't? But *Phases and Stages* was a fictional account of the sorrow that comes with the ruins of romance.

This was a period when the musicianship in my band also got deeper. In fact, my band—Bobbie on piano, Mickey on harp, Paul on drums, Bee Spears on bass, and the great Grady Martin on guitar—cut another version of *Phases and Stages*. Wexler liked the Muscle Shoals sessions better—and that's the one that came out. Some were calling it my "breakthrough record." I had to laugh. In my mind, I thought I had broken through way back in the fifties when I was a radio star in Vancouver, Washington.

Austin turned out to be the perfect place for me. For a while I thought of opening a club of my own called Nightlife, but when some promoters offered me an interest in the just-opened Texas Opry House on South Congress, that felt like a natural fit. It was a whole complex—a huge dance hall that held a couple of thousand, another room that held five hundred, plus a pool, a cabana, and some adjacent apartment houses that were soon called "The Willie Hilton." The Opry House became my go-to performance platform and my hangout headquarters.

"If you're so comfortable there," said Wexler on a visit to Austin, "why not cut a live album?"

In the summer of 1974, that's just what we did. And suddenly radio was playing my live versions of "Whiskey River," "Me and Paul," and "Bloody Mary Morning" more than the studio ones. Also recorded "The Party's Over," a song I'd written during my dark nights and days driving around the Houston ship channel and cut for RCA. But this live rendition was the one that really revived the song. Don Meredith, one of the commentators for *Monday Night Football,* would sing it every time the score got lopsided. Dandy Don kindly reminded the national audience that the song was written by his good pal Willie Nelson. It was a great plug.

We started packing them in at the Opry House from the start. There might be a little trouble now and then between a longhair and a cowboy, but that was rare. I'm not sure I would have called our music "progressive country"—the term used often by FM radio—but here in the seventies I did feel like we were making progress in bridging the generation gap that had opened up in the sixties.

If things were more peaceful—and they were—that didn't stop Paul English from his longtime habit of packing heat. Like me, Paul was the product of the old-school sawdust-on-the-floor Texas roadhouse circuit and was always ready to defend me and his bandmates.

I was ready for the second Fourth of July picnic, this one held in 1974 at the Texas Motor Speedway. Leon Russell came back, along with Jerry Jeff Walker, Doug Sahm, the Lost Gonzo Band, Nitty Gritty Dirt Band, and Greezy Wheels. Some folks got a little loaded and decided to have an RV race on the speedway. There were a few wrecks, a few cars caught fire, but overall the crowd, estimated at a whopping 75,000, had a ball, proving to the world that this picnic was all about peace, love, and good music of all stripes.

Begun as an experiment, the picnic proved popular enough to be an annual event. I didn't see it as a moneymaker. If anything, it was a love maker. After paying production costs and musician fees, there was little if anything left over.

Because Neil Reshen was managing Waylon as well as me, he'd sometimes hint that Waylon was having a hard time with all my success in Austin. It wasn't like Waylon and I had a falling out. We were good friends and would remain so till the day he died. But sometimes close buddies can get a little competitive. Waylon saw how my picnics were drawing people from all over and getting national publicity. He saw how my Texas Opry House was one of the hottest venues in the country. I'd never called myself King of Austin, but Waylon heard others use that phrase. I had the feeling that he thought I was getting too much sugar for my own good.

So when he was booked into the Texas Opry House to record a live album of his own, he had a devilish look in his eye. The song he wanted to sing, right there in my own house, was something he called "Bob Wills Is Still the King."

The lyrics told the story of how he had grown up in the

honky-tonks of Texas and was raised on western swing. But then, looking at me, he sang, "It don't matter who's in Austin, Bob Wills is still the king."

He described the Grand Ole Opry and how Nashville was the home of country music. He sang, "But when you cross that ol' Red River, hoss, it don't mean a thing. Because once you arrive in Texas, Bob Wills is still the king."

To make sure I didn't miss his point, his final verse talked about how Texas was the "home of Willie Nelson, the home of western swing. But Willie will be the first to tell you, Bob Wills is still the king."

The crowd went wild.

When he came offstage, he came right up to me. He was looking to see if I might be wounded.

"What do you think of that song, Willie?"

"I think it's a hit, Waylon."

"You mean it?"

"It's one of your best."

"And what about the lyrics?"

"Right on the money."

Waylon looked a little disappointed. He was gearing up for an argument, and I wouldn't give him one. Truth be told, I really did like the song. And besides, he'd sung the gospel truth: far as I was concerned, Bob Wills *was* still the king.

Besides, if I had illusions about being royalty, I didn't need Waylon to knock me off my throne. Life was there to do just that. As much as Austin helped reinvigorate my performing career and Jerry Wexler helped reshape my recording career, there were some unexpected bumps along the way. One came from Wexler.

He called me from New York and put it plainly.

"Atlantic is closing their Nashville office," he said.

"Why in hell would they do that?" I asked.

"The people above me don't see us making significant money in the country field."

"Even with good sales from my first two Atlantic records?"

"They won't let me develop a roster of country artists. They want to close down the whole operation."

"Where does that leave me, Jerry?" I had to ask.

"It'll be next to impossible to promote your records right without a presence in Nashville. You're better off somewhere else. I could hold you to your contract that obligates you for two more albums, but I won't. I wouldn't do anything to hurt the progress you've made. I'm gonna release you, Willie. I'm urging you and Neil Reshen to find another label with a strong Nashville operation. I'm suggesting that you look to one of the majors, like Columbia."

When it came to record producers and execs, Jerry Wexler broke the mold of the greedy exploiter. He put music first. He put friendship first. And even though our business relationship had ended, the trust he'd earned sure hadn't, and our friendship would continue forever.

So there I was—without a label or a producer.

"You nervous?" asked Paul.

"Hell, no. Why should I be?"

"No goddamn good reason ever to be nervous. I was just wondering how you felt, Willie."

"Feel fine, Paul. Feel like I'm on the verge of writing a bunch of new songs."

"What are they about?"

"Have no idea."

Paul laughed and said, "That's good, Willie. 'Cause the less you know about your songs, the better they turn out."

What I didn't know was that these songs, put together in the form of a short story, would be another one of those unexpected but beautiful breakthroughs.

21

PURE SUNSHINE AND PURPLE JESUS

I TRIPPED.

Along with millions of other experimenters, I wanted to see where these hallucinogens would lead. I was curious. I was happy to be alive in the coming Age of Aquarius, and I sure as hell didn't want to miss out on any of the spiritual fun.

Could I expand my mind?

Could I lose my ego?

Could I see beyond the veil and escape mundane reality?

Could I realize some cosmic vision?

It was a hippie friend who gave me my first tab of acid.

"What exactly is it?" I wanted to know.

"Pure sunshine. Straight from a chemist in San Francisco."

I liked the name. I quickly swallowed it whole.

"Big mistake, Willie," said my pal. "You were supposed to cut it up and only take a third. A third is five hundred micrograms. Fifteen hundred micrograms will put you on the moon."

"Oh well. Like the space traveler said: 'That's one small step for a man, one giant leap for mankind.'"

I wasn't concerned until I remembered I had to do a concert in two hours. The first hour was all euphoria. I felt washed over with a golden glow. Couldn't stop smiling. Hour two was when the bliss took a strange turn. When I walked onstage, I didn't feel like my feet were my own. As I started singing, my voice sounded like it was coming from inside a cave. Didn't sound like my voice at all. My hands no longer felt like hands. They felt like claws. I had trouble gripping the guitar. The roar of the audience sounded like the roar of a thousand angry lions. The flickering lights out in the crowd took the form of fiery figures. Was I freaking? Were there demons out there?

Paul sensed that I was tripping. His steady sense of time got even steadier. Mickey, Bee, and Bobbie brought me back by slowing down the tempo. They surrounded me with their loving sound. They surrounded me with their loving hearts. They kept me from going off the deep end.

Once offstage, though, I was increasingly uncomfortable. Forms were changing before my very eyes. The stars had turned into burning torches. Fireflies were laughing like hyenas.

"Just go with the flow, Willie," someone said. "Don't try to control nothing."

I took the advice. I sat back and watched the light show unfold. Just when I thought the show might be over, there came another explosion of crazy colors and inhuman sounds.

Growing impatient, I had enough sense not to panic. I wanted out of the acid universe, but realized I couldn't simply exit this psychedelic theater. The more I wanted to come down, the worse it'd get. Struggling to get back to my normal mind would only make things worse. So I sat still and chilled. Eventually the merry-go-round stopped turning and I got off. When I did, my first thought was, *This was interesting, but never again.*

I didn't fault the other trippers who used acid to blow their minds in their search for a deeper truth—or just 'cause they wanted to try a new high. For my part, though, experimenting with LSD convinced me that I had already found the high that worked for me. My love affair with pot became a long-term marriage. It was, by far, the smoothest of all my marriages. Pot and I got along beautifully. Pot never brought me down, never busted my balls. Pot got me up and took me where I needed to go. Pot chased my blues away. When it came to calming my energy and exciting my imagination, pot did the trick damn near every time I toked.

After Atlantic shut down its Nashville office and let me out of my contract, it didn't take long for other labels to come a-courting. Articles about this change in country music were appearing all across the nation. Magazines were putting me on the cover and my audience was growing by leaps and bounds. I went with Columbia, the biggest record company in the world. This signing, though, was different. In the past, I had no stipulations. It was just, *Give me the money.* But my experience with Jerry Wexler had shown me that I could—and should—control whatever happened in the studio. I needed to have the creative freedom to mold my music and shape my sound in whatever form felt right to me.

When the suits at Columbia heard my demand, they hesitated. They had their own Nashville machine with a strong track record of turning out hits. They asked my manager, "Who is Willie Nelson to challenge our ways?"

"Tell them I'm not challenging anything," I said. "Tell them it's simply my way or the highway."

I got my way.

My way came just in time 'cause I was on the brink of a writing spree. But little did I feel it at the time: being on the brink of writing and actually doing the writing are two separate things. After signing with Columbia, I entered a period when I felt blocked. Maybe that's because I knew I'd have to turn out some material right quick.

To take a break, Connie and I went on a skiing trip to Steamboat Springs, Colorado. This was the winter of 1975. Because I didn't want to rush the vacation, I decided to drive. The skiing was invigorating and the cold mountain air did me good. On the long haul back I started thinking it was time to get serious about pulling some new songs outta my feeble brain. Connie happened to mention an old song—"Red Headed Stranger"—that I had played as a deejay back in Fort Worth and sung to all my children when they were small. I saw the song as an old cowboy movie. I felt the story deeply. I could picture this old preacher who murdered his wife and spent the rest of his life wandering the land, looking for consolation that never comes.

I could see how the movie might start. I could hear the words inside my head.

It was the time of the preacher when the story began
With the choice of a lady and the love of a man
How he loved her so dearly he went out of his mind
When she left him for someone she'd left behind
He cried like a baby, he cried like a panther in the middle of the night
And saddled his pony and went for a ride
It was the time of the preacher in the year '01
And now the preaching is over and the lesson's begun

I took my time, all the while staying focused on the preacher's feelings. I thought that when he discovered that his wife was gone, he'd relate to an old Eddy Arnold song, "I Couldn't Believe It Was True."

As I drove over a ridge and looked at the landscape below, I suddenly imagined how the preacher and his wife might have met.

The bright lights of Denver are shining like diamonds
Like ten thousand jewels in the sky
And it's nobody's business where you're going
Or where you're coming from

And you're judged by the look in your eye
She saw him that evening in a tavern in town
In a quiet little out-of-the-way place
And they smiled at each other as he walked through the door
And they danced with their smiles on their faces

The song "Denver" became part of the story, together with other songs that fit the sad mood of the piece. Hank Cochran's "Can I Sleep in Your Arms" was the kind of tune the preacher would use to sing himself to sleep. I could also hear the preacher doing a beautiful old ballad by Fred Rose, "Blue Eyes Crying in the Rain," that had been sung by everyone from Hank Williams to Gene Autry to Conway Twitty. It was another song about lost love whose mantra—"Love is like a dying ember and only memories remain"—expressed the overall theme and tied all the loose ends together.

The story stayed loose, the songs were a little scattered, and just for good measure I slipped in other elements, like "Just as I Am," a hymn that Bobbie and I played in our childhood church. To show the preacher's desperation, it seemed like my story needed a prayer. "I looked to the stars, tried all the bars," said "Hands on the Wheel," the last song in the set, "and I've nearly gone up in smoke." Finally, though, the preacher could get his hands on the wheel of something real. And he was coming home. Home might be a dream. Home might be death. Or home might just mean the end of the record.

When it came time to record, I think Columbia expected me to fly into Nashville, New York, or L.A. and cut the songs in a state-of-the-art studio with triple-scale sidemen. Instead, I asked Mickey Raphael to find us some low-key place off the beaten track. He told me about Autumn Sound in Garland, a sleepy suburb east of Dallas. I used my own band. Bucky Meadows dropped by and played both piano and guitar. We did it down and dirty. The arrangements were lean. The accompaniment behind my voice was sparse. We cut every song in just a few takes. I was modeling the style on old albums made by Eddy Arnold and Ernest Tubb where all you heard was a singer and a guitar. The feeling couldn't have been more relaxed. When we were through, I was satisfied that the preacher's story had been told right.

When I signed with Columbia they advanced some $60,000 toward making a record that they were sure would cost me $40,000 to cut. I don't think the Autumn Sound sessions cost more than $2,000. I got to use the balance—$58,000—toward buying better equipment for our road show. So far, so good.

But when the chief Columbia bigwig heard the tracks, he said, "Why are you turning in a demo?"

"Ain't no demo," I explained. "This is the finished product."

"Can't be. It's too rough. It's too raw. It does not sound like a finished record."

"What's a finished record supposed to sound like?"

"Anything but this. The songs feel disconnected. The mood is too down. And the sound is far too flat. You need to go back in and polish it."

"That ain't gonna happen," I said.

"You're shooting yourself in the foot, Willie."

"Maybe so, but the contract couldn't be plainer. I turn in the music I wanna turn in. Your job is to sell it."

"You're making our job impossible."

"Well, let's see what the public has to say."

The public said yes, we like this *Red Headed Stranger.* We like this sparse sound. We like this sad story. And we like the way Willie sings that old song "Blue Eyes Crying in the Rain" so much that we'll send it all the way to the top of the charts. That single went number one and the album soon went gold. One week the execs were calling the record my ruination; a week later they were calling it my breakthrough.

I found myself playing a slew of new venues. I sang with the Dallas Symphony Orchestra before a huge crowd of wine-and-cheese yuppies. I did an arena tour with the rock band Poco. I headlined the ultrahip Troubadour before an L.A. audience of industry insiders. Columbia was so stoked at our record sales that they gave me my very own custom label that I named Lone Star.

Rather than stay to record my follow-up in Hollywood, I went right back to Autumn Sound in Garland, where I recut some of my old compositions like "Healing Hands of Time," "Crazy," and "Night Life." I also revived one of my favorite Lefty Frizzell numbers, "If You've Got the Money I've Got the Time." The music magazines were saying I was breaking through new barriers when, in fact, I was simply singing some old songs.

Didn't matter what the magazines said. I was grateful

for the attention. Grateful for new opportunities. Grateful for a lucrative multiyear contract to play Caesars Palace in Vegas.

And just when I thought things couldn't get any better, a good friend got elected president of the United States.

22

FUNNY THING HAPPENED ON THE WAY TO THE WHITE HOUSE

I WAS ON A GRUELING TOUR with Hank Cochran. It was 1977, and we played ten straight nights—sometimes two shows a night—before we got a two-day break. That's when Hank and I decided to make a beeline for the Bahamas, where we could go out on Hank's boat for a little deep-sea fishing.

We were so late in getting to the airport, though, that our luggage didn't get on our flight. No big deal.

Arriving in the Bahamas and clearing customs, we rented a car. It was then that I realized that getting our luggage might well turn into a big deal. I'd slipped a small bag of weed in the pocket of a pair of jeans. That got me to worrying. But since worrying never has solved anything, I let the worry go.

Next morning we got a call saying that our luggage had arrived. All we had to do was come by the airport and claim it. When Hank and I got to customs, I saw that the agent had a look in his eye, as if to say, *We caught you red-handed, motherfucker.* But maybe I was just being paranoid. Why would customs care about such a minuscule amount? They were looking for dealers coming in with tons of the shit, not someone bringing barely enough to roll a few joints. All I had to do was relax and be cool.

"Is this your suitcase?" asked the agent.

"Believe it is."

"You believe, or you *know* it is?"

"It's mine. And it was awfully nice of you to take care of it for me. I wanna thank you. I'll be on my way."

Ignoring my bullshit, the agent got sterner. That's when I knew I was fucked. "You won't be going anywhere, Mr. Nelson," he said.

"What's the problem?"

He opened the suitcase. The jeans were on top. He reached into the pocket and pulled out the pot.

"This is the problem," he said.

There was no chance to call a lawyer. Even if there was, I didn't know any lawyers in the Bahamas, and neither did Hank.

"Don't worry, Willie," said Hank, who loved to joke as much as I did. "I'll come visit you."

Next thing I knew I was whisked into a van and driven to the pokey and put in a cell. I was bummed out, but I couldn't say that I was panicky. Hank was my buddy. He'd find a way to fix this.

Sure enough, he came to see me during visiting hours.

"They set bail at some ridiculous amount," he said. "Between you and me, we don't have the cash. I'm gonna have to get it wired from back home."

"Hurry," was all I said.

"Brought you something to tide you over."

I was hoping it was a brownie laced with pot, but it was only a six-pack of beer. For the most part, I'd given up drinking. But in this instance I'd make an exception. If I was gonna be sitting in a dank, dark jail cell all day, might as well get plastered.

When Hank returned a few hours later with enough money to make bail, I was ripped.

The good news got better when he said, "Not only are they letting you out, but there's a good chance the judge will drop the charges."

The second we left the jailhouse and the sunlight hit my eyes, I hollered hallelujah and jumped off the porch of the jail. Given my inebriation, I took a nasty tumble and broke my left foot. I spent the next five hours in an emergency room. When I left, I was walking on crutches. Hungover and hobbling, I appeared before a judge. Hank had found a lawyer who started telling his honor about all the charitable work I did back in the States. His honor didn't give a shit.

"We're letting your client go on one condition," said the judge. "He's never to return to the Bahamas."

"Deal," I blurted out before the attorney had a chance to speak. And that was it.

Two days later I was hobbling into the White House on crutches. President and Mrs. Carter had invited me to perform.

They had also invited my family to spend the night. I'd campaigned for Jimmy Carter during the presidential run in 1976 and we'd become good friends. The Carters reminded me of the people I'd grown up with in Abbott.

Before my performance in the Rose Garden, the president came up to greet me.

"I'm glad everything turned out well for you in the Bahamas, Willie," he said. I was relieved that he didn't ask about my accident. His warm smile and quick wink gave me the idea that he knew—and didn't seem fazed in the least. My little concert went off without a hitch.

That night we had dinner with the Carters. Lots of farm talk. The president spoke about growing peanuts and I told some stories about my adventures as a pig farmer. It was an early evening, and Connie and I kissed the girls good night in the Martha Washington bedroom before we retired to the Lincoln bedroom. My head was spinning.

A few days ago I was in the pokey. When you're in the pokey, you're feeling mighty insecure. Now I found myself in the most secure place in the world. I was about to fall asleep in the center of world power. Except I couldn't fall asleep. That's when I heard a gentle knock on the door.

It was a friend of mine who happened to be a White House insider.

"I was guessing you'd still be up," he said. "It's early for you. Thought I'd give you my own tour of this place. What do you say?"

I said yes.

Winding our way through back staircases, we made it up to the roof.

"Best view of the city," proclaimed my pal. "Private, quiet, and absolutely serene."

He pointed out all the sights: the Washington Monument, the Jefferson Memorial, the Capitol, the Watergate apartment complex. The night air was cool and the sky glowed with glittering stars. I felt aglow, a picker from Abbott sitting on top of the world.

To top things off, my friend pulled out a joint.

"Think it's time to burn one, Willie, if you don't object."

"Think it's cool?"

"If it wasn't I wouldn't be offering."

I accepted the offer. The smoke took the edge off my excitement.

Getting stoned on the roof of the White House, you can't help but turn inward. Certain philosophical questions come to mind, like...

How the fuck did I get here?

The answer was obvious: through the front door. By invitation from the man who runs the place.

But how the fuck did he *get here?*

By bettering himself. He went from farming to politics and got real good at it. He found a way to help out the average Joe.

In my own life I'd tried to get good at my job. I found a way to entertain the average joe.

Okay, maybe I was ego-tripping. But given where I was sitting—on the roof of world power—who wouldn't be?

There I was, smoking weed and watching the city lights flicker like fireflies, thinking back to where I had started, thinking of the twists and turns of my crazy career, thinking how I had somehow managed to stay half sane. I had to offer up a prayer that consisted of no more than two words:

"Thank you."

Back in Austin, I had even more reason to be grateful when Ray Charles came to town. I'd been appreciating brother Ray for years, but had never gotten the chance to meet him. As the Austin music craze heated up, he was booked at all the big venues, including the Texas Opry House. We had a chance to spend some time together and became friends for life.

I told Ray I thought his records from the early sixties were single-handedly responsible for dramatically broadening the audience for country music.

"Willie," he said, "I really wasn't trying to broaden a damn thing. I was just singing songs I've always loved. As a kid growing up in the Florida backwoods, I loved listening to *The Grand Ole Opry*. The natural fact of the matter is that I'm country—*deep country*."

Like Jimmy Carter, Ray was a man I felt that I'd known my whole life. Naturally I was flattered when he said he was a Willie Nelson fan. It was especially flattering because Ray was so sincere. Not only did he never sing a false note, but he never said a word he didn't mean. He gave off supercharged electric energy. In his attitude toward music, I saw him as a kindred soul. He wouldn't stay boxed in. He once said, "They called me an R & B artist, so I put out a jazz album. Then they started calling me a jazz artist, so I sang country. Now they don't know what the fuck to call me. And that's just the way I like it."

Ray and I had similar histories with producers.

"Some producers think they know more about me than I know about myself," he said. "That's bullshit. I'm the best student of my own style. Hell, I've been studying myself forever. Same way you've been trying to figure out how to match your voice with your guitar, Willie, I've been working on matching my voice with my piano. Might sound like I'm bragging, but I don't need no motherfucker in the studio with fancy ideas about how I should sound. Best producer I ever had was Jerry Wexler. And do you know what he did? He made sure the studio's electric bill was paid and left me alone. He said, 'Go on, Ray. Last thing *you* need is advice about music.' "

When I told Ray I'd had a similar experience, he wasn't surprised.

"You're different, Willie," he said. "And it's your job to protect that difference. Producers want you to sound like the last hit you had. But hell, I see that as old history. Right now I wanna make new history."

Ray also loved to laugh. He had a wicked sense of humor.

When he learned I liked chess, he invited me over to his hotel suite. We met in the well-lit foyer. Ray had me follow him to the living room, which was pitch-dark, I guess to even the playing field. The chess pieces were marked in braille. Not knowing braille, I got my ass kicked.

Another time I was with Ray, Roger Miller—one of the funniest guys in the world—walked up behind him, put his hands over Ray's eyes, and said, "Guess who?"

Ray, who knew sounds and voices better than anyone, knew exactly who it was.

In putting together these yearly picnics, I knew exactly who I was *not*. I was not a detail man. Once I see the big picture, I count on others to make it happen. The big picture of my party for America's big bicentennial back in 1976 couldn't have been clearer: a good-size city of fun-loving fans—over a hundred thousand strong—would come to hang out and hear good music. I'd pick the artists to make that music and make a little music myself. That's it.

But that ain't "it," 'cause the logistics are overwhelming. As a guy who doesn't like being overwhelmed, I'll separate myself from the pre-picnic commotion till it's time to go onstage. That's good and bad: good 'cause I preserve my peace of mind, but bad if the wrong people start running things.

Those wrong people, of course, are in my employ. And that's where we come to another area where some say I'm lacking. Having grown up around hustlers, having liked hustlers, and having hustler blood running through my own veins, I'm especially tolerant and even fond of certain hustlers.

In the era when I came up, you couldn't survive the music business without having a hustler in your corner. And when I say hustler, I don't exactly mean a cheater, although hustlers have been known to cheat. I mean someone who's hustling to make sure your deal gets done, whatever your deal happens to be. In the case of the picnic, the deal was enormous. In 1976, the deal meant accommodating a crowd estimated at 150,000. We had secured the town of Gonzales, fifty miles outside Austin. The usual crew of my buddies were on board: Kinky Friedman, Roger Miller, Waylon and Jessi Colter, Kris and Rita, George Jones and Leon and Mary Russell.

But a few of the town leaders got ornery, complaining about the hippies descending on their hamlet. Manager Neil Reshen and promoter Geno McCoslin, busy partying on Peruvian powder, forgot to get a permit and we wound up paying a big fine. Even worse, Mother Nature got pissed and brought down the heavens on our heads. We had to put a huge tarp over the stage. (At another rain-soaked picnic, this one in Liberty Hill, Paul English pulled out his pistol and shot straight up into the overhead tarp containing rainwater. Instant drainage.)

Beyond the nasty weather, there were supposedly some nasty altercations when a motorcycle gang roared through the crowd. Rumors circulated that a man had drowned in a stock pond not far from the picnic grounds.

I didn't see any of this. I was so busy promoting the event back in Austin that I didn't make it back in time to play my set. But I did get to sit in with Waylon.

The press hit us hard. They called us unprepared, unorganized, and unprofessional. Of course I regretted any harm or any injuries suffered by anyone. And I also couldn't deny responsibility for putting people like Neil and Geno in charge.

In Neil's case, I was still under the illusion that he was the kind of savvy manager I needed to protect me from the music industry wolves.

In Geno's case, he had booked me back when I couldn't get myself arrested. He'd saved my ass during down times in my career. He'd been loyal.

Loyalty is a strong element of my character. A love of the unexpected is another. When someone close to me said, "Come on, Willie, admit it. You like things a little chaotic, you like not knowing what's going to happen, you feed on explosions, you like it wild and crazy," I couldn't deny it.

Yet even my worst critics couldn't argue with the fact that, in spite of unfortunate occurrences and bad weather, a whole lot of people still had a whole lot of fun.

Those same critics predicted that this would be my last annual picnic. I didn't pay them no mind. I knew better.

I also knew that the pressure of my hectic career was getting to my wife and hurting my family life. I wanted to do right by Connie and the girls, just as I've always wanted to do right by everyone close to me. But as my success in Austin got bigger, so did the demands on my time. More and more people came round, looking for my attention. I was easy to reach. Everyone knew where I lived. Our Fitzhugh Road ranch was an open house to the world. I was no good at turning down requests. I'd play any benefit if I thought the cause was half just. I'd been taught that if you could help out a neighbor, you do it.

Connie was convinced I was helping out too many friends and neighbors. After she and I had enjoyed some great vacations in Colorado, she argued that it would be the perfect place for a permanent escape.

I wasn't all that sure. I loved the Austin area. I loved my home state. It was the very act of coming home that had allowed me to have this recharged career. Texas was my base. If I was gonna move somewhere to escape the crazy crowds, why not move back to Abbott? To my way of thinking, Abbott was the calmest spot in all the world.

Connie didn't see it that way. If we moved to Abbott, she argued, she and the kids would get even less privacy. Night and day, everyone would be at our door.

I don't like arguing with women. Fact is, I don't like arguing—period. If Connie wanted Colorado, well, let's move to Colorado. Colorado has fresh mountain air. Colorado has beautiful vistas. Colorado has small towns where no one would find us. Connie found a hundred-acre ranch with a twelve-room chalet right there on the property.

She said it was perfect.

I said it was too far from Austin.

She said if I had my own jet, Austin would be only an hour away.

I got my own jet.

We got the property in Colorado.

I went back on the road. And back to the recording studio. This time I was determined to make things run smoothly.

"Your life ain't ever gonna run smoothly, hoss," said Waylon when we went to cut a song by Bobby Emmons and Chips Moman called "Luckenbach, Texas (Back to the Basics of Love)."

"Why do you say that?" I asked.

"Look at the lyrics of this goddamn song."

I did.

The story starts out with an introductory announcement that gave me a chuckle.

The only things in life that make it worth living
Is guitars to tune good and firm-feeling women
I don't need my name in the marquee lights
I got my song and I got you with me tonight
Maybe it's time we got back to the basics of love

Then it's off to the races...

Let's go to Luckenbach, Texas
With Waylon, Willie, and the boys
This successful life we're living
Got us feuding like the Hatfields and McCoys

"Don't you see, Willie?" said Waylon. "Until you get back to Luckenbach—or Abbott—or wherever the hell you came from, things ain't ever gonna run smooth because the outside world is too fucked up and filled with confusion."

"I was thinking about going back to Abbott," I admitted, "but it didn't work out."

"Of course it didn't. That's 'cause life ain't letting you. The best you can do is sing this song and pretend that you're going back."

I sang the lyrics that said...

Between Hank Williams's pain songs and Newbury's train songs
And blue eyes crying in the rain
Out in Luckenbach, Texas, ain't nobody feeling no pain
So, baby, let's sell your diamond rings, buy some boots and faded jeans
This coat and tie are choking me
In your high society you cry all day
We've been so busy keeping up with the Joneses
Four-car garage and we're still building on
Maybe it's time we got back to the basics of love…
Let's go to Luckenbach, Texas
With Waylon, Willie, and the boys
This successful life we're living
Got us feuding like the Hatfields and McCoys

I loved the song. Loved that my duet with Waylon hit the number one country slot and crossed over into the top-twenty pop chart.

Waylon was a smart son of a gun. He knew me well. He knew that I'd prosper with Neil Reshen, the manager we now shared. He knew that this outlaw persona fit me perfectly, just as it fit him. But he also knew that, given my predilection to please those around me, the pressures of show business would have me hopping in five different directions at once.

"You're trying to do too much and trying to please too many," said Waylon. "Doesn't that worry you?"

"Nope."

"How come, hoss?"

"'Cause one way or the other," I said, rolling a fat one, "it's all gonna work out."

"And what makes you so goddamn sure?"

I took a hit and held it in. When I exhaled, I said, slowly but deliberately, "It's a matter of faith, Waylon. And I got enough faith to last me this lifetime and whatever lifetimes come next."

Waylon just laughed and called me crazy.

23

AGAINST THE GRAIN

I'M SENTIMENTAL AND NOSTALGIC. I try to live in the present tense, but I'm always aware of the power of my past. I do that by honoring my heroes.

Lefty Frizzell, maybe the greatest of all the honky-tonk singers and writers, was one of my heroes. When he passed away during the summer of 1975, I made up my mind to do an entire album of Lefty material. A year later I had picked the tunes and was ready to roll. As you might have guessed, the label tried to stop me.

"It's not a commercial idea, Willie," were the first words I heard.

"Didn't say it was."

"You're the hottest country artist out there. Now's the time you want to expand your market, not contract it."

"Were it not for Lefty, I wouldn't have a market. He paved the way."

"Look, Willie. Nothing against Lefty. Lefty was great. He

was a Columbia artist. But three years ago his sales were so weak we had to drop him."

"Even more reason to honor him," I said. "You guys got some making up to do."

"We urge you to think about this."

"I have, and the more I think, the more I'm dead set on doing it."

I called the album simply *To Lefty from Willie,* and I did some of his best stuff, including "Always Late (with Your Kisses)" and "Mom and Dad's Waltz," and something by Jerry Jeff Walker and Jimmy Buffett called "Railroad Lady," the last song Lefty ever recorded. One of the songs, "I Love You a Thousand Ways," made the top ten on the country chart, convincing me of something I already knew: the label really didn't know shit.

What I did know was that it was time to take a break from Colorado. Thought it would be fun to live on the Southern California coastline. So in the summer of 1977, Connie, the girls, and I moved into a nice condo in Malibu.

I fell into an easygoing routine. Get up, have my coffee, and head to the beach for a brisk jog. Then it was back to the condo for lunch, a little nap before an hour or two of business calls.

An alarming call came in early June. I learned that the Drug Enforcement Administration had raided Waylon's office in Nashville and found a packet of cocaine that had been shipped to him from Neil Reshen's office in Nashville. Waylon was arrested.

This was distressing news, not only because Waylon and Neil were friends, but because I'd recently helped Waylon get into rehab. Mark Rothbaum, Neil's loyal assistant, had done the same for Neil. Apparently, though, the rehab didn't take. The boys were back snorting more blow than ever.

I wondered how in hell they could get out of this mess.

The answer was Mark. A sharp young man with a brilliant future before him, Mark nonetheless took the rap for Waylon and Neil. As the sender of the coke, he claimed the drug was his. The irony was thick: Mark, who eventually became a world-class Ironman triathlon athlete, didn't even do drugs. But he wanted to protect his boss and Waylon, an artist he loved. And he did. The law didn't touch Neil or Waylon. Mark wound up in a Connecticut prison.

Acts of valor are rare. Mark's unselfish behavior impressed me deeply. It came at a critical time in my career. The very week Mark was being incarcerated, I learned that I was being liened up by the IRS. For the past four years, Neil had asked for tax extensions. Although he told me otherwise, he had never paid a single cent of the taxes. It was time to let Neil go.

By now Mark knew my operation as well as anyone. I trusted him implicitly and decided to let him take over for Neil. Did it bother me that my new manager was in jail? Not in the fuckin' least. Hell, I was proud of him for being in jail.

In fact, I went to his Connecticut prison to play a benefit. By then Mark was editing the prison newspaper and doing all sorts of good work. The warden was so impressed that he let Mark use his office—and his phone—to book gigs for me. Miles Davis had also fired Neil and, like me, turned his career over to Mark.

Imagine: a thirty-year-old managing Willie Nelson and Miles Davis from jail, and doing a kick-ass job.

Mark also turned into a legal beagle, studying up on his case and finding a precedent that convinced a federal court judge to reduce his sentence from a year to two months. During his eight weeks in prison we spoke every day.

Just as I had gone from prison in the Bahamas to the White House, Mark did the same. Turned out that the day of his release I was putting on another concert at 1600 Pennsylvania Avenue. Mark had made the concert arrangements with the Carter administration and was sprung just in time to attend.

From that day forward, Mark has been by my side. On more occasions than I care to count, his keen intelligence has saved my sorry ass.

Back in the summer of 1977, I faced another decision: how to follow up my Lefty Frizzell album. Waylon and I had recorded "Mammas Don't Let Your Babies Grow Up to Be Cowboys," which proved to be a huge crossover hit. Naturally the Columbia execs were looking for more of the same. But I wasn't thinking that way. All during that Malibu summer, I was thinking back to songs that had inspired me coming up—not

Jamming with my good friends Rosalynn and President Jimmy Carter along with my sons Luke and Micah

My main man, manager Mark Rothbaum, with Hillary Clinton

Governor Ann Richards and Dennis Hopper honoring my hometown

His Holiness the Dalai Lama enjoying a good laugh

A happy man behind the wheel of a pickup

A happy man with a happy horse

One of life's enduring pleasures—playing poker with Merle Haggard *(Danny Clinch)*

Kris and Merle, buddies for life *(Danny Clinch)*

Back alley of the Apollo Theater, NYC, with two blues masters: B.B. King and Eric Clapton *(Photographed by Jonathan Becker)*

Miles Davis, a creative giant

Bob Dylan and Paul Simon, American originals

I have great respect for Neil Young as an artist and a humanitarian.

Jack White, superb guitarist, producer, and musical preservationist

Honorary degree at Berklee School of Music, with Kris, Carole King, and Annie Lennox

The great Ray Charles: I cherished his music, I cherished our friendship.
(Courtesy of the Ray Charles Foundation)

Harmonizing with beautiful Bonnie Raitt

As much as I like George Clooney, I liked the singing style of his aunt Rosemary even more.

Relaxin' at home in Hawaii with Woody and Owen

I earned my 5th degree in Gongkwon Yusul at the Master Martial Arts school under Tae Kwon Do master Sam Um.

Trigger, my closest ally and best friend

country songs, but Tin Pan Alley standards sung by singers like Frank Sinatra.

Jogging on the beach, watching the sunsets, toking, and dreaming of days gone by.

Coming back from a morning run, I happened to run into Booker T. Jones. He and his wife had a condo in the same building where I was staying with Connie and the girls.

We got to talking. I knew his work from Booker T. and the MG's, the great rhythm section that not only had huge hits like "Green Onions" but was the main support system of the Stax/Volt soul music labels and the backing band for Otis Redding and Sam and Dave.

When he mentioned that he had a few keyboards at his place, I went over to try out some material. Booker is a schooled musician, well versed in all the genres, so he knew every song I wanted to sing—"Stardust," "Blue Skies," "All of Me," "Unchained Melody."

For all our differences, Booker and I were linked by our love of the blues in general and our love of Ray Charles in particular. When I had just the slightest hesitation about singing "Georgia on My Mind," a song so closely associated with Ray, Booker encouraged me.

"Ray did it his way," he said, "and you'll do it yours. None of these songs belong to any particular singer. They belong to the world."

Booker was right. Much as I loved Sinatra singing "Blue Skies," Roy Hamilton doing "Unchained Melody," and Margaret Whiting interpreting "Moonlight in Vermont," I was set on creating my own interpretations.

When we had mapped out ten songs, I decided to use a home studio in the Hollywood Hills set up by Brian Ahern, then married to Emmylou Harris. In addition to Booker serving as supervisor and playing keyboards, I brought along the usual crew: Jody Payne on guitar, sister Bobbie on piano, Bee on bass, Paul and Rex Ludwig on drums. Mickey recorded his bluesy harmonica solos in the tiled bathroom, taking advantage of what he called "the great natural reverb."

Booker kept it basic. No soaring string sections, not a single backup singer. We did the whole thing in little more than a week. Yet I never felt rushed. I had lots of space to maneuver and calmly meditate on the meaning of these timeless songs. I had lots of time to caress the melodies in my own way. I had the freedom to let my guitar say what needed to be said.

In singing "Moonlight in Vermont," for example, I discovered something that, for all the times I had heard the song, I had never noticed: none of the words rhyme. Doesn't that go against one of the basic rules of songwriting? Isn't some rhyme always necessary? The answer is no. "Moonlight"'s storytelling is so enchanting, its lyrics so poetic and its melody so lush, that I can't imagine anyone complaining about—or even noticing—the lack of rhyme. It's a masterpiece, and masterpieces are defined by results, not rules.

The boys at Columbia? You guessed it: they did not think this new album that I was calling *Stardust* was anything close to a masterpiece.

"They're songs from a forgotten era," said the top man. "What's the point of digging up these old chestnuts?"

"The point is simple," I explained. "When they came out,

they were hits. People loved these songs. They were so good they lasted. And now there's three or four new generations of fans who haven't heard them. I don't think it's a stretch to say that those fans are bound to love this music. Fact of the matter is, I think it's goddamn obvious."

"Listen to reason, Willie. These new generations you're talking about look at you like an outlaw guru. They want you to sing edgy cowboy songs. Or Grateful Dead or Bob Dylan songs. They relate to you because you're a nonconformist. Believe me, they don't want to hear you doing songs they associate with their fathers or grandfathers. Don't indulge yourself. Listen to reason."

"I'm listening to my heart," was all I said.

"Then at least take these basic tracks and let a producer work them up so they'll get airplay. Right now they sound like demos."

I didn't bother to say that I'd heard that same criticism about *Red Headed Stranger.* What was the point? Knowing that my contract guaranteed me creative freedom, the executive realized his argument could go only so far. I didn't want to be disrespectful, but I also didn't want to hear any more bull.

"I like this record," I said before leaving. "I like the way we framed these songs. If you're right and people think they're old-fashioned, that still won't change my opinion."

When I didn't put my likeness on the cover of the album and instead used a painting of a starry constellation, the powers that be grew even more incensed. I didn't care. I thought the picture reflected the mood of *Stardust.*

Before the album was released, I played it for an audience of one: Waylon Jennings. He and I were in Austin, shooting the shit in the suite I kept as a hideaway at the old Hotel Gondolier on the banks of Town Lake. Waylon listened to the whole thing without saying a word. When the last song, "Someone to Watch Over Me," was over, his eyes were filled with tears.

"Goddamn, hoss," he said. "I never knew these tunes were so fuckin' beautiful. Where'd you find them?"

"There's a big book full of them, Waylon. If the album sells, I can make my living singing in cocktail lounges for the rest of my natural life."

The album came out in the spring of 1978. Even though I was confident that the project would find success, I had no idea of the level of that success. The singles "Blue Skies," "All of Me," and "Georgia on My Mind," hardly country songs, became top-five country hits. *Stardust,* hardly a country album, rose to number one on the country charts. And then it crossed over into pop territory. The big surprise was how long *Stardust* stayed on the charts: over ten years. More people heard it, more they liked it. Last time I looked, the damn thing had sold over five million copies.

I appreciated the kind words from the critics. But what pleased me most was the damage done to narrow-minded thinking. Conventional wisdom said that country music fans wouldn't go for pop standards, and it insisted that my new young audience wouldn't go for old songs. Wrong on both counts.

Stardust broke down barriers and busted up categories. Its blockbuster sales success put me in a position where I never had to argue with record execs again. From then on, without discussion, I just kept recording what came to me naturally, without forethought or analysis.

After *Stardust,* my mood sure was up. I didn't wait long to release another record, a live one called *Willie and Family Live,* a two-LP package of a show at Lake Tahoe. By the time that one hit the stores, I was back in the studio doing an album of all Kris Kristofferson songs. And because we had enjoyed such smooth sailing with *Stardust,* I brought back Booker to produce a Christmas album. I named it after my holiday song that Roy Orbison had sung back in 1963: *Pretty Paper.*

If everything was working, why not try a little bit of everything? Before the seventies came to an end, I initiated a project I'd been wanting to do for years: a collaboration with Leon Russell. While we were in the studio, there was a lot of press speculation. The assumption was that we'd aim our music at the "youth market," the audience that Leon had reached long before I had left Nashville for Austin.

That assumption could not have been more misguided. The truth was that in picking songs, Leon and I shared the same attitude. He was as steeped in nostalgia as me.

The result, *One for the Road,* was a double album of everything from Gene Autry's "Ridin' down the Canyon" to Cole Porter's "Don't Fence Me In" to George Gershwin's "Summertime," with an old blues tune like "Trouble in Mind," a pop ballad like "Tenderly," and a honky-tonk favorite like "The Wild Side of Life" thrown in for good measure. The first single turned into a number one hit on the country charts: our version of "Heartbreak Hotel," the song my mentor Mae Axton had written for Elvis Presley.

Leon and I took *One for the Road* on the road, playing dates to multigenerational audiences all too happy to hear us slip and slide over the overlapping genres of country, soul, pop, and sloppy rock and roll.

Musically, I couldn't have been happier. As I moved into middle age—I turned forty-five in 1978—I looked back with wonder and gratitude.

What to make of my trip from Abbott to Waco to San Antonio to Fort Worth to San Diego to Portland back to Fort Worth to Houston to Nashville to Bandera to Austin to the snowy heights of Colorado?

Surely I was blessed. Surely some benevolent force was protecting me. Given all my stupid mistakes, it was amazing that I hadn't gone under, in more ways than one.

Lots of people who love the Lord die young for no fault of their own. I don't think it was the Lord who kept me from falling off the cliff or down the well. In my own weird way, I knew to avoid certain pitfalls. I knew how to survive.

More than mere survival, I was looking at new horizons. Beyond music, I had my eye on something else.

That something else went back to my childhood, when I'd take my bike from Abbott to the Best Movie Theater in West to watch Roy Rogers ride the range.

I thought about movies and how the singers that I admired—Bing Crosby, Gene Autry, Frank Sinatra, and Elvis—had made the move to the silver screen.

If I fell on my ass, so what? At least I'd have fun trying. It was a temptation I couldn't resist.

PART FOUR

OVER THE RAINBOW

Back to the Future

> **"WILLIE NELSON**
> **HOMELESS AND BROKE**
>
> He's lost his cars, his band, his houses, his money, and his clothes."

I've never given a flying fuck what the scandal sheets say about me—especially *The National Enquirer.* So when that low-rent rag put me on the cover and blew up my misfortune—along with headlines about Cher's plastic surgeries and psychic predictions for 1991—I didn't even know about it until my phone started ringing. Friends and neighbors were worried, thinking that I was standing on the corner hawking pencils or, like the man in my Christmas song, on the street selling pretty paper.

Truth is, the band never disbanded. Being the loyal and loving dogs that they were, they worked for less money. I still had a roof over my head and was living more comfortably than nine-tenths of the world's population. I'm not saying I wasn't in a serious financial stew. I sure as shit was. But I had my health and my fighting spirit.

First thing I did was tell the naysayers—those crying out like Chicken Little that the sky was falling—to get out of my face and shut the fuck up.

I'd heard enough. Not for a minute was I considering throwing in the towel and declaring bankruptcy. I'd decided to go along with the plan devised by Mark Rothbaum and supported by my attorneys Joel Katz and Jay Goldberg and tax expert Larry Goldfein. I was going to fight the IRS.

I had to face facts: my resources were few. The IRS's resources were unlimited. They had billions on their side. They had at their command an army of killer lawyers whose only aim was to destroy me.

When it came time to question me—a two-day ordeal scheduled at the IRS offices in Austin—I got an idea.

By then I had Honeysuckle Rose II, the second incarnation of my custom bus with a Western scene painted on the exterior.

"Let's roll up to Austin in the bus," I told my team, "and park it right in front of their building."

That's what we did.

The first sessions started at about eleven. I showed up in my usual jeans, T-shirt, and jogging shoes. I expected to be facing some sharpshooter from New York City. But they threw me a curve. The attorney was a good ol' boy from my part of Texas.

"You don't mind if I call you Willie, do you?"

"Not at all."

"Feel like I've known you all my life."

"Feeling's mutual."

He looked down at my jogging shoes and said, "Well, Willie, you're living proof that we Hill County boys know a comfortable pair of shoes when we see 'em. Wish I could dress comfortably as you. Meanwhile, it's an honor to have you up here."

I liked this guy. How couldn't I? We knew a ton of folks in common, and the chitchat went on for some time. But I also knew that having someone from my part of Texas to do the questioning was a way to throw me off guard. Despite the man's easy charm, I stayed on guard. I gave my usual monosyllabic answers. I stuck to what I knew and only what I knew. Their strategy didn't work. Meanwhile, mine did.

My strategy was to position my bus so that by lunchtime all of downtown Austin knew where it was parked. By the time we took our twelve-thirty break, there was a huge crowd of fans lined up outside Honeysuckle Rose II. One by one I let them on the bus, signed whatever they wanted me to sign, and let them take as many pictures with me as they liked. That took nearly three hours. When we got back up to the IRS offices, I apologized for the delay.

By the second day, the Austin crowds had grown so big that police were brought in to keep the lines orderly. Not only that, but the clerks and secretaries at the IRS were sneaking out to come to the bus for autographs of their own.

When the last session was over and I still hadn't veered from my usual answers of "Yup," "Nope," and "Don't rightly recall," the lawyer asked one last question.

"You sure you secretly never went to one of those fancy law schools back east, Willie?"

"Never went further than Abbott High. Abbott is where I got all my smarts. I was one of those Fighting Panthers. Fact is, I still remember the sign over the school gym that said, 'A winner never quits and a quitter never wins.' Been trying to live by those words ever since."

"Well, Willie," he said, "I'd say you're doing a pretty good job."

That's when I got another pretty good idea:

While I didn't have the past-due tax money the Feds were demanding from me, I had something else: my music. I could always sing for my supper. I could make a couple of records and give all the proceeds to the IRS. I'd even call them *The IRS Tapes* and *Who'll Buy My Memories?* The feds went along with the plan.

I cut down on production costs by being the only musician. I simply sang and accompanied myself to a selection of twenty-four songs. Just bare-bones Willie singing the blues.

I picked the tunes that fit my mood: "It's Not Supposed to Be That Way," "Permanently Lonely," "Home Motel," "Yesterday's Wine," "Wake Me When It's Over," "Remember the Good Times," and especially "What Can You Do to Me Now?"

Sony, the label that then had me under contract, kicked in some money. The record was mainly marketed via a television commercial. On the cover was a picture of myself wearing a black cowboy hat and a T-shirt that said "Shit happens."

The record sold enough to keep the IRS at bay—at least for a while.

24

SILVER SCREEN

I MET ROBERT REDFORD AT A benefit in New York City. The next day, we found ourselves sitting next to each other on the plane back to Los Angeles. We got to talking. He told me about this movie, *The Electric Horseman,* that he and Jane Fonda were about to make with director Sydney Pollack.

"Ever thought about doing a movie, Willie?" he asked.

"Sure. But let me ask you this, Bob: is acting anything like having a conversation?"

"That's exactly what it's like."

"Well, I believe I can do that."

"You're a natural, Willie. As a singer and musician, you're naturally relaxed. As an actor, I think that same quality would come through."

I thanked him for the kind remark. The more I thought about it, the more I was inclined to make the move. But how?

Figured the simplest way was the best. Pick up the phone,

call the boss, and ask for the job. In this case the boss was Sydney Pollack.

I'd never met the man, but he sounded glad to hear from me.

"How can I help you, Willie?"

"Put me in that movie you're making with Bob and Jane Fonda."

He laughed, not scornfully but sweetly.

"Come to think of it," he said, "you might be right for the part of Redford's manager. Would you mind reading for it?"

"Be my pleasure."

The reading was easy. The part was easy. I played myself. In fact, in every movie to follow, I played myself. Or as that great sidekick cowboy Slim Pickens would soon say, "No one plays Willie Nelson better than Willie Nelson."

I didn't plan and I didn't rehearse. I learned my lines, but tended to bend them my own way—or borrow from writer friends. In *The Electric Horseman,* Pollack loved the line I spewed: "Gonna get myself a bottle of tequila and find me one of those Keno girls who can suck the chrome off a trailer hitch and kick back." Still not sure how that made it past the ratings people. Wish I could claim credit, but I'd found it in a novel by my buddies Bud Shrake and Dan Jenkins, who were happy to loan it out. For the most part, though, I did what Redford had predicted I'd do: I said what came naturally.

Reviews were great. I sang what I thought was an appropriate song on the soundtrack, "My Heroes Have Always Been Cowboys," as well as "Mammas Don't Let Your Babies Grow Up to Be Cowboys."

The film did brisk business, I got good reviews, and just like that, I was sitting in a dark theater and staring up at myself on the silver screen, another one of those crazy boyhood fantasies turned real.

The hustler in me got all worked up. Movies were not only easy to do, but the exposure gave me an even bigger audience, not to mention good money.

Just as I'd always wanted to do it my own way with music, I wanted to take the same approach with film. I'd work up my own projects. The first that came to mind was "Red Headed Stranger." Connie had been right: ever since I sang it to my children, I'd always seen that song as a movie. If people were calling me a natural actor, I sure as hell would call that song a natural film script.

Took the idea to my friend Bud Shrake, but Bud was hesitant.

"How you gonna make a hero out of a man who shoots his woman to death for stealing a horse?"

Bud suggested I try another writer friend in Austin, Bill Wittliff, who wrote a beautiful screenplay that Universal liked. My idea was to make the movie with their money through my production company. Of course I'd play the Red Headed Stranger.

Universal didn't see it that way. They saw Robert Redford in the role. They also wanted me to leave Columbia Records for their label, MCA. Welcome to Hollywood, where strings are always attached.

Being a practical man, I couldn't dismiss their offer out of hand. Redford could easily play the part. I called Bob to see what he thought of the script. He liked it but said he needed time to make a decision.

Well, two years later Bob still hadn't made up his mind. By then Universal had lost interest and I was back where I started. I had a good screenplay but no financing. And of course I was not about to break Hollywood's golden rule: *When making a movie, never use your own money.*

With patience, I figured, the stars would be aligned and the Red Headed Stranger would have his day.

In the meantime, other roles came my way. In *Honeysuckle Rose,* I starred as Buck Bonham, a Willie Nelson–styled character torn between his love for his wife, Dyan Cannon, and his girlfriend, Amy Irving—a delicious dilemma if there ever was one. Sydney Pollack was the producer.

At one point Sydney, director Jerry Schatzberg, and I were flying to some location in a private plane.

"This movie could use a song, Willie," said Sydney. "What do you say?"

I was always willing, ready, and able to write a song.

"What do you think it should be about?" I asked.

"Being on the road."

Nonchalantly, I threw out a line at them: "On the road again."

Sydney and Jerry looked at each other for a second or two. Then, at the same time, they said, "That's it!"

"But do you have a melody?" asked Sydney.

"I will by the time we get to the studio."

By the time the plane landed, the lyrics were written.

On the road again
Just can't wait to get on the road again

The life I love is making music with my friends
And I can't wait to get on the road again
On the road again
Goin' places that I've never been
Seein' things that I may never see again
And I can't wait to get on the road again
On the road again
Like a band of gypsies we go down the highway
We're the best of friends
Insisting that the world keep turning our way

As promised, the melody clicked in shortly thereafter.

Independent of the film, the song wound up with a life of its own. Even got nominated for an Academy Award for Best Original Song. Became a big hit on its own—so big that when it was time to air the movie on TV, they changed the title from *Honeysuckle Rose* to *On the Road Again.* That simple song, a part of my nightly repertoire ever since I wrote it back in 1979, has had a longer battery life than the film it was written for.

The studios took a liking to me. In *Barbarosa,* written by Bill Wittliff, I played the lead character, a badass cowboy, and costarred with Gary Busey. The press had been calling me an outlaw for so long, I figured I might as well get paid to play one.

And in *Songwriter,* I was Doc Jenkins, the most autobiographical Willie Nelson character of all. That's 'cause it was written by Bud Shrake, who knew me so well. The story has Doc all mixed up with hardheaded producers, crooked promoters, and sexy women. He means well. All he wants is a simple life with his wife and children, but he just can't resist the temptations of the road. That sounded awfully familiar. I was having fun, but my costar Kris Kristofferson proved to be a singer who, unlike me, had honest to God acting chops.

At about the same time my movie career kicked off—the tail end of the seventies—I was able to buy the old Pedernales Country Club together with a large parcel of land. Thirty miles outside Austin, this acreage was the perfect spot. There was lots of room for friends and family to camp out as long as they wanted. This was also where I'd build my recording studio.

Having my own private nine-hole golf course was the icing on the cake. The course was rocky and rough, but who cared? My golf game was rocky and rough. In the summertime, my usual golf outfit was shorts and jogging shoes, and no shirt.

Deer loved to roam over the course, and I didn't mind.

One time on the golf course, I was on the fourth hole when one of the golf hustlers I invited to play intentionally whacked a line drive into the ribs of a doe.

"Great shot, huh?" he asked.

"So fuckin' great," I said, "that I don't ever wanna see your ass on this course again."

I sent him packing.

I had a rule: If you wanted to hunt deer, you had to climb a tree and jump down onto the deer. That was the only way you were allowed to bring a deer down. I'm glad to report that no one even tried.

At Pedernales, I'm big on protecting our deer, wild ducks, geese, and turtles. No one's allowed to hunt rabbits. It's a golf course, but it's also a game park where the animals have just as much right to be there as us.

When it came to golf, I tried my dead level best to improve my game. Even had pros like my good buddy Lee Trevino give me tips. Tried meditation. Tried visualization. Played dead sober and played seriously stoned. And yes, I did get better. I had days when my swing was poetry itself, when my drives were long and true and my putting super-precise. On such days I convinced myself that I had finally learned the game.

But like a wily woman, golf has a mind of her own. Golf will fool you. She'll get you to thinking that you understand her. Golf lures you into believing you've tamed her. Golf will even have you convinced that you've conquered her.

And then, just when your confidence is higher than a kite, golf will fuck you up. In one stroke, you'll forget everything you've learned about a good swing. Your drives will hook out of sight and your putts will miss the mark by a mile. Once having pleased you, golf will tease you, turn on you, and frustrate you to where you're smashing your club into trees. You'll vow to quit, but you'll be back the next day.

My good buddy Coach Royal and I would shake things up by something we called speed golf. We were known to play thirty-six holes in four or five hours. Wasn't that we played well—just fast, as if speeding up the game would somehow calm our addiction. It didn't. Just made us wanna play more.

I'm convinced that the only way to survive the sport is the same way you survive a woman: with humor. And humility. If you eventually accept the sad fact that you're never gonna win, you'll be fine.

I tried to inject some humor at Pedernales. Humor is always a saving grace. My good friend singer Don Cherry loves to talk about being on the links at Pedernales when he and his wife were having a hellish time getting along. Before he took a shot, he looked down at the ball and said, "If that was only her head!" Then he drove the ball a country mile, straight down the middle.

I teed up next, and when my shot actually outdistanced Don's, I turned to him and said, "I never liked her either."

Yes, sir, humor helps. Also helped posting a few rules and etiquette for the course. For instance: no more than twelve in your foursome; no bikinis, miniskirts, or sexually exploitative attire allowed, except on women; no gambling, except if you're broke or if you need a legal deduction for a charitable or educational expense.

25

ALWAYS

BACK ON DECEMBER 5, 1978, my dad died. Ira Doyle Nelson was only sixty-five. The cause was lung cancer. He'd been a heavy smoker his entire life. Towards the end he'd needed oxygen, night and day. It hurt my heart to see him suffer. A strong and determined man, he fought for his breath till the very end. The ordeal was long and painful.

I don't want to list the many friends and loved ones who have died of this disease. I don't want to go into a tirade against tobacco. This isn't the time or place to go into the history of an industry that for decades hid the truth about its product's deadly properties. Better to simply remember my dad as a good man, a good fiddler, a good mechanic, and a well-meaning human being who loved his children and grandchildren.

His decision to leave me with his mom and dad had been a wise one. Even though he didn't raise me and Bobbie, he was always there when we needed him. We were never estranged.

It didn't matter that we didn't have a traditional father-son relationship. Didn't matter that months could go by when we weren't in touch. The love and concern were always there. During his final years, it comforted us both that we lived in Austin and were closer than ever.

On November 9, 1979, we lost Mama Nelson. Five years earlier, when she was no longer able to care for herself, we moved her from Abbott to a nursing home in Fort Worth. By then she was in her late eighties. It wasn't easy to see this fiercely independent woman lose her physical strength. She never did lose her spiritual strength. Her faith was absolute. Her frailty did nothing to weaken her conviction about the goodness of God. Some people preach the Word; others live it. Mama Nelson lived it. When Daddy Nelson died and left her with two young grandchildren, she had relied on the Word to see her through. The Word galvanized her spirit and her resourcefulness. She taught music, she cooked in the school cafeteria, she gardened, she did whatever was required to keep body and soul together—and she did it all with grace.

When I ventured out into the world, playing in the local bars and juke joints of Hill County, she had her reservations. She had never stepped foot in a bar. She could have been discouraging. She could have been judgmental. But Mama Nelson was neither of those things. Her thing was love. Love trumped everything.

She knew that the musical talent God had given Bobbie and me couldn't be contained in a small hamlet like Abbott. It couldn't be contained in our Methodist church. Not only did she allow our musical adventures to lead us into a wider world, but she gave us her blessing. I'm forever grateful that she lived to see our success. She lived to come to many of our shows, every one of which concluded with a hymn—"Amazing Grace" or "Will the Circle Be Unbroken" or "In the Garden"—that we had learned from her.

The spirit of Nancy Elizabeth Nelson is eternal and a source of inspiration to me, now more than ever.

It was special to me to be close to both of them at the end. Everything felt as together as it had ever been. And my new perch near the Pedernales turned out to be a good location for the Fourth of July festivities in 1979 and '80. Got to jam onstage with two of my favorite artists from two different generations: Ernest Tubb and Leon Russell. With me in the middle, we were able to close all generation gaps. Merle Haggard was there along with Charlie Daniels, Johnny Paycheck, and Asleep at the Wheel.

To be honest, not all my neighbors were pleased. But their beef wasn't really what you might expect.

"Been meaning to ask you something about these goddamn crazy picnics of yours," said one old-timer who lived nearby in the Austin hill country.

"Shoot," I said.

"Are they supposed to be rock concerts or country music jamborees?"

"Damned if I know."

"When I saw all these hippies running all over your golf course, I thought, *Oh shit, I'm staying away.*"

"That's your right."

"But then I look up and here comes Ray Price's tour bus. Hell, Willie, I been listening to Ray Price since he took over Hank Williams's band after Hank died."

"I was in Ray's band," I said. "I was a certified Cherokee Cowboy."

"Then you know better. What in hell do you think you're doing with hippie-dippie assholes?"

"Same thing I did with Ray Price. Playing music."

I wanted to do more than play music on my Pedernales property; I wanted to record there. With surroundings so serene and a vibe so relaxed, it was the perfect spot for a studio. Where else could I record in the morning and, while the engineers were mixing, step outside and shoot nine holes in the afternoon?

Turned out that there was a bankrupt restaurant on the grounds that I was able to buy out of receivership. My idea was to convert it to a studio. At the time I'd been working with Chips Moman, a crackerjack producer who had his own studio in Memphis where he'd cut records for some of the biggest names in music. Chips and his crew knew how to build a studio from scratch that would put out the kind of soulful sound that I was looking for. Our original name for the facility was Cutt and Putt.

Some professional friends had reservations.

"You need some separation between your home life and recording life. Don't shit where you work."

"Does a bear shit in the woods?" I asked. "Well, I'm no different. I just wanna be comfortable and do what comes naturally." Plus I was pretty used to having everything together by now.

In less than a year the Pedernales Recording Studio—the more formal name—was up and ready to roll. It was a world-class facility.

Chips produced the first album I cut there. True to my fashion, the song selection broke traditional boundaries. I sang a song that Chips had written with Dan Penn and that Jerry Wexler had produced for Aretha, "Do Right Woman, Do Right Man." I sang it nice and slow and it felt great. Felt like I understood the story.

I did *not* understand the story of "A Whiter Shade of Pale." I knew it'd been a hit by a group called Procol Harum. But that's all I knew. Now *that's* a song where the words made no sense, unless it had something to do with an acid trip.

"You know what these lyrics are about?" I asked Waylon Jennings, who, at Chips's suggestion, sang the song with me as a duet.

"I have no fuckin' idea, hoss."

"You wanna sing it?"

"Why not?"

I believe Waylon and I did a good job, proving that the singers don't always have to understand what they're singing about. Sometimes all you need is a strong melody to pull you in.

I covered an old Everly Brothers smash from 1960, "Let It Be Me," and recut one of my favorite end-of-the-night sad songs, "The Party's Over," written during another era in my life but still relevant to practically every evening in the life of a wandering troubadour.

Then Merle Haggard dropped by one of the sessions. We were discussing doing a duets album together, and Chips brought in a song that had been sung by Brenda Lee and Elvis. I hadn't heard either version.

Very first time I listened to "Always on My Mind," written by Chips's guitarist Johnny Christopher along with Wayne Thompson and Mark James, I knew I wanted to record it.

"Wouldn't mind saving it for our album," I said to Merle. "We could sing it together."

"I don't hear it," said Merle. "You go on and do it alone. I don't think it'll work as a duet."

I'll never know whether Merle was right or not. That's because the song became the title of the album and a hit single. Went to number one on the country charts and crossed over to the top five on the pop charts. Turned into one of the biggest records of my career.

And turned out that when Merle and I did get together to cut that album, we had a monster hit of our own.

Mark Rothbaum likes to say that Merle and I are like two bookends holding up a shelf full of music. I take that as a compliment. Merle is all about authenticity. What you see is what you get. Doesn't matter that he came out of Bakersfield and I came out of Abbott. Our roots are the same. We share the same musical heroes, the same human values. Merle is my brother and a man who appreciates the good herb as much as I do.

When Merle came to Pedernales to cut an album with me, I figured it'd be a breeze—and it was. If anything, Merle's more kicked back than I am, and that's saying something. We got Chips to supervise the sessions. We did one of Merle's great tunes—"Reasons to Quit"—and a couple of mine: "Half a Man" and "Opportunity to Cry." Before we knew it, we'd sung down something like twenty songs, but Chips, who has a sixth sense about these things, kept saying that he didn't hear a hit. Far as I was concerned, all twenty tunes were hits. But that's just my nature. If it sounds good to me, I figure it'll sound good to most folks.

Nonetheless, Chips kept looking for more songs and we kept recording. Didn't mind because singing with Merle is always a treat.

At some point in this process my daughter Lana called me up late at night to say she'd found a song she thought I might like. It was Emmylou Harris singing something written by Townes Van Zandt, a wonderful Austin writer.

"Daddy," said Lana, "you ever hear 'Pancho and Lefty'?"

"Don't believe I have, darling."

"Well, let me come over and play it for you now."

"Right now? It's awfully late."

"The song's awfully good."

Lana ran over. One listen told me that she was right. I loved Emmylou's version—I love anything Emmylou does—but I could hear how the song lent itself to a duet sung by two men. It had two male characters. Pancho was a Mexican bandito, Lefty his pal. When Pancho is killed by the Federales, he may or may not have been betrayed by Lefty. I loved the line that said, "The dust that Pancho bit down south, ended up in Lefty's mouth." I loved the song's essential mystery. I saw it as a great Western, and I couldn't wait for Merle to hear it.

Went straight to Merle's bus that was parked outside the Pedernales studio and woke his ass up.

"What's so fucking important?" he wanted to know.

"This song."

When I played it for him, he liked it but wanted to go back to sleep. "We'll do it tomorrow after the band's learned it."

"The band's already in the studio, Merle," I said. "Chips and the boys are waiting on us. I got them to work an arrangement. We're good to go."

Reluctantly, Merle dragged himself out of bed.

Didn't take us more than one take to run down the vocals. It was like we'd been singing the song for years.

Next day I was on the golf course, working off my energy and excitement from last night's session.

On about the fourth hole, here comes Merle.

"Hey, Willie," he said. "Been thinking about that 'Pancho and Lefty' song. It really is something, but I'm not sure my vocal was all it should have been. Let me run into the studio and take another crack at my part."

"Too late, Merle," I said. "We already sent the fucker to New York. They heard it and think it's a smash."

It *was* a smash. Went all the way to number one. And the album, named *Pancho and Lefty,* wound up selling millions. Even better, my daughter Lana directed a great video version of the song.

* * *

Not everything I recorded sold millions. Far from it. Did an album called *Somewhere over the Rainbow* with a *Stardust*-like lineup of songs. Didn't sell like *Stardust*—nothing did—but I didn't care. I got to sing more of the old standards that I loved.

I also got to go off and do jazz projects, inspired by my good friend Jackie King, a master guitarist who'd played with everyone from bebopper Sonny Stitt to blues shouter Joe Turner. We cut a record called *Angel Eyes* and, just to be different, played the old cowboy tune "Tumbling Tumbleweeds" together with a swinger, Bob Wills's "My Window Faces the South." No spectacular sales, but I got to play with Jackie King, an artistic pleasure unlike any other. We even went to Japan, where the record was first released, to perform it live.

Japan has strict drug laws. Getting caught with a skinny joint could mean a year in the can.

"Don't fuck around," said my manager, Mark, who, as something of a joke, turned up at my Tokyo hotel room with a pound of hemp seed.

"What the hell am I going to do with hemp seed?" I said.

"Strain it," he said, "and maybe you'll get a buzz."

Hate to confess it, but I actually did strain the shit and rolled it into a joint. I smoked it all the way down.

"You get a buzz?" Mark asked.

"No," I said, "and that proves the difference between hemp and pot."

* * *

Because money was plentiful, the eighties was a time when I could relax in the studio and do what I wanted. I loved duets because duets are a beautiful expression of friendship. They're a way to have a musical conversation with a buddy. Because Pedernales was off the beaten trail and so relaxed, my buddies loved to come there. I welcomed them all.

I was honored when Ray Charles traveled to Pedernales to sing a duet with me on "Seven Spanish Angels." He sang the shit outta the song, which felt like a Western movie, a sad refrain about gritty gunfighters and death on the lonesome Texas prairie. Became a big hit.

In my studio, I had to laugh when Ray ran his fingers over the board and started telling the engineer about how to better manipulate the controls. Before anyone else, Ray was also into computers. Years later he was the first guy to email me.

I was in London listening to the radio when I heard a singer I liked. He had a distinctive lilt in his voice. After asking around, I found out his name was Julio Iglesias. Might be interesting to do a duet with him. Something different. Didn't matter to me if he was little known.

"Little known!" exclaimed Mark. "This guy's one of the biggest-selling singers in the world. He's number one in Latin America. He's huge in Europe, huge in Asia."

"So much the better," I said. "See if he wants to sing with me."

He did. He picked out a song with English lyrics. It was something called "To All the Girls I've Loved Before." Apparently the writers—Hal David and Albert Hammond—had composed it with Sinatra in mind.

"Ask him if he'd mind cutting it at Pedernales," I told Mark.

Turned out he didn't mind at all. He'd fly in on his private jet.

"You might want to cool it with the joints, though, Willie," said Mark. "Julio's a Spanish lawyer."

A day before he arrived, I still hadn't heard the song.

Coach Darrell Royal, who was hanging around the studio, asked, "Don't you need to hear the song to see if you wanna sing it?"

"Hell," I said, "a guy who sells that many records worldwide is bound to have good taste."

Turned out Julio had great taste. He arrived in grand style. There were at least a dozen dudes in his entourage. When he showed up at the studio, he was wearing all white. Nice-looking guy. Perfectly mannered.

"Hope you don't mind the down-home atmosphere in here, Julio," I said, "but we believe in relaxing when recording."

"I thoroughly approve."

"Good." And with that I lit up a fat one.

No objections from Julio. He was focused on singing. He had a suggestion or two on how I might phrase the lyrics. The suggestions were good, and I took them to heart.

Me and Julio were simpatico. Maybe it was his suggestions that made the song go to number one. If that was the reason, more power to him. More power to me for having a hit duet with a European artist commanding an international market.

I'd done so many one-off duets by now that the record label wanted to put 'em together in a compilation record.

"What do you think we should call the album, Willie?" asked one of the suits.

"*Half Nelson,*" I said.

The man laughed and said that seemed suitable. The title stuck.

Can't tell you how much I liked sticking around Pedernales. I'd wake up in the morning, wander over to the studio, never knowing who might drop by. Say hello to Hank Snow. Or Roger Miller. Or Webb Pierce. Or George Jones. Or Kenny Rogers. Or Hoyt Axton.

When old friends like Faron Young, the man who had helped me get going by singing "Hello Walls," showed up, I was all smiles. Didn't matter that his career had cooled off. Happens to all of us. If I could do anything to help, I was ready. My studio was his for the asking. Styles might change, but great country singers like Faron and Ray Price are forever.

Other artists from different fields, like Bon Jovi and Aerosmith, came not to sing with me but to cut tracks of their own. I was gratified that they had that kind of confidence in my studio.

In 1983, the year I turned fifty, my mother, Myrle, died. Once again, it was that ol' devil called lung cancer. It was another painful death, another gruesome reminder of how tobacco poisons our bodies.

Mom was one of the great characters. She was as far from

traditional as any mom could get. She was fiercely independent and full of self-confidence. This was one woman who did her own thing. At the time of her passing, she was living in Yakima in the state of Washington.

Even though she left us in Abbott shortly after I was born, I never felt as though she'd left us at all. She was always popping in when we'd least expect her. Always had a smile on her face. Always had an encouraging word.

During my early life when I needed a fresh start and ran out to Eugene to see her, she welcomed me with open arms. No matter where she was, I knew I could count on her. Later, when I had some success, she'd come to the shows and loved being introduced to the crowd. She'd come onstage and sing with us during the finale. I was proud to show her off. There was one happy time at Caesars Palace in Vegas and another down in Houston when she came marching in the moment we broke into "Up Against the Wall, Redneck Mother."

Until cancer caught her, Mom stayed young and vital.

She once wrote me a note that said how proud she was that I'd made something of myself. She talked about her lifelong determination to be self-reliant.

"You have the same quality, son," she wrote, "and because of that quality you can go to sleep every night knowing that everything's all right. Lots of men are always looking over their shoulder, worrying that their bad deeds are coming back to bite 'em in the butt. You don't have those worries. You're real loyal to your friends and you're real good to your fellow man. I've never seen you hate on anyone, son, and everyone can feel that you want the best for them. I've always wanted the best for you. You found a formula for living that suits you just fine. If I had anything to do with finding that formula, I'm mighty glad."

Mom had everything to do with my finding that formula. She lived a life that said, *Go your own way, chase your own dreams.*

I was lucky to have such a mother.

I was lucky to be surrounded by such a strong family. Lucky to have a spread like Pedernales. Lucky to have the studio and the golf course and the great camaraderie with cherished companions.

Yet for all this good fortune, something was tugging at my heart. I felt the need to reconnect, to go somewhere I hadn't been for too long.

I still felt a hankering to go home.

26

"BURN THE FUCKER DOWN!"

I WAS BACK IN ABBOTT, the only place on planet Earth where my heart can truly rest in peace.

Austin is cool. Colorado is high and mighty. The California coast is something to behold. The world is filled with spots of great natural beauty. And even though no one in their right mind would put Abbott in that class, I'd never be in my right mind if I hadn't been raised right in Abbott.

Abbott gave me stability. It rooted me in the land and in the people—good-hearted and well-meaning people—who anchored me in love. One of those people was my old running buddy Zeke Varnon, the dominoes demon and poker-playing devil who gave me some of my first glimpses into the wild side of life.

It was the eighties, and Abbott was celebrating its centennial birthday. I was asked to play a benefit to raise funds for a big birthday party, and I jumped at it. Good opportunity to go home and renew old friendships. Walking around town, it hurt me to see that the little house where Bobbie and I had been raised by Mama and Daddy Nelson was gone. But I noticed that the house of Doc Simms, the physician who had brought me into this world, was still standing. Wasn't luxurious by any means, but it was a good solid two-story house. Hadn't changed much in all these years. Doc was long gone but his relatives had held on to it. When I asked whether they'd be willing to sell, they were only too happy to see the house stay in the hands of a son of Abbott.

"See if they'll take five thousand dollars over their asking price," I told the real estate agent.

With the deal done, I felt like I was really back home. Got some old furniture, fixed up the wiring, put in a new air conditioner, and was ready to go. From then on, I always kept a month's worth of clothes in Abbott—meaning I could go into hiding in my hometown whenever the world of show business got to be too much.

Some years later someone put up a billboard on Highway 35—the heavy traffic interstate that runs from Dallas to Austin—that said, "Abbott, home of Willie Nelson." Abbott sits right off 35, and the last thing I wanted was a bunch of tourists running around Abbott to find out where I lived.

I was playing poker with Zeke and complaining about how the billboard blew my anonymity when Zeke said, "Well, what do you think we should do about it?"

"Burn the fucker down!" I said.

Zeke didn't blink. "Good idea."

So like two teenagers, we snuck out to the interstate. We

stopped to buy a can of gas. A cop came by, recognized me, and said, "Hey, Willie. What are you guys up to?"

"We're going to burn down a sign," I said.

He just laughed and went on his way. He didn't believe the truth.

We then drove over to the sign, soaked it with gas, and lit it with a match. It started to burn but then stopped. Must have been treated with some anti-inflammatory fluid. Pissed me off. So we poured more gasoline and lit another match. Still no go. We went home frustrated.

Next day I learned that the sign actually did catch fire some time after we left and had to be extinguished by the lone Abbott fire truck. Not only that, but an innocent teenager was picked up and charged with arson.

I called the police and told one of the boys to let the kid go.

"How come, Willie?" he asked.

"It was me and Zeke who set that blaze."

"Why would you do something like that?"

"I didn't like the sign. I didn't want the attention."

"Well, hell, Willie, you should have told us that. We would have taken it down for you."

"Was more fun to try and burn it," I said.

The kid was set free and—at least for a while—I didn't have to worry about unwanted visits from strangers.

Margie Lundy was no stranger to me. I'd known her all my life. She owned the Nite Owl beer parlor just outside town, one of the first places where I was paid to play music. I loved Margie.

She'd been charged with killing her brother-in-law but claimed self-defense. Her lawyer asked if I'd testify as a character witness on her behalf.

Hell, yes.

"She's a jewel," I told the jury. "One of the kindest, most loving people I've ever known. Never heard anyone say a bad word about Margie. If Margie killed him, he must have had it coming."

The prosecutor went after me. What kind of witness is Willie Nelson, a man known to smoke dope and chase women?

Glad to say that during the trial it was proven that Margie's brother-in-law had attacked her in her sleep and she had acted in self-defense. The good people of Hill County set Margie free.

Being back in Abbott, even for short periods of time, let me reassess, regroup, and figure out what I really wanted to do.

After my Fourth of July picnics had been moved to big stadiums in New Jersey, Syracuse, and Atlanta, I moved the party back to Texas in 1984 and '85 to Southpark, a huge outdoor venue outside Austin. The mid-eighties picnics—with Waylon and Kris and Johnny Cash and Faron Young—were some of the best.

It was also in the mid-eighties that I finally got serious about making a movie out of *Red Headed Stranger.* Felt like I'd been fucking around with that project long enough.

By now it was obvious that neither Universal nor Robert Redford was gonna green-light the project. So I bought the rights back and, together with writer Bill Wittliff, became a producer. That meant finding our own money. Don Tyson, the poultry mogul from Arkansas, stepped up to the plate. He joined my limited partnership and threw in a quarter of a million, enough to get us started. Fifteen other investors put in $50,000 each to get us the million dollars needed to make the film.

Once Bill's script was ready to go, I fulfilled my longtime dream of playing the stranger himself and got Morgan Fairchild to play my wife. Katharine Ross played my other woman. I put a couple of guys from the band—Bee Spears and Paul English—into the film along with lots of other pals like Austin lawyer Joe Longley. It was a homegrown affair.

Not knowing what I was doing, it made sense that I'd run out of money before finishing principal photography. When that happened, Carolyn Mugar, a good friend from Boston, came to the rescue with a cool half million.

Naturally we were shooting at Pedernales, the only logical place for a true-blue Willie Nelson Western. Right next to my golf course, I built an 1870s frontier town. We put up the facades of a bank, stables, stores, and a church. Eventually we actually built a freestanding saloon that was later named World Headquarters. To this day you'll find me there playing poker and dominoes while bullshitting with the boys.

"What are you naming this town, Willie?" I was asked when the set was completed.

"Luck," I said. "Gonna put up a sign that spells it out: 'When you're here, you're in Luck. When you're not here, you're outta Luck.' "

All during the production, I was in Luck. The filming went smoothly and the final cut impressed all my backers. They were even more impressed when Shep Gordon, the famous rock manager, decided to buy the finished product, paying enough so that my investors got reimbursed with a 25 percent profit on their money.

Looking at the film today, I still marvel at the beauty of Neil Roach's fine photography. The costumes are authentic as hell. The action scenes keep you at the edge of your seat. And the acting—if you don't mind me playing another version of myself—is pretty goddamn good. Most importantly, I got the thing made. And when it was all over, I got to keep my frontier town intact. I was still in Luck.

Getting rerooted in Abbott did something else for me. It reminded me that I'd started out as a member of the Future Farmers of America. Being back home allowed me to see how the small farmers were doing. The answer was, not well.

In 1985, I was talking to Bob Dylan at a Live Aid concert.

"This is a great thing, Willie," he said. "But wouldn't it be great if we could do something like this to help out small farmers in America?"

Dylan's question hit me hard. I started researching exactly what was happening in American agriculture. In the late summer of that same year, I went to do my annual concert at the Saint Louis fair, where Illinois governor Jim Thompson always showed up. Big Jim and I would sit around, eat a bowl of chili, drink a beer, and talk about the world. This time I told him about Dylan's remark. Having heard from my farmer friends about their life-and-death struggles, I was concerned.

Big Jim shared those same concerns. He said that the situation for the family farm had never been worse.

"Well, sir," I said, "we're going to do something about it. We're going to raise some serious money."

"When?"

"Right now. I'll put on a show to raise money, and get my friends to help out."

"Who do you think you can round up?"

"I can think of a couple of pickers and singers willing to help."

"If you want to put on the show in Illinois, I'll help with the arrangements."

"Let's do it," I told Big Jim.

I called Dylan, Neil Young, and John Mellencamp and asked them to perform. They all agreed. The show sold out in twenty-one days. And only weeks later—in September—I was standing onstage at the University of Illinois's Memorial Stadium in Champaign, staring out at some eighty thousand fans. Everyone showed up. Beyond Bob, Neil, and John, there was Billy Joel, B.B. King, Waylon, Kris, Merle, Roy Orbison, Charley Pride, Bonnie Raitt, Loretta Lynn, June Carter, and Johnny Cash. We wound up raising $7 million for family farmers.

It didn't stop there. The fate of the small farmer was a topic I couldn't ignore. More I read, more motivated I became to help publicize their plight. I went to Washington to testify before a Senate committee, telling them how in recent years we'd gone from eight million small-family farmers to two million. Every week hundreds of farms were going under. The legislation was woefully inadequate. They had one bill called Freedom to Farm, but its provisions were so lame that the farmers called it the Freedom to Fail bill.

"If we abandon the farmer," I testified, "we're abandoning the essential values that made America great. It's all about our relationship to the land—how we cultivate it, how it yields goodness and provides us with sustenance. And it's not just economic sustenance. It's spiritual sustenance. It's our heart. We need to make sure that our heart stays strong. We need to stand up for the farmers—today, tomorrow, and as long as it takes to guarantee their survival."

I set up a hotline back at Pedernales where farmers in need could call, voice their complaints, and get some guidance about where to find relief. The calls came in by the thousands.

I also vowed to make Farm Aid a yearly event. When the first one was such a huge hit, I asked my good friend Carolyn Mugar to serve as executive director. It was Carolyn's leadership that turned the shows into an institution respected the world over.

In 1986, I turned my annual Fourth of July picnic into a Farm Aid benefit. We held it at Manor Downs, a racetrack outside Austin. The lineup was the most freewheeling and multigenre ever: we had everyone from Stevie Ray Vaughan to Rick James to Julio Iglesias to the Beach Boys to Los Lobos.

I'm not saying that my friends and I single-handedly saved the farmer or stopped the suffering of those looking to make a living off the land. We did not. In this postmodern world of corporate greed and government indifference, the family farm continues to struggle. But the struggle is a noble one. And I'm proud to be part of it—and that after thirty years, we're still going strong.

27

FALLING IN LOVE

BACK IN ABBOTT, OL' ZEKE and I were talking about midlife crises.

"They say it happens to a man when he's in his forties or fifties," said Zeke.

"Well, I'm fifty-two," I said, "and I haven't had no crisis yet."

"Are you kidding? You've had one after another. You just don't call it that."

"What do I call it?" I asked.

"Falling in love. Every time you fall in love it's another goddamn crisis."

I started to argue with Zeke, but stopped.

Reason I stopped was 'cause I knew my old friend was right.

But before I start yakking about the next great love affair in my life—the one that continues to this day—I should point out that my oldest love, and the one to which I've been truest, was always music. I never cheated on music and music never cheated on me. Music has always been the connection that led to my deepest friendships. If I meet a musician who has different political and religious views than mine, those differences dissolve the minute we start to play. The musical discussion never involves bitterness or jealousy. It's all about working together in the cause of beauty.

I say all this because on paper, the combination of me, Waylon, Kris Kristofferson, and Johnny Cash might not make a lot of sense. Waylon, of course, was a wild man, not known for taming his tongue. He'd say anything to anyone anytime he pleased. Johnny was a straight-up patriot. I say that without prejudice. Johnny championed the cause of the Native American back in the early sixties, when to do so was hardly in fashion. His album *Bitter Tears: Ballads of the American Indian* took a hard look at the injustices suffered by the various tribes. Johnny had a high political consciousness, but one that came out of a traditionally conservative tradition. On the other hand, Kris was a firebrand liberal, a former Rhodes scholar and longtime opponent of American adventurism abroad.

Then there was me and my peculiar politics. I wasn't a card-carrying member of any political party, but I did have my causes. I was a flag-waving advocate of legalizing pot and utilizing cannabis in dozens of positive ways. I had my save-the-family-farm crusade that I'd plug at every opportunity.

Not since the days of Ray Price and his Cherokee Cowboys, though, had I been a member of a communal touring group.

That all changed when Johnny called me to say he was putting together a TV Christmas show to be filmed in Montreux, Switzerland, for worldwide viewing.

"I want you, Willie, and I want you to bring Waylon and Kris."

Didn't at all mind being a guest on someone's television show.

"It's more than a one-shot," Johnny added. "I want the four of us to cut a record together in Nashville before the show airs so we have something to sell during the holiday season."

When I didn't say yes immediately, John prodded me. "Hell, Willie, you've recorded with everyone in the world except me. Don't you think it's time?"

"I do, John," I said. "Let me talk to the boys."

Waylon was willing, but Kris was hesitant. He wasn't sure he'd fit in.

"You can use the occasion to pitch us some of your new songs," I said.

That's all Kris needed to hear. He was in.

Chips Moman, who ran the recording session, showed us an original by Jimmy Webb called "The Highwayman." There were four verses, one for each of us. All I had to do was read the first one to know that the song would work perfectly.

I was a highwayman, along the coach roads I did ride
With sword and pistol by my side
Many a young maid lost her baubles to my trade
Many a soldier shed his lifeblood on my blade
The bastards hung me in the spring of '25
But I am still alive

Kris played the part of a sailor, Waylon a dam builder, and Johnny a starship commander.

You wouldn't think that our four uneven voices would blend. But they did. They fit together like a jigsaw puzzle. The song and the album were hits.

During a photo session to promote the show, the photographer asked, "Of all places, why in the world are you guys taping a Christmas show in Montreux, Switzerland?"

Before anyone had a chance to respond, Waylon spoke up.

"Because that's where the baby Jesus was born."

Our successful show gave birth to another Highwaymen project, a remaking of the old classic Western *Stagecoach*.

Kris, who had become a bona fide leading man after making *A Star Is Born* with Barbra Streisand, was reluctant. He didn't like the script. Johnny and Waylon were willing 'cause they thought it'd be fun, another way to bolster the Highwaymen myth. I went along 'cause of my love of Westerns. They gave me the title of executive producer, but only 'cause they thought I'd keep Kris in line. I couldn't. Every time he spoke to the press, he spoke candidly.

"The screenplay is shit," he said, "and I expect the film to be no better."

Johnny became quickly disillusioned on account of how shabbily the production company was treating the Native American actors. I stepped in to make sure that treatment improved.

As the lead actors, we ourselves were treated shabbily. We'd get up at the crack of dawn for early morning shoots, get in our costumes, go through makeup, and arrive on time only to learn that the scene had been scrapped. That happened again and again.

All I wanted was to make merry and keep things light.

In one scene a female character, played by Bing Crosby's daughter Mary, was giving birth. Before they had a chance to pull out the baby, I pulled out a live rabbit. Everyone howled. Everyone, that is, except the director.

The most memorable thing about *Stagecoach* wasn't the movie itself. It was a beguiling young lady applying the makeup.

Meet Ann Marie D'Angelo. Everyone called her Annie.

By then I was separated from Connie, who, like Martha and Shirley before her, had tried her level best to put up with me. No easy task. My years with Connie were not notable for fidelity on my part. I don't say that to be prideful. I say it to be truthful. The plain truth was that, despite my love for Connie and loyalty to my children, I had wandered off more than once. It got to where Connie had had enough.

I had no defense. By then I was famous for avoiding marital confrontations. Can't quite recall the sequence of events—whether Connie kicked me out or whether I just took a hike. Either way, by the time I showed up in Tucson to make *Stagecoach,* my marriage had collapsed.

I met Annie in the makeup trailer. She was pretty, she was smart as a whip, and she sparkled with energy. She was also super self-assured. I loved talking to her.

Our first conversation involved my hair. It was on the long side. The producers had implored her, as the chief makeup artist, to ask me to cut it. They thought it was out of character with Doc Holliday, the man I was playing.

When she made the request, though, I could tell that her heart wasn't in it.

"What do you really think of the idea of my cutting my hair?" I asked her.

"Personally, I think it's unnecessary and ridiculous."

I couldn't help but smile—and so did she.

That was the start of a friendship. I really wanted to be more than friends but I learned that when it came to dating men, Annie had rules: no celebrities, no divorcés, and no one with kids. I struck out on all three counts.

One night during the shoot the whole crew decided to go to a jazz club. We rode over there on my bus. That's when I asked Annie if she knew how to play dominoes. She didn't but was eager to learn. Her brilliant mind went right to work and she caught on fast.

Jazz clubs are good places to get to know a lady.

Jazz is a make-it-up-as-you-go-along kind of music. I see courting the same way. You go with the flow. It helps when the musicians on the bandstand are playing a bluesy tune. The blues might be sad, but the blues are sexy. And when you don't play the blues too loudly, you don't drown out the conversation of a man trying to get to know a woman.

From the get-go, I knew Annie was special. She was fine, but also feisty.

"Where's all that fire come from?" I asked as we sat alone at a corner table.

"Sicily. My father's people are hot-blooded Sicilians. My mother's family is from Ofena, Italy, near L'Aquila."

"Right there we have a lot in common," I said. "I grew up right next to Italy and Aquilla."

"I thought you grew up in Texas."

"I did. Italy, Texas, and Aquilla, Texas, are little towns close to Abbott, where I lived. I visited them all the time."

She laughed.

It's always great when you can make a lady laugh, and vice versa. Annie and I loved each other's humor. Over the course of making this movie, we were together from early morning, when she applied the makeup, to late at night, when she removed it. It was during these long days that we realized how much we loved spending time together. Didn't take long to realize we were falling in love.

She told me how she'd grown up in L.A., where, through her cousin Joe Laird, she wound up working at the old Desilu Studios. From there, she became one of the industry's leading makeup artists, working on film projects all over the map. She was a strong and independent woman who had the kind of honest tell-it-like-it-is attitude that I admired.

She told me the story about how once, while working on an Elmore Leonard film in Detroit, she was alone at the end of a long night's shoot. It was 2 a.m. Everyone had left, no cabs to be found, and she faced a long walk alone through a bad neighborhood back to her hotel.

"It was probably a silly thing to do," she said, "but I did it. About two blocks before I got to the hotel, two guys started following me. I picked up my pace. So did they. The faster I walked, the closer they came. I was almost at the hotel but knew I couldn't make it before they caught up with me. So I turned and faced them. I actually moved closer to them and said, 'Where the fuck is the hotel entrance?' They weren't expecting that. They ended up walking me to the door, where the concierge, on seeing these thugs, freaked out."

Because Annie had a keen sense of right and wrong, she had to be convinced that I really was free, that my marriage was long over, and that my celebrity and status as a dad would in no way hurt our relationship.

Annie was perceptive. Not only did she have a highly developed sense of world politics, but she knew her personal politics. She was an expert on reading people. Once she saw that I was sincere, I saw that I had a chance.

Then, like the old song says, love walked right in. When that happened, everything fell into place. Love is the great persuader. It's love that changes minds and melts hearts. It's love that brought Annie and me together, and it's love that, nearly thirty years later, has kept us together. When it comes to romantic relationships, that's a record for me. Took me damn near a lifetime to get it right.

28

KEEP ON TRUCKIN'

AT THE START OF THE EIGHTIES, I did a tour with Bonnie Raitt on a few of the Hawaiian Islands. That's when I fell in love with Maui. I bought some beachfront property in a sleepy little town called Paia. Things are pretty kicked back all over the island, but Paia has its own super-relaxed vibe. Folks there leave you alone and aren't too impressed with show business. My kind of place.

Maui has this spiritual quality. It's in the air, the mountains covered in mist, the exotic plants, the wildlife, the sea, the sky, the wise *kupuna* who tells stories that connect the mysteries of nature to the mysteries of man. It's a place whose natural beauty has me thinking on the eternal questions. Doesn't matter that I don't have the answers. The questions themselves are inspiring.

"I got a question for you, Willie," said my friend Zeke, calling me in Maui from back in Texas.

"What is it?"

"I know you've fallen in love with that island. But you don't plan to stay there forever, do you?"

"Just for a spell," I said. "What's on your mind, Zeke?"

"That Fourth of July picnic of yours. You've held it about everywhere but Abbott. What's wrong with Abbott? Abbott ain't good enough for you?"

"You know better than that. But I'm thinking you must have some scheme up your sleeve. What is it, Zeke?"

It wasn't Zeke's scheme. The scheme belonged to Zeke's buddy Carl Cornelius, who owned and operated Carl's Corner, a big truck stop just outside Abbott. Actually, it was more than a truck stop. Next to the restaurant Carl had opened a topless bar. Nearby were expansive grounds large enough to accommodate thousands of fans. I liked the idea of hosting the picnic a stone's throw away from the place of my birth. I also thought if the headquarters was Carl's Corner, we might as well dedicate the event to America's truckers. I'd been singing the praises of the farmers. Why not praise the hard-working truckers who, like the farmers, keep our economy rolling?

Zeke and Carl went all out. They put up billboards with huge pictures of themselves—and me—advertising that this would be the greatest picnic in the history of the civilized world. My friends turned up and it turned out fine. The lineup included Jimmie Vaughan and his Fabulous Thunderbirds, Delbert McClinton, David Allan Coe, Merle, Kris, Dwight Yoakam, Joe Walsh, and a host of others. That was 1987, the same year that Farm Aid III took place in Lincoln, Nebraska. And I started up in Vegas.

* * *

You might think Vegas would be incompatible with my fondness for the spirituality of Hawaii and the ruggedness of Pedernales. But I'm a man of many parts, and Vegas always managed to satisfy several of those parts. I'm not much of a casino gambler. I prefer playing poker and dominoes with good friends at home. But I certainly appreciate that hustler energy that drives a place like Vegas. The excitement behind taking risks and waging big money has been in my blood long as I can remember. Besides, if you're in the entertainment game, there's no way to avoid Vegas. Steve Wynn, one of the city's visionaries, became a good friend. It was Steve who arranged for one of my celebrated dates of the eighties: the time I played the Golden Nugget with Frank Sinatra as my opening act.

I don't say that to brag. Wasn't my idea. It was Steve's. He felt that since I was selling more records than Sinatra, I'd be a bigger draw and was entitled to top billing. I would have been happy with second billing, though. As I told Steve, Sinatra's my favorite singer.

When I was introduced to Frank before the show, I was surprised when he said, "You're *my* favorite singer, Willie."

Unfortunately, he had to cut his show short because of throat problems. Some said it was because he didn't want to open for me. But that's bullshit. Like me, Frank wasn't hung up on being the headliner. He was the consummate pro.

I told you that I ain't much on casinos, but there was one exception. It had to do with Tom Preston, who went by the name of Amarillo Slim. Slim claimed to be the world's best dominoes player. I knew that to be a lie. Zeke Varnon of Hill

County, Texas, held that high honor. After Zeke, I considered myself second best. So when Slim challenged me to a match at a Fremont Street casino, I couldn't resist. The stakes were high. Can't remember the exact figure, but it was hundreds of thousands. Later Slim claimed that Steve Wynn backed me and promised me some fancy car if I beat him. Not true. Steve wasn't even there. He had nothing to do with it. It was just me and Slim.

Slim won, but only because he cheated. He had some guy sneaking looks on me and giving away my moves. I figured Slim was gonna cheat, but I also figured I could beat him anyway. Hurt my pride when I lost.

To show you I wasn't all that pissed, I agreed to write a blurb for his book, *Amarillo Slim in a World Full of Fat People: The Memoirs of the Greatest Gambler Who Ever Lived:* "Every one of Slim's tall tales had me in stitches except, of course, the time that country cowboy took me for a pretty penny playing dominoes. I would never make another bet with Slim, but I'd bet everything that Slim's memoir is the best I've ever read."

In truth, I never bothered to read it.

The Highwaymen turned out to be much more than a one-shot deal. We recorded a bunch of albums and did a bunch of tours, several of them around the world. Rumors spread that Waylon, Johnny, Kris, and I were having ego problems and fighting like cats and dogs. The rumors were bullshit. We saw it as one nonstop transcontinental party. Our wives, our kids, our friends—everyone got along. In spite of the size of the entourage, we traveled the world as one big happy family. I don't mean that we didn't get a little cranky from time to time. Hell, we were getting up there in age. Old pickers tend to get a little cranky. For the most part, though, it was smooth sailing. On and off, the Highwaymen had a solid ten-year run.

Funny thing happened when we were booked to play the Astrodome in Houston. We were the opening act for a livestock show, biggest in the world.

Out of nowhere we get hit by a lawsuit. Turns out another group had called themselves the Highwaymen before us. Some college kids at Wesleyan University took the name and even had a hit with a version of "Michael, Row the Boat Ashore" back in 1961. One of the Highwaymen, Stephen Trott, had become a U.S. circuit judge. Judge Trott hired a lawyer who tried to get a court to issue a restraining order to keep us from performing at the Astrodome.

My manager, Mark, a man who relishes a good fight, brought in heavyweight lawyer Jay Goldberg to argue our case.

Jay stood before the court and said, "Your honor, the plaintiffs have come today with a powerful argument. When seventy thousand fans show up at the Astrodome next month, they will surely arrive with an impassioned expectation of seeing the Highwaymen. I don't mean Willie Nelson, Waylon Jennings, Johnny Cash, and Kris Kristofferson. Those seventy thousand fans have shelled out their hard-earned money to see the *original* Highwaymen, the group from Wesleyan that performed thirty years ago and have not performed since. As the plaintiffs have so ably argued, this is the group synonymous with the name Highwaymen. According to them, they are the artists most readily associated with that brand.

"Your honor, I can only imagine the anger and dismay of the audience when, instead of seeing Judge Stephen S. Trott and his four associates take the stage, the fans see Willie, Waylon, Johnny, and Kris. I'd venture to say we're even running the risk of a riot. I'm surprised that the plaintiffs failed to argue that, if only for the public's safety, these faux Highwaymen must be barred from the Astrodome."

The judge got a kick out of Goldberg's sarcasm and seemed ready to dismiss the case against us. I felt sorry for the original Highwaymen, though, and came up with an idea. I asked my partners whether they'd go along with my plan.

"What you got in mind, Willie?" asked Waylon.

"Let's get the original Highwaymen to open for us at the Astrodome."

Waylon laughed. So did Johnny and Kris. They loved the plan. And so did the original Highwaymen. The rodeo fans got to hear "Michael, Row the Boat Ashore," and everyone lived happily ever after.

Unlike the original Highwaymen, I never stopped recording. When a pal once asked me why in God's name I put out so many albums, I said for the same reason a cow puts out so much milk. What's in you gotta come out.

In 1989, I came out with *A Horse Called Music*. Got my

good friend Fred Foster, who had produced "I Never Cared for You" back in my Nashville days, to supervise the sessions. The busier I became, the more I was amenable to outside producers—as long as they understood me.

Understanding me was simple. First off, present me with songs that suit my style. That's not much of a chore since I see my style as suitable for all sorts of songs. Secondly, surround me with musicians who respect melody. I'm a melody man. I'll elaborate on a melody now and then, but not all that much. I like stating the melody plain and simple. Simplicity is always the key. Get in there. Sing the song. Get out. I'm not big on a hundred takes and a thousand overdubs. My kind of singing isn't meant to be perfect. It's meant to reflect the imperfections of a human being like me. After a couple of takes, that reflection is pretty accurate.

I'm also most comfortable around my own musicians. That means Bobbie and Mickey Raphael, Paul English and Bee Spears and Grady Martin. You add some more if you want to. Just make sure they understand the basics of my sound. If I lose the rawness, I lose myself. You can surround me with strings—I'm inspired by strings as much as any singer—but don't drown me in strings. Use strings sparingly.

Fred Foster understood all this. He wanted to recut some of my old stuff like "I Never Cared for You" and "Mr. Record Man." I'm always pleased to sing my old songs. In a strange way—and I don't say this to be bragging—they never sound old. They just sound like me.

He also brought me a new song by Beth Nielsen Chapman.

From what Fred said, she'd given him some songs for me and he didn't think enough of them to pass them on. He told her to go home and think long and hard about my life—and then custom-write a song that fit my story. She came up with something she called "Nothing I Can Do about It Now." Fred flew down to Pedernales and played it for me while we were driving around the golf course. The lyrics got to me.

I've got a long list of real good reasons
For all the things I've done
I've got a picture in the back of my mind
Of what I've lost and what I've won
I've survived every situation
Knowing when to freeze and when to run
And regret is just a memory written on my brow
And there's nothing I can do about it now
I've got a wild and a restless spirit
I held my price through every deal
I've seen the fire of a woman's scorn
Turn her heart of gold to steel
I've got the song of the voice inside me
Set to the rhythm of the wheel
And I've been dreaming like a child
Since the cradle broke the bough
And there's nothing I can do about it now.
Running through the changes
Going through the stages
Coming round the corners in my life

Leaving doubt to fate
Staying out too late
Waiting for the moon to say good night
And I could cry for the time I've wasted
But that's a waste of time and tears
And I know just what I'd change
If I went back in time somehow
But there's nothing I can do about it now

I thought the song might sound even better if Beth sang the chorus with me. She did and I believe her extra touch was one of the reasons we wound up with a number one hit.

I'd also written a new tune that fit the mood of the record. That mood had me looking inward. The story could apply to many of my past romances. Or maybe to many of yours. I called it "Is the Better Part Over."

Is the better part over?
Has a ragin' river turned into a stream?
Is the better part over?
Are we down to not quite sayin' what we mean?

And after thinkin' it over
Wouldn't you rather have the endin' nice and clean
Where love remains in all the closing scenes?
Is the better part over

Why hang around
For an ending that's laden with sorrow?

We've both been around
We've both seen that movie before

And as much as I love you
I can't live while fearing tomorrow
If the better part's over
Then why should we try anymore?

29

"LISTEN TO THE BLUES THEY'RE PLAYING / LISTEN TO WHAT THE BLUES ARE SAYING"

THOSE ARE LINES FROM "NIGHT LIFE," a song I wrote from what feels like a hundred years ago. From an early age I knew the blues contain truth. They are an honest expression of the human condition. All the artists I loved most, from Hank Williams to Django Reinhardt to Ernest Tubb to Ray Charles, played the blues. They played the blues because they had the blues. They played the blues to purge themselves of the blues, knowing all the while that the blues were sure to come back.

For all the joys of falling head over heels in love with Annie, the period that followed our meeting was marked by some heavy blues. It wasn't that we weren't happy together. As a couple, we were happy in the extreme. We felt like two souls who'd been searching for one another our whole lives. Our connection was powerful on every level—spiritual, intellectual, and physical.

It was only right that one of my favorite ministers, Father Taliaferro, married us in September of 1991. Both of our baby boys were present at the wedding. Lukas Autry had been born on Christmas 1988 and Jacob Micah in April of 1990. Two beautiful blessings.

For a while I thought that I'd raise my new sons the same way I'd been raised—in Abbott. I moved us all into the old house I'd bought from the estate of Doc Simms. Annie fixed it up and made it comfortable for all of us. It was another way for me to reestablish my roots and return to the scene of my early years. If I had been happy there, there was no reason why my wife and sons couldn't be, too.

Unfortunately, that proved to be a fantasy.

It wasn't the fault of the good people of Abbott. They couldn't have been nicer. They treated us no differently than anyone else in town. There was no need for heavy security. It was just plain ol' Abbott, where folks respected their neighbors' privacy.

But word got around. It always does. Folks outside Abbott learned where I was living, and not just because of that dumb old billboard. I should have seen that coming. But in my fantasy that my kids could lead the simple life I had once led, I ignored reality. Because anyone could pull into Abbott and come right to my front door, we got some uninvited guests. If I was around, I could handle it. But when I was on the road, which was frequently, Annie was feeling vulnerable. And, in fact, she was. We moved back to Austin when, in the middle of the night, a drunk in a truck pulled up yelling for Willie and backed into the house. We kept Doc Simms's house—we own it to this day—but soon saw that it couldn't be our main residence.

I'd bought and sold a private jet because it proved to be not only expensive but impractical. Bad weather kept it grounded to where I'd missed several gigs. Since I have a cardinal rule against missing gigs, I went back to Honeysuckle Rose. Like the ever-reliable postman, my bus made it through all sorts of shitty weather.

But even my beloved bus had its limitations. Riding the highways of America to play a couple hundred one-nighters a year was getting to me. So when my good friend Mel Tillis offered to lease his theater in Branson, Missouri, the new mecca of live country music, the idea appealed to me. I made a commitment for six months of shows. That meant six months when I could stay off the road and be in Branson with Annie and the boys. Sounded great.

Turned out terrible. The people of Branson were hospitable but their town of four thousand had no real infrastructure. The main drag was always gridlocked. Nothing worked—not even my schedule. I thought eliminating travel would make life easier. I was dead wrong. I'd forgotten the old adage about teaching old dogs new tricks. This old dog was used to traveling. Staying put drove me up the wall, especially since it meant living in a hotel suite.

I hadn't realized how the road had conditioned every inch of my mind, body, and soul. Going to the same auditorium twice a day turned what had always been a pleasure into a grind. I felt like a factory worker on an assembly line.

Tried to shake things up by pitching a big sleeping tent in my hotel room and pretending I was out in the woods. When that didn't break the monotony, I considered making a bonfire and burning down the building. Cranky, restless, pissed at myself for having made this crazy long-term commitment, I somehow made it through the ordeal without completely losing my mind. With her good sense, sweet Annie kept me sane. As soon as legalities allowed it, I got the hell out of Dodge. Minute I was back on that bus and sailing down the highway, I breathed a big sigh of relief.

The Branson period was difficult for reasons other than feeling trapped in one place. It happened just months after I lost my son Billy. He was only thirty-three. The cause was a terrible accident. All I can do is grieve. I'll be grieving the loss of Billy for the rest of my life.

I haven't discussed my children at any length in this book. That's because of my strong feeling that, while I have every right to tell my story, I don't have the right to tell theirs. I can say how deeply I love them. I can say how they, each of them, possess enormous talents. I can let them know that I'm proud of them. And I can express deep regret for not spending more time with them. I believe the children of entertainers—especially the children of wandering troubadours—pay a big price. Sharing your dad with the world isn't fun. And when that dad has moved through three tumultuous marriages and is on his fourth—well, that's no picnic. I regret the pain that my lifestyle has caused my kids.

At the same time, I'm grateful for their patience with me. I'm proud to say that I'm close to all of them, just as I was close to Billy. All of them have shown me more love than I deserve.

When she was in her early thirties, Susie, my second daughter, chose to write a book about herself and her relationship with me. It was beautiful. If my other children—Lana, Paula, Amy, Lukas, and Micah—choose to do the same, I'll support their efforts. But it's their choice. Until then, I will protect their privacy. Other than touting their talents—as any proud father would—I will let my children determine when, where, how, and if they want to go public with their stories.

When Billy left us, he took his story with him. It is an unnatural and unspeakably painful act for a father to bury a child. I will remember Billy always and in this, my attempt to tell my own tale, I want the world to know that this good boy, this good man, this good son will live forever in the hearts of those who knew and loved him so well.

The blues thickened, as they can do.

Losing Billy came the same year that I learned I was on the brink of losing my land and all that was on it. That was the year the IRS came down on me.

Compared to the loss of a son, material losses seemed insignificant. But they had to be dealt with. I was responsible for many more livelihoods than just my own. I finally had to face a financial nightmare that had been chasing me for years.

I could close my eyes and pretend it all wasn't happening, but it was. I could plug my ears and block out some of the noise, but those voices came through anyway.

Those were the voices that were saying, in different ways, the same fuckin' thing.

They were saying I was through.

PART FIVE

SPIRIT

The Future Is Now

In tae kwon do, the head-high spinning kick is a beautiful maneuver. I love doing it. Between kicks I was taught to relax. That split second between action and inaction is crucial. As the world seemed to be tumbling down around me, tae kwon do did more than keep me toned. It showed me how to keep kicking.

Some see the golf course as an arena of frustration. Not me. When my money woes were weighing down everyone around me, I saw golf as a great escape. Didn't matter if I misdirected my drives or fucked up my putts. Out on the links, I had learned to laugh at my frustrations rather than let them laugh at me. Golf had a way of soothing my soul.

How can you explain why a man threatened with bankruptcy would take off for two or three days to go on a poker-playing marathon? I didn't need to explain. Just needed to do it. Just needed to find a way to keep my fears for the future from overtaking my mind. Playing poker, I had no fears. All focus was on the cards, the angles, the odds, the bluffs, the dares, the motionless silent dance between me and my opponents.

My understanding was that by clinging to my faith, I'd find the wisdom to effectively deal with those lawyers.

"You still don't have the resources, Willie," advisers were telling me. "Make a clean break of it. Just admit that you're dead broke and benefit from the bankruptcy laws."

"That would mean burning too many people," I said. "I don't see myself doing that. I can still make good money singing songs. Long as that's the case, I don't have any business not honoring my past debts."

"You're naive."

"More stubborn than naive. Either way, I ain't caving. I'm moving on."

The two albums I had made to satisfy Uncle Sam—*The IRS Tapes* and *Who'll Buy My Memories?*—hadn't stopped selling.

"It hasn't sold enough to pay off your taxes," a naysayer reminded me.

"That's not the point," I countered. "The point is that the IRS knows I'm trying my best to honor my debts. I'm singing for my supper. That's all I can do."

Then, miracle of miracles, things started to turn around.

After negotiation, the IRS dropped proceedings against me for a reduced payment of $6 million.

In the end, all the animosity melted, and that's a beautiful thing.

Thanks to the brilliant big-picture strategy developed by Mark Rothbaum and Larry Goldfein, the IRS was no longer my adversary. In fact, the IRS proved to be downright reasonable. Adding to my good fortune, friends who had bought my properties when they were being auctioned off made sure I got them back.

When it's on us, seems like the storm will never pass. But it always does.

30

HIGH

I'M WRITING MY LONG STORY at a time when the tide has finally turned. The idea of legalizing marijuana, whether for medical or recreational reasons, is more popular than ever. The majority of rational people have concluded that the plant is not a menace to society but can actually do good. This has been my argument for a good half century.

But twenty-five years ago, that argument was falling on deaf ears. In the early nineties, I campaigned for Gatewood Galbraith, a Lexington attorney running for governor of Kentucky on a let's-legalize-pot platform.

He and I traveled across Kentucky in a Cadillac powered by hemp oil. Didn't matter to me that he won only 5.3 percent of the vote in the Democratic primary. When he ran the second time, in '95, I joined his campaign and was happy to play a benefit. He boosted his primary percentage to 9 percent. Come '99, he switched to the Reform Party and I was right there with him. In the general election, he garnered 15 percent of the vote. I saw that as progress.

I kept hearing warnings and criticisms. Folks said that I shouldn't associate myself with pot and potheads and bogus pot-related products. I didn't think any of it was bogus. I thought it was good. And I didn't give a shit whether the association hurt me or not.

I couldn't betray marijuana any more than I could betray a family member or lifelong friend. That's because marijuana had never betrayed me. Unlike booze, it had never made me nasty or violent. Unlike cocaine, it never sped me up or fired up my ego. Instead, it mellowed me out. Unlike acid, it never scrambled my brain. It calmed my brain. Unlike tobacco, it didn't cause the cancer that had killed my mother and dad.

I owe marijuana a lot. As I write these words on the verge of age eighty-two, I think I can fairly make the claim that marijuana—in the place of booze, cocaine, and tobacco—has contributed to my longevity.

Back in 1994, when the world was still looking down on weed smokers, I had spent a few days in Abbott. It was one of those times when I went home just to relax and play poker with the boys. Saturday night I was driving back down to Austin when, somewhere around Waco, I got tired and figured, rather than risk a wreck, I'd pull over, climb in the backseat, and take a little snooze. Soon I was out like a light.

Next thing I knew a couple of highway patrolmen were banging on the window. There were flashlights pointed at my eyes.

"Good evening, officers," I said.

The flashlights probed the inside of the car from top to bottom, stopping at the open ashtray.

"What's in the ashtray?" asked one of the officers.

"A joint," I answered.

"Are you in possession of any more illegal substances?"

"I think so," I said. "Look under the passenger seat."

He did and discovered a little more pot.

Off to the McLennan county jail in Waco.

I was charged with a class B misdemeanor that carried a six-month jail sentence and a big fine. I got out on $500 bail.

The court hearing didn't happen till the following March, on the same day I was supposed to sing at the Grammys in L.A. I decided to skip the Grammys and have my day in court. My lawyer pointed out that the officers had switched off their video and audio recording system during the search. They also never offered any reason for searching my vehicle.

The judge threw out the state's case and sent me on my way.

In order to avoid any hard feelings, I came back to Waco to play a dance, free of charge, for the Sheriffs' Association of Texas. Just wanted to let the police officers know that it wasn't them I disliked; it was the outmoded law against pot. I make a practice not to talk much at my performances. I'll introduce a tune and that's it. But on this night, playing before the sheriffs, I made an exception. In short order, I simply said that it'd be better for everyone if we legalized marijuana, regulated it and taxed it like we tax cigarettes. There was only scattered applause.

Compared to the injustices suffered by others, I didn't suffer at all. Ray Charles told me a story about how one of his sidemen was caught with one skinny joint in Houston back in the fifties and, as a result, spent a year in the pen. When it comes to persecuting people for pot, there's a long list of horror stories. The thing that gets me is, why? Why waste precious law enforcement resources on bullshit?

I never wasted any time in the studio. I was always eager to cut another album, especially the one called *Across the Borderline.*

Bob Dylan and I cowrote and sang a duet called "Heartland." People are always asking me about my relationship with Dylan. Well, there isn't much to it. He and I did a tour together, but during those weeks on the road our paths hardly crossed. We were friendly—and we surely respected each other—but Bob is private and I'm not pushy. Forgot which one of us suggested that we collaborate. Doesn't matter 'cause it was a good idea. He sent me a track and I sent him back a verse of lyrics. He added on some lyrics, and from then on we completed the song through the mail. We had similar views about what was happening in America, so the theme emerged from both of our hearts.

There's a home place under fire tonight in the heartland
And the bankers are takin' my home and my land
from me
My American dream
Fell apart at the seams
You tell me what it means

I was reluctant to sing "Graceland" 'cause I thought Paul Simon had nailed it in his original version. But Paul insisted and was also gracious enough to give me another song—"American Tune"—that carried the same Simon signature of deep soul.

I sang Peter Gabriel's "Don't Give Up" with Sinead O'Connor, and Turner Stephen Bruton's "Getting Over You" with Bonnie Raitt.

The album was filled with brilliant songs by brilliant writers. I especially loved John Hiatt's highly original "(The) Most Unoriginal Sin."

I added a few originals of my own. The one that has lasted longest was built on a contradiction. I like contradictions. I like what the great American poet Walt Whitman wrote in *Leaves of Grass:* "Do I contradict myself? Very well, then I contradict myself, I am large, I contain multitudes." The contradiction that interested me had to do with movement. Moving through my sixties, I realized that even when I was still, I was still moving—which was why I called the song "Still Is Still Moving to Me."

Still is still moving to me
I swim like a fish in the sea all the time
But if that's what it takes to be free I don't mind
Still is still moving to me, still is still moving to me

And it's hard to explain how I feel
It won't go in words but I know that it's real
I can be moving or I can be still
But still is still moving to me, still is still moving to me

When *Across the Borderline* came out, it did fine. "Still Is Still Moving to Me," the first single, was a solid hit. The album didn't sell millions, but it sold hundreds of thousands. I was pleased, but the Nashville division of Columbia/Sony wasn't.

This was the same period when my contract was up. I didn't think much about it. For the past eighteen years, starting with *Red Headed Stranger,* I'd been churning out best-selling records for the label and naturally presumed they'd pick up my option.

But then during a meeting in Nashville they told my manager Mark they were going to drop me. I wasn't there but from what I heard Mark nearly lost it. When the executive announced the news, Mark lunged at him and was ready to punch him out before someone restrained him. Mark's my great defender, and I appreciate his passion, but this was one instance when I didn't share it. To be honest, I didn't really give a shit.

The label had purged one exec who was loyal to me and hired another who wasn't. This new man looked at country music and saw stars like Garth Brooks and Alan Jackson dominating the charts. My sales were respectable; theirs were spectacular. I could understand how this young lion might see me as dead weight.

"It's outrageous," said Mark. "Especially in light of the fact that you've made these people millions."

"The operative word," I said, "is 'made.' That's past tense."

"But you're more creative than ever, Willie."

"No need to preach to the choir. And no need to be all that

surprised. I knew this was a cold-blooded business back forty years ago when I recorded for Pappy Daily down in Houston. With these big corporations, it's only gotten colder."

"At the very least they owe you respect."

"The only thing those bean counters respect is beans. You're taking it personally, Mark. I'm not. I'm not worried about a thing. I got my own studio. I got new songs on my brain. I got the willingness to record 'em. And I got faith that we'll have an easy time finding new friends willing to put 'em out."

As irony would have it, it was old friends who put out my new stuff, which was made up mainly of old songs. Mark got me a one-shot deal with Liberty, the label where I had recorded back in the sixties. Liberty was now a division of Capitol Records. I decided to go back to a *Stardust* vibe. Rather than use my facilities at the Pedernales ranch, I flew to L.A. and worked at Capitol's famous studio, where Frank Sinatra and Nat King Cole had recorded. I turned production duties over to Jimmy Bowen.

Big arrangements with big strings let me shed new light on old songs like "Funny How Time Slips Away," "Crazy," and "Night Life," as well as newer songs like "(How Will I Know) I'm Falling in Love Again" and the title track, "Healing Hands of Time."

Someone asked, "Are you healing from the way the last label gave you the boot?"

"Hell, no," I said. "I'm not even thinking about that. Life's always about healing. That's because life is always filled with hurting. If we don't heal, we turn cynical and bitter. Healing is what lets us push past the pain."

To sing old standards like "All the Things You Are," "Oh, What It Seemed to Be," and "I'll Be Seeing You" was part of the healing. It didn't matter that these songs had been sung a thousand times before by a thousand different singers. In fact, that made it better. It was evidence that these old melodies and old lyrics, like old prayers, had proven their power. They touched people's minds, they stirred people's hearts, they stirred up emotions about long-lost pains and pleasures once forgotten and now remembered.

When someone suggested that I dress up in a formal tux for the cover photo, someone else said, "That'll mess up Willie's image. He'll never do it."

So naturally that's just what I did. Even combed my hair and gathered it in a ponytail. I figured messing up my image was a good thing.

Also figured that, after doing this lush album with a thousand strings soaring behind me, I'd go the other way. I'd strip down naked. Rather than hire out a producer to do the planning, I'd plan the thing myself. My plan was to keep it super-simple. Go back to my Pedernales studio. Go back to bare bones. Get to the *Spirit,* which was what I called the record.

It came about because the family band was off for a few weeks. Sister Bobbie and I had done a show—just the two of us—in Santa Fe that reminded me of when we had been little kids falling in love with music. That love was suddenly refreshed. I wanted that sense of rediscovery on my next record.

So in the studio it was just me and Bobbie with sparse accompaniment. There was nothing electric. The lights were low and the mood was nostalgic. The words I wrote for "Your

Memory Won't Die in My Grave" best sum up the feeling I needed to express.

Been feelin' kind of free, but I sure do feel lonesome
Baby's takin' a trip, but she ain't takin' me
I've been feelin' kinda free, but I'd rather feel your arms
around me
'Cause you're takin' away everything that I wanted

There's an old hollow tree where we carved our initials
And I said I love you and you said you love me
It's a memory today it'll be a memory tomorrow
I hope you'll be happy someday
Your memory won't die in my grave

The other titles convey that same sense of loss: "I'm Not Trying to Forget You," "Too Sick to Pray," "I'm Waiting Forever," "I Guess I've Come to Live Here in Your Eyes."

One of the beautiful things about making music with Bobbie is how her abiding faith washes over me. That faith led me to write,

I thought about trees
And how much I'd like to climb one
I thought about friends
And how rare it is to find one

I thought about you
The most gentle, sweet, and kind one

I thought about you, Lord
I thought about you

I thought about life
And the way that things are goin'
I thought about love
And the pain there is in growin'

And I thought about you
The one who is all-knowin'
I thought about you, Lord
I thought about you

I thought about you
And the songs that I keep singin'
I thought about you
And the joy that they keep bringin'

Wrote another one called "We Don't Run." Friends asked me whether I was talking about a woman or God. Truth is, I don't like to answer those questions. Don't like to explain my own songs because maybe the song will say something to you that wasn't my intention. Well, if that's the case, I couldn't be happier. Once the song comes out of me, it's yours. You make of it what you will. Don't want my explanation to get in your way.

We don't run, we don't compromise
We don't quit, we never do

We look for love, we find it in the eyes
The eyes of me and the eyes of you
You are the road, you are the only way
I'll follow you forevermore
We'll look for love, we'll find it in the eyes
The eyes that see through all the doors
There is a train that races through the night
On rails of steel that reach the soul
Fueled by fire as soft as candlelight
But it warms the heart of a love grown cold

So if you ask me if my song is about an earthly love or a divine love, I'll say I don't know. You tell me.

Few years back I wrote a song called "Angel Flying Too Close to the Ground." Some folks said it was about a lost love of mine. Some folks even wanted me to name the love. So just to confuse everyone, my bass player, Bee Spears, dressed up in ballet tights and during a gig at Caesars Palace in Vegas he came flying in on suspended wires just behind my head.

"Was Bee the angel you were writing about?" someone wanted to know.

"He sure as hell was tonight."

Spirit, the album that came off like a quiet conversation between me and sister Bobbie, not only had a different sound than the big orchestrations of *Healing Hands of Time,* but it had a different look. In the cover photo, I wasn't exactly sporting formal evening wear. I had my cowboy hat, my headband, and my old disheveled look.

"This one reviewer says he doesn't like the way you keep

changing up your music and your image," an associate told me. "He thinks you're confusing everyone. What do you think?"

"I think that's good."

"It's good to be confused?"

"It's good to change. If the change brings about confusion, who cares? Confusion makes you think. And that's another good thing."

Some other folks were questioning my choice of hiring Daniel Lanois to produce my next record. They thought he'd be too far-out, too experimental and distant from the kind of music I made. I disagreed. I had heard the album he produced for Bob Dylan, *Time Out of Mind,* and his work with Emmylou Harris, *Wrecking Ball,* and I knew he'd be perfect.

He was. Daniel is all about ambience. He creates deep, dark, brooding moods. He found an old abandoned movie theater in Oxnard, California, where he set up the recording equipment. He wanted to capture an open and arid feel, complete with echoes of ghosts from the past. Like me, he was inspired by mystery. Uncertainty didn't bother him.

On the album we called *Teatro,* Daniel had Emmylou Harris shadow me on the choruses. Emmylou sang beautifully, giving the stories a haunting shade of blue. Daniel also made good use of Bobbie and especially Mickey Raphael's soulful mouth harp, which, like Emmylou's voice, followed me wherever I went.

Daniel encouraged me to go back to my earliest days and revisit some of my earliest songs.

"Those are some of the deepest blues songs you've ever written," he said. "Let's see what they sound like in this broken-down old theater."

So I went back and got "Home Motel"—"just a place to stay, a crumbling last resort when day is through. . . . My home motel on Lost Love Avenue." I revisited "I Never Cared for You" and "Darkness on the Face of the Earth" and an old one I wrote with Ray Price, "I've Just Destroyed the World (I'm Living In)."

To contrast the old and the new, Daniel had the good sense to employ the brilliant young jazz pianist Brad Mehldau, who sprinkled his own style of fairy dust on all the right spots.

The result was a radically different sound. Lanois created an aura of an era long past, as though we were going back in time to locate something that had been lost long ago. Most producers would work to make my old songs sound new. But Daniel managed to make them sound even older. And deeper. And stranger. And I couldn't have been happier.

The last cut was something new, an instrumental mixing the bluesy feeling of Django with a sense of romantic love. Because the love in my life had been so powerfully renewed by my wife, Annie, I named the song after her.

The nineties were about to fade into the sunset. We were about to slip into a new century. And soon I'd slip out of my sixties and into my seventies.

I looked back at this past decade with some satisfaction. When it came to the IRS, I had dodged a bullet. The Highwaymen tour had gone around the world. Not only was it musically satisfying, but it was a source of great personal pleasure.

And Annie and I had decided to make Maui our main home. Seemed like the calmest place to raise the boys. In Paia, no one made a fuss over us. Naturally we'd continue to spend time at the Pedernales ranch. Because Pedernales had the horses, the golf course, and the studio, I couldn't go more than a month or so without visiting my Texas homestead. And of course we'd always drop by our house in Abbott to say hello to my oldest friends and revisit my deepest memories.

31

RAINBOWS

THE FIRST SIX DECADES OF my life had been filled with drama. Watching the pink-purple sunset from my living room in Hawaii, I couldn't help but hope that the coming years would bring less drama.

For now, I just wanted to kick back, enjoy a smoke, and listen to the waves splash against the shore.

But beautiful as it was, I couldn't sit there for long.

Something started calling to me.

It was that same "something" that had always been calling.

New music.

Old music.

New songs to sing in old ways.

Old songs to sing in new ways.

Any way you looked at it, I had to get up and get going.

I heard a new riff in my head.

I heard a different kind of lick.

That's when I knew it was time to pick up Trigger and see where this new lick would lead.

And of course it led where it always led:

Back out on the road.

Maui isn't the only place where I've seen rainbows radiant enough to bring tears to my eyes.

From the bedroom in the back of my bus, I've looked out the window as we wound our way over the Rockies. In the aftermath of a thunderstorm, I've seen double arcs of dazzling light. Driving up the rugged coast of Maine, through the Louisiana swamps, along the 636-mile highway that links Dallas to El Paso, I've witnessed rainbows that seemed to stretch halfway across the world.

Each time I see one my reaction is the same:

My heart starts to sing. I see that miracles surround us. Just when we think our lives are monotonous and predictable, miracles pop up out of nowhere. The miracle of a rainbow turns dullness into brilliance. It's a miracle that says light comes out of darkness. I need to remind myself of that miracle because, as a writer, darkness has been one of my main subjects.

I've spent a lifetime expressing the emotions that come with lost love. I expressed those emotions as a child—in poems and songs—even before I had experienced the feelings themselves. Can't tell you why. Maybe it was the music I heard on the radio, whether Hank Williams or Big Bill Broonzy. Or maybe it came from missing my mother and father, who had wandered off early to find their own fates. Whatever it was, it put me in touch with loneliness and heartbreak. My early hits—the songs that established my name in the music game—all had a strong tinge of sadness. And yet it wasn't sadness that saw me through my day. It was optimism. It was a belief that, no matter how dire or confused my circumstances, a rainbow might just light up my sky.

As I approached seventy, I didn't at all feel like an old man. So in order to usher in the new century, I decided to do a record, suggested by my daughter Amy, mainly of children's songs. As a kid, Amy used to watch the Muppets and listen to Kermit the Frog's "Rainbow Connection," the song Paul Williams wrote about people of all kinds looking for that elusive link of love. I sang other kids' songs like "Won't You Ride in My Little Red Wagon" and "Ole Blue." In order to please the adults, I added grown-up stuff like "Playin' Dominoes and Shootin' Dice" and Mickey Newbury's powerful "The Thirty-Third of August."

Rainbow Connection was one of the simplest albums I ever made. It was a production that followed the creed "less is more." Not so with *The Great Divide,* a huge Hollywood production that cost hundreds of thousands of dollars. The producer was Matt Serletic, who was coming off a superhit with Carlos Santana's *Supernatural,* a record that sold tens of millions of copies and won a Grammy for Album of the Year.

Other than the title cut, which I wrote with jazz guitarist Jackie King, Matt had me singing other people's songs. There were duets with Lee Ann Womack, Kid Rock, Sheryl Crow, Brian McKnight, and Bonnie Raitt. Taken together, the overall sound reminded me of an epic Western movie. There was a heroic quality to many of the stories, like "Last Stand in Open Country" and "Don't Fade Away."

A friend asked me about the record.

"You're always saying how much you love simplicity, Willie," he said. "You're always talking about how much you wanna get back to the basics, and how you're your own best producer. Yet here you are, turning the record over to someone else who's working up these tunes to a fever pitch. I don't understand."

"Who doesn't like success?" I asked. "If every now and then I can hook up with a highly successful producer, why not? He puts it all together for me. As long as I can relate to the songs and the arrangements, I got no problem putting someone else in charge. My job is easy. Just go in there and sing."

"And what about your integrity?"

"My integrity is what it's always been: a flexible thing, just like my music. It can bend this way and that. Even during those years in Nashville, when I was being produced in ways that didn't suit me, I went along with the program. Never felt like I was compromising my integrity. Always took the attitude that said, 'Hell, maybe I'm wrong. Maybe this producer can get a hit out of me. Maybe I just gotta get out of my own way.' Today my attitude hasn't changed. If Matt Serletic can help keep me on the charts, I'd be a fool not to give him that chance. I suppose there are some artists who really don't give a shit about being popular, but I ain't one of them. Never have been. Never will be."

The Great Divide turned out to be a great seller. I liked the way it sounded, I liked the way I sang inside all those big arrangements and alongside those intriguing duet partners. By then I had my own label, Lost Highway, and found a distribution deal with Universal Music. In the spirit of being open-minded and eager for ongoing hits, I'd continue to let other successful producers organize some albums for me. But that didn't get in the way of my producing albums of my own, done without regard for commerce. Done just 'cause it felt right to do 'em—albums with old friends who needed a helping hand and new friends whose music appealed to me. In short, I did just about everything with everyone. That might sound like a peculiar way to go about strengthening a career in its sixth decade, but that's me.

Early in this new century I lost two friends, two brothers who meant the world to me. Waylon Jennings died in 2002 and Johnny Cash a year later.

I looked at Waylon and Johnny as giants. They were rugged individualists and great American heroes. They each had paid deep down dues, lived through one storm after another, and survived to tell the good news. They were true to their craft, true to their friends, and spokesmen for everyday people.

Waylon was a firecracker. Essentially a sweet and loving man, he could go off like a rocket. He could be ornery. He could even be a little sneaky. But he was all heart. When it came to taking on the country music establishment, he had the guts and self-confidence to lead the way. If it weren't for Waylon, I might still be back in Nashville looking to please the wrong people. Waylon said, "Hoss, first we got to please ourselves. Once we do that, the fans will follow us—not those guys in suits sitting behind their big desks." Waylon had guts and grit and a singular style that put some hard rock into honky-tonk.

Johnny was a gentleman. Above all, he was a believing Christian. Many were the times when he told me that it was only his love for Jesus that saw him through. You could feel that love in everything he sang. He was a man of compassion. He championed the disadvantaged. He was one of the first artists who made it a practice to visit prisons and treat those inmates with respect. Like Waylon, he was also a brilliant writer whose songs will never die. At the center of his soul was a gentle calmness. In spite of the craziness that surrounds show business, Johnny found a way to steer a steady course. I not only loved singing with him, I loved being around him because of the self-assurance he projected. His national television show was a landmark in the history of country music.

Waylon and Johnny will live forever as two of the most beloved artists in our musical history. I'm thankful for the circumstances that led me to befriend them both.

A friend dies and you move on. You climb back on the bus, you go back onstage, you do your show, you do your job, but it's never the same. A part of you is missing. During my seventies, I lost many parts of myself. My two bass players—David Zettner and Bee Spears—died young, each in his early sixties. They had been with me forever. They were great musicians and loyal friends. I loved them like sons.

Grady Martin, a genius guitarist and my longtime cohort, also passed away, leaving a million beautiful musical memories in his wake. Jody Payne, a brilliant rhythm guitarist for years, was gone too.

I also lost my good friend Floyd Tillman. We got to cut one last record together. That was a thrill. We joked about how I had stolen the opening notes of "Crazy" from Floyd's "I Gotta Have My Baby Back."

"Hell, Willie," said Floyd, "I probably stole those same notes from someone else."

Floyd was a pioneer of the music of my childhood, western swing. He had been the lead guitarist for Adolph Hofner and his Pearl Wranglers down in San Antone.

I looked on these losses as a natural part of aging. Yet I looked on them with great sadness. The old saying goes, "We're born to die." Even if I believe the opposite—that is, when we die we're born again—that doesn't mean death doesn't sting. It stings hard and leaves us at a loss for words.

When I'm at a loss for words, the best thing I can do is reach for Trigger, pick out some melody—old or new, doesn't matter—and start singing. That's the only way for me to process grief. The contradiction never ceases to work: you sing the blues to lose the blues. You lift the burden by transferring it into a song. I'll be damned if I know why or how that miracle takes place, but it always does.

As I walked through my seventies and started losing friends, I felt an even more urgent need to make music. Every year I looked forward to the Fourth of July picnic and the Farm Aid concert. Never missed a one. It was a chance to connect with old pals and make new ones.

"These landmark events that have been going on for

decades," wrote one critic, "have become a permanent part of the American landscape. And the musical eclecticism that characterizes them is due largely to the generosity of spirit that is, in fact, the hallmark of Willie Nelson's musical aesthetic."

Fancy words—but it felt good to read 'em.

And it felt good to keep working. In these past ten years or so, as I moved from my seventies into my eighties, I performed on average some 150 one-nighters a year. Didn't see it as a burden, but a blessing.

Sure there were times when the hassle of travel had me saying I was gonna quit. But after a week or two on my ranch in Texas or at my place in Paia, I got to itchin' and scratchin' and knew what to do. I knew it was time to go out on the road and sing for my supper.

The other day, just to shock me, my manager, Mark, came on the bus with a grocery bag filled with CDs. He placed them on my desk. Piled high, they totaled around twenty-four.

"Look 'em over," he said.

I did. They all carried my name. I knew them all.

"These are the records you've turned out," said Mark, "in these past ten years alone. You've been averaging two albums a year."

I had to smile. It was Mark's way of patting me on the back. He knew me well enough to know I hadn't kept count or realized that the last decade's output has been the strongest in my career.

I looked over the CDs. Each one brought back good memories.

Milk Cow Blues was a blues record with me playing with everyone from B.B. King to Dr. John to Susan Tedeschi.

Countryman, produced by Don Was, was my first all-reggae album. Better late than never.

It Always Will Be was an old-fashioned Nashville record of duets with my daughter Paula, Lucinda Williams, and Norah Jones. I'd heard Norah and her band the Little Willies back in New York. Norah became a great friend. One of her band members gave me my greatest compliment when he said, "Willie Nelson plays guitar like Django with one finger."

You Don't Know Me: The Songs of Cindy Walker was a special project. I'd known Cindy for fifty years. She was one of the best country writers of all time. I know that Ray Charles, who had a huge hit with "You Don't Know Me," felt the same. Fred Foster, who also knew Cindy, produced the record and put me together with Buddy Emmons on steel and Johnny Gimble on fiddle—musicians who, like me, understood the country music tradition of the forties and fifties that Cindy represented with such tender beauty.

Cindy, who was nearing ninety, heard the record and, according to Fred, said, "I've had many fine recordings, but Willie's are the only ones I've believed."

I didn't have a chance to thank her for that comment because just a few weeks after the record was released, she went on to glory.

Last of the Breed was an album that put me together with my old boss Ray Price and my forever friend Merle Haggard.

I'd probably keep doing records like *Last of the Breed*

forever if my manager, Mark, didn't kick my ass to make sure I stay current. Not that I mind, because staying current usually involves another series of duets. Whether it's Shelby Lynne or Toby Keith or Joe Walsh or Rickie Lee Jones or Lee Ann Womack or Ben Harper or Carole King or Toots Hibbert or Los Lonely Boys, I'm always ready to harmonize.

I liked the title *Outlaws and Angels,* another duets collection, because I've slipped in and out of both of those categories.

Another category I always believed applied to me is jazz. I'm no Barney Kessel or Wes Montgomery or Jackie King, but I hear jazz as clearly and love it as dearly as I do any music. So when I had a chance to collaborate with Wynton Marsalis and do a live record at Wynton's Jazz at Lincoln Center, I didn't hesitate. I ran up to New York and brought my man Mickey Raphael along with me. When it comes to jazz, Mickey can stand alongside Toots Thielemans as one of the best of all improvisers. The record, *Two Men with the Blues,* was the start of what would prove to be a beautiful musical relationship with Wynton.

Just as I would never abandon country, gospel, or jazz, I would never abandon the love for the Great American Songbook that I first expressed on *Stardust.* I did another similar session that they called *American Classic,* produced by a renowned expert in the field, Tommy LiPuma. It included a duet with Diana Krall, Tommy's protégé, and another with Norah Jones.

I never stopped writing tunes but was always keen to sing songs by other writers that I thought needed to be sung. One such song by Ned Sublette, was called "Cowboys Are Frequently Secretly Fond of Each Other." I loved the lyrics and was proud to sing 'em.

Well, there's many a strange impulse out on the plains
of West Texas
There's many a young boy who feels things he can't
comprehend
And a small town don't like it when somebody falls
between sexes
No, a small town don't like it when a cowboy has
feelings for men

And I believe to my soul that inside every man
there's the feminine
And inside every lady there's a deep manly voice loud
and clear
Well, a cowboy may brag about things that he's done
with his women
But the ones who brag loudest are the ones that are
most likely queer

Cowboys are frequently secretly fond of each other
Say, what do you think all them saddles and boots was
about?
And there's many a cowboy who don't understand the
way that he feels for his brother
And inside every cowboy there's a lady that'd love to
slip out

And there's always somebody who says what the others just whisper
And mostly that someone's the first one to get shot down dead
So when you talk to a cowboy don't treat him like he was a sister
You can't fuck with a lady that's sleepin' in each cowboy's head

In recent years another song came out that I didn't sing but couldn't help but love. It was written by Bruce Robison, who took the old cliché "What would Jesus do?" and turned it into "What Would Willie Do?" Normally I'd have to argue against any comparison between me and the perfect man, but Bruce wrote the thing as a joke and suddenly I started hearing it all over the radio. I'd be lying if I said I didn't get a kick out of it.

I was lost in trouble and strife, I heard a voice and it changed my life
And now it's a brand-new day, and I ain't afraid to say
You're not alone when you're down and out
And I think you know who I'm talking about
When I don't know how I'll get through
I ask myself what would Willie do

What would Willie do, well he'd travel so far with nothing but a song and his old guitar
And a tour bus and some semitrucks, thirty crewmen and a little bit of luck

Well he loves all the people, the ugly and the
randy
If you don't believe me take a look at the family
And they'll tell you that it's true
When skies are gray what would Willie do

Well long ago he came unto us, his words were simple
but they went right through us
And the whole world sang along, but then they didn't
want to hear his songs
He was gone and we thought we'd lost him
But he grew his hair and he moved to Austin
And all of the people smiled, they came to hear him sing
from miles
Like a miracle all those rednecks and hippies
From New York City down to Mississippi
Stood together and raised a brew
When it's all gone wrong what would Willie do

One of the most beautiful things in my life has been watching how each of my children—Lana, Susie, Billy, Paula, Amy, Lukas, and Micah—has expressed artistic talent.

They've all come onstage to sing with me; they've all done me proud by realizing their own creative projects.

In recent years, Lukas has formed a band, the Promise of the Real, and Micah put together a group, Insects vs. Robots. Both bands have appeared at my shows around the world.

Whenever I get a chance to make music with my kids, I have to stop and express gratitude for that privilege.

* * *

Another late-life privilege has been my association with Buddy Cannon, a great musician/producer/writer in Nashville. Buddy's become my main go-to writing partner. He's inspired my own creativity, and working with him, I find myself—in my eighties—composing and recording more than ever. It was Buddy who put together my latest duet project, *To All the Girls...*, where I'm singing with no fewer than eighteen lovely ladies, including Dolly Parton, Loretta Lynn, Rosanne Cash, Shelby Lynne, Mavis Staples, and my daughter Paula.

Most recent record I cut with Buddy was *Band of Brothers*, which came out in 2014. In terms of record sales, I would have guessed that by now I'd be irrelevant, an old relic who's damn lucky to have any label—in this case, I was back on Columbia—release my stuff. So when the album debuted at number one, I had to scratch my head.

"No big mystery," said Buddy. "It's a hit because it's your philosophy. People like the way you think."

"But I'm thinking that my thinking isn't all that clear."

"That's what they like about it. Neither is theirs."

Here's how my thinking went with "Band of Brothers."

We're a band of brothers and sisters and whatever
On a mission to break all the rules
And I know you love me 'cause I love you too
But you can't tell me what to do
I sure don't know where we're going
And I'm really not sure where we've been
And if I can take you all with me

I'd sure like to go there again
When all the songs have been written
And when all the music is played
When the curtain comes down we'll be around
To make sure the musicians are paid
'Cause we're a band of brothers and sisters and whatever
On a mission to break all the rules
And I know you love me 'cause I love you too
But you can't tell me what to do

It wasn't just the songs I wrote with Buddy that made *Band of Brothers* a big hit. I also sang a sly and clever tune by Billy Joe Shaver called "Hard to Be an Outlaw." I related. I related even more to "The Songwriters," written by Gordie Sampson and Bill Anderson.

We get to break out of prison
Make love to our best friend's wife
Have a beer for breakfast in Boston
Drink rum in Jamaica that night
We get to tell all our secrets
In a code that no one understands
We get to shoot all the bad guys
And never get blood on our hands
We're heroes, we're schemers, we're drunks and we're dreamers
We're lovers and sometimes we're fighters
We're students, we're teachers, we're the devil, we're preachers

We're true love, but mostly one-nighters
We're the songwriters
Half the world thinks we're crazy
And the other half wants to be us
And they're jealous 'cause we get to hang out
In the back of some big star's tour bus
We're old boots and T-shirts and blue jeans
We're cables and strings and E chords
We only get dressed up in November
When they hand out some writers' awards
We're heroes, we're schemers, we're drunks and we're dreamers
We're lovers and sometimes we're fighters
We're the truth, we're the lies, we're stupid, we're wise
We're true love but mostly one-nighters
We're the songwriters
We write bridges, we cross them and burn them
Teach lessons but don't bother to learn 'em
Our mamas all know what we're doing
Why we stay out all night long
I told mine I was a drug dealer
She said, "Thank God you ain't writing songs."

32

ABBOTT

IN THE BACK OF MY BUS, rolling up I-35, heading from Austin back home to Hill County. Got a little time to myself. A little time to reflect back and see if I can make sense of these eight long decades I've spent on planet Earth.

My lungs aren't what they used to be, so instead of burning joints I try to restrict myself to inhaling vapors. These e-cigarettes, packed with THC, will do the trick. Hell, I even smoked one the other day on the big commercial jet flying out of Maui. No one said a word.

It's been especially satisfying to see public opinion turn in favor of legalizing pot. The arguments advocating the many good uses of that plant have finally prevailed. For agriculture, for pain relief, for clothing—for the good of the environment and the good of the creative mind—my money's on pot. To have lived long enough to see it being decriminalized from coast to coast brings me deep satisfaction.

Before I get off the marijuana bandwagon, there's one last

story I need to tell. Happened back in 2006. It was my last—and funniest—run-in with the law. I'd played a benefit concert in Montgomery, Alabama, with Ray Price, celebrating the birthday of Hank Williams. I was on my bus, hurrying to get back to Texas so I could attend the funeral of Governor Ann Richards, a wonderful lady who'd been a good friend. Somewhere in Louisiana we got pulled over.

"Got anything in there?" the officers asked.

"Got lots of stuff," I said.

The officers came on the bus. Ben Dorcy, who'd been working for me for over a half century and was eighty-three years old, was sound asleep on the couch.

"What's wrong with him?" one of the officers asked.

"Nothing," I said. "He's dead."

The officer didn't laugh. He and his cohort did their search and found the stuff they were looking for.

"'Fraid we're gonna have to take you in, Willie," they said.

"Figured as much. I know you gotta do your job, but busting us is like busting an old-age home."

They still didn't laugh. The hassle of the arrest caused me to miss Ann's funeral. Took us a while, but we got out of the mess—the kind of mess that today, a decade later, is less likely to happen.

Bottom line is that I've seen some progress in my time. Not long ago millions of gay folks were hiding in the closet and living in fear. Now they're free to come out, create their own path, and even marry. That's a beautiful thing.

I'm not saying things are perfect, but I am saying they're better than when I was coming up. I still see the need to protest, especially on behalf of the small farmer and especially on behalf of our environment. If we fuck up this planet any more, we fuck up the future of our kids and grandkids. Global warming is serious as sin. I'll play just about any damn benefit where the money goes to protecting our earth, water, and sky. I still believe in taking strong stands.

Only last month my boys and I joined Neil Young in a rally against the Keystone XL pipeline, which the oil industry is hell-bent on building, a project certain to do far more harm than good. More than ever, our planet Earth is suffering from mindless abuse. That pisses me off something fierce.

"You're mad as hell about all this environmental neglect," a friend said to me the other day, "but why aren't you equally as mad about the state of the music industry?"

The question made me stop and think. Among my peers and younger musicians, I hear lots of groaning. Many of the complaints are justified. Record sales are in the toilet. Technology has made it harder for artists to get our fair share of revenue. In the old days you had to buy a piece of sheet music, a 78 shellac record, a 45 or 33⅓ rpm vinyl record, a cassette, an eight-track, or a compact disc. Now, in the digital age, you don't have to buy a thing. With streaming subscription services like Spotify, you can listen to anything you want, whenever you want, and on whatever digital device you want. As a result, artists' and songwriters' royalties have been drastically downsized.

In short, high tech has made music accessible in ways we could never have imagined. It's something of a free-for-all.

Does this anger me? Does this alarm me?

I'd have to say no, and here's why. I like the idea that it's easier than ever for fans to get hold of the music they love. It's good that there's more music on more media outlets than at any time in the history of the world. Some of those outlets have been especially friendly to me. On Sirius radio, for instance, there's Willie's Roadhouse, a channel devoted to classic country that pays special attention to my material. It's commercial-free, so the music is practically nonstop. And even if the royalty payout isn't what it was compared to back in the day, I can live with this new reality—but it would be nice for artists to get their fair share.

I can live with it because my approach to making my living hasn't changed since I started out back in the dark ages. My approach is that the wandering minstrel makes his living from wandering—from playing joints and dives, dance halls and clubs and county fairs. I've never counted on income from radio play or record sales—not then and not now. I've always assumed that whatever I got would be watered down by the radio stations and the record companies doing the auditing.

Back in the fifties, the system was rigged against artists getting their fair share of airplay money and record sales. Today it's a different system, but the result is the same. Before that money trickles down to us—the artists and writers—it gets diluted by formulas that defy understanding.

So I go back to basics. I put my faith in one thing and one thing alone: my ability to perform for the people. I see records as advertisements for my shows. The only money I've ever counted on is the money I make when you buy a ticket to my show. And if hearing my record on your laptop or your smartphone motivates you to come see me, I'm a happy man.

I'm not saying my thinking is all that sophisticated. There are ways you can analyze how digitalizing music is chopping up the industry into little microchips and fucking the music makers out of the kind of money we made in the past. But that was the past, and this is the present, and present reality has us going back to basics, even further back than the invention of radio, when the essential relationship between the artist and the audience couldn't have been simpler:

You pay to hear me play.

I still believe in the rightness of that relationship.

When you whittle away all the bullshit, I've been living on that righteous relationship since I first left Abbott and rode my bike down to West to join John Rejcek's polka band. Since then, a million things have changed and yet, when it comes to getting out there one night and the next in the hopes of entertaining people, nothing has changed at all.

I reflect on my life now, and it's pretty simple. I'm home in Hawaii or Texas for a couple of weeks, reconnecting with family and friends, playing golf, playing cards, relaxing. But after a while I get to thinking about my music and my fans and I'm eager—and happy—to climb back on the plane and the bus and go back out there to entertain those people who, though I may not know their names, are an essential and loving part of my family. The fans *are* my family.

One little anecdote proves my point.

You might have heard the story on public radio a few years back. It went all over the world and got some of the highest ratings in the history of the show called *This American Life.* Seems a guy in Austin named Josh listed his phone number under the name "Willie Nelson" as a prank and soon started getting my calls. Seeing my name listed in the phone book, folks from all over began to leave messages for me on his answering machine. Some of these calls were just curiosity seekers; others were people asking me to play for their charities. Many of the messages were very personal and serious.

"Willie," said one lady, "I live in Abilene and don't want nothing from you. I'm about to move on outta here and just wanna hear your voice one more time before I die."

"Willie," said a man, "my wife's dying of the same liver disease that killed my mother. And just like my mom, we can't get a transplant. We're too far down on the list. Can you help us, Willie? Can you call me back today?"

"Willie," said a young woman in Montana, "our twelve-year-old boy has a rare form of cancer and is going through a lot of painful treatments. When he was a little baby and wouldn't stop crying, we'd put on your records and suddenly he'd calm down. All his young life he's loved your records. Right now, after the pain of his chemotherapy, he started crying like a baby. We know it's a mighty big favor, Willie, but if you could just sing a short little song to him over the phone, it would make all the difference in the world."

When I finally found out about these calls—and there were hundreds of them—I got the number and called Josh myself. He was surprised to hear from me.

"I'd like to meet you in person," I said. "I'd like you to come backstage after my next show in Austin."

Well, Josh came back and apologized for taking my name. He said he did it as a prank, but that he was really a fan. I didn't raise my voice—raising my voice is not my style—but I didn't hide my anger. I was boiling inside.

"Far as I'm concerned," I said, "this is not an amusing prank. You gave these folks, who are already connected to me through my music, the idea that they could connect to me over the phone. These are sincere folks, proud folks, folks willing to pour out their hearts, folks looking for a little love, kindness, and understanding. Folks who need to be comforted. Folks who need to be heard. Shame on you, son, for fooling them. That's a cruel thing to do. You've let these people down. When it comes to my fans, I've never ever let them down. And never will. So you go on your way and let this be a lesson to you. True fans need to tell stories and hear stories that touch their souls—and that's no joke. Whether those fans live in West Virginia or West, Texas, they're my family."

Talking about West, Texas, we're just about to pass it now. I look out the window of my bus speeding up I-35 and see the exit sign. That means we're only minutes away from Abbott.

We ride over the railroad tracks and pull up to my house. On the walls of the living room are framed movie posters from the Hillsboro Theater, now shut down. Looking at those old Gene Autry and Lash LaRue pictures brings me pleasure and takes me all the way back to a time when this tiny town of Abbott was the center of my universe. I make myself a cup of coffee and turn on the TV. By coincidence, there's a commercial advertising "Willie Nelson Week." One of the cable channels is broadcasting all my Westerns. Who in the hell would have thought I'd ever make enough movies to merit something like that? Another reason to smile.

The black coffee kicks in and makes me restless. I go out on the front porch and sit for a spell before deciding to walk a few blocks down to the Abbott United Methodist Church. The historical plaque says that services were first held here in 1883 by the Rev. G. W. Swofford. You're going to laugh, but the only reason this church is still standing is 'cause me and sister Bobbie bought it a few years back. We bought it 'cause we heard it was going to be torn down. We couldn't let that happen. When I was a little boy, I didn't have the understanding that a church could be bought and sold. I thought God owned all the churches. And I thought that this church, which so comforted my little-boy soul, would stand forever.

I look at it now and love what I see. It's a plain white-painted building with a pretty steeple. Inside there are a half-dozen pews that stretch all the way from one side to the other. There are pretty stained glass windows in white and pink. At the altar, there's a large wooden cross, stark and plain.

I sit in one of the pews. I'm alone on this weekday morning and I'm enjoying the solitude. I have all the time in the world to let my memories fly this way and that.

My eyes are closed, my prayers are aimed towards the heavens, but in my gut, I don't feel worthy of so much good fortune. I sing okay, I play okay, and I know I can write a good song, but I still feel like I've been given a whole lot more than I deserve.

On April 29, 2015, I turn eighty-two. That's another big blessing, longevity—one I never expected. It's one thing to be eighty-two, but it's another to have the energy to keep touring the globe. That energy isn't fueled by anything I can generate on my own.

The fuel is love—love of people, places, animals, plants, water. Love of sound, love of space, love of fireflies and star-filled skies. Love of life. Love of home.

To some, coming home means the end of the journey.

But to me it means the start of another journey, a journey without end.

THE BEGINNING

ACKNOWLEDGMENTS

I would like to thank my wife, Annie, my sister Bobbie, Mark Rothbaum, David Vigliano, David Ritz, my editors at Little, Brown—John Parsley and Malin von Euler-Hogan—my whole family, including all the musicians, crew, friends, and loyal fans who have made my life worth living.

—Willie Nelson

I would like to thank Willie, Annie, Mark Rothbaum, John Parsley, and David Vigliano; my family: Roberta, Alison, Jessica, Jim, Henry, Charlotte, Alden, James, Isaac, Esther, and Elizabeth; and my friends: Harry Weinger, Alan Eisenstock, Herb Powell, John Tayloe, and Patrick Henderson.

—David Ritz

INDEX

INDEX

INDEX

INDEX

INDEX

INDEX

CREDITS FOR SONG LYRICS

"Band of Brothers"
Words and Music by Willie Nelson and Buddy Cannon
© 2014 Warner-Tamerlane Publishing Corp., Act Five Music and Run Slow Music
All rights on behalf of Warner-Tamerlane Publishing Corp and Act Five Music administered by Warner-Tamerlane Publishing Corp. *Used by permission of Alfred Music.* All rights reserved. All rights for Run Slow Music administered by BMG Rights Management (US) LLC. All rights reserved. *Reprinted with permission of Hal Leonard Corporation.*

"Bloody Mary Morning"
Written by Willie Nelson
© 1970 Full Nelson Music Inc.
"Crazy"
Written by Willie Nelson
© 1961 Sony/ATV Tree Publishing
"Denver"
Written by Willie Nelson
© 1976 Full Nelson Music Inc.
"Funny How Time Slips Away"
Written by Willie Nelson
© 1961 Sony/ATV Tree Publishing
"Goin' Home"
Written by Willie Nelson
© 1971 Full Nelson Music Inc.
"I Gotta Get Drunk"
Written by Willie Nelson
© 1963 Sony/ATV Tree Publishing
"I Never Cared for You"
Written by Willie Nelson
© 1964 Sony/ATV Tree Publishing
"I Still Can't Believe You're Gone"
Written by Willie Nelson
© 1974 Full Nelson Music Inc.
"In God's Eyes"
Written by Willie Nelson
© 1961 Sony/ATV Tree Publishing
"Is the Better Part Over"
Written by Willie Nelson
© 1978 Full Nelson Music Inc.
"It's Not for Me to Understand"
Written by Willie Nelson
© 1963 Sony/ATV Tree Publishing
"It's Not Supposed to Be That Way"
Written by Willie Nelson
© 1974 Full Nelson Music Inc.
"Me and Paul"
Written by Willie Nelson
© 1989 Full Nelson Music Inc.
"Mr. Record Man"
Written by Willie Nelson
© 1961 Sony/ATV Tree Publishing
"On the Road Again"
Written by Willie Nelson
© 1989 Full Nelson Music Inc.
"Pretty Paper"
Written by Willie Nelson
© 1962 Sony/ATV Tree Publishing

CREDITS FOR SONG LYRICS

"Remember the Good Times"
Written by Willie Nelson
© 1971 Full Nelson Music Inc.
"Sad Songs and Waltzes"
Written by Willie Nelson
© 1964 Sony/ATV Tree Publishing
"Shotgun Willie"
Written by Willie Nelson
© 1973 Full Nelson Music Inc.
"Still Is Still Moving to Me"
Written by Willie Nelson
© 1989 Full Nelson Music Inc.
"These Are Difficult Times"
Written by Willie Nelson
© 1976 Full Nelson Music Inc.
"Time of the Preacher"
Written by Willie Nelson
© 1976 Full Nelson Music Inc.
"What Can You Do for Me Now"
Written by Willie Nelson and Hank Cochran
© 1970 Sony/ATV Music Publishing LLC & Full Nelson Music Inc.
"Where's the Show"
Written by Willie Nelson
© 1971 Full Nelson Music Inc.
"Your Memory Won't Die in My Grave"
Written by Willie Nelson
© 1978 Full Nelson Music Inc.
All rights administered by Sony/ATV Music Publishing LLC., 424 Church Street, Suite 1200, Nashville, TN 37219.
All rights reserved. Used by permission.

"Cowboys Are Frequently Secretly"
a/k/a "Cowboys Are Frequently Secretly (Fond of Each Other)"
Words and Music by Ned Sublette
Published by Ned Sublette Music (ASCAP)
© 1981, 2006 Ned Sublette. All rights reserved. Used by permission.

"Family Bible"
Written by Walter M. Breeland, Paul F. Buskirk, and Claude Gray.
Used courtesy of Glad Music Publishing & Recording LP and Pappy Daily Music LP. All rights reserved. Used by permission.

"Heartland"
Words and Music by Willie Nelson and Bob Dylan
© 1993 Warner-Tamerlane Publishing Corp., Act Five Music and Special Rider Music
All rights on behalf of Warner-Tamerlane Publishing Corp and Act Five Music administered by Warner-Tamerlane Publishing Corp. *Used by permission of Alfred Music.* All rights reserved. All rights on behalf of Special Rider Music administered by Special Rider Music. International copyright secured. All rights reserved. Reprinted by permission.

"I Thought About You, Lord"
Words and Music by Willie Nelson
© 1996 Warner-Tamerlane Publishing Corp. and Act Five Music
All rights administered by Warner-Tamerlane Publishing Corp. *Used by permission of Alfred Music.* All rights reserved.

"Luckenbach, Texas (Back to the Basics of Love)"
Word and Music by Bobby Emmons and Chips Moman
Copyright © 1977 Universal-Songs of Polygram International, Inc., and Sony/ATV Music Publishing LLC. Copyright renewed. All rights controlled and administered by Universal-Songs of Polygram International, Inc. All rights reserved. Used by permission.
Reprinted with permission of Hal Leonard Corporation.

"Night Life"
Written by Walter M. Breeland, Paul F. Buskirk, and Willie Nelson

CREDITS FOR SONG LYRICS

© 1962 Sony/ATV Tree Publishing and Glad Music Publishing & Recording LP, Pappy Daily Music LP
All rights on behalf of Sony/ATV Tree Publishing administered by Sony/ATV Music Publishing LLC., 424 Church Street, Suite 1200, Nashville, TN 37219. All rights reserved. Used by permission. All rights on behalf of Glad Music Publishing & Recording LP, Pappy Daily Music administered by Glad Music, Inc. All rights reserved. Used by permission.

"Nothing I Can Do About It Now"
Words and Music by Beth Neilsen Chapman
© 1989 WB Music Corp. and Macy Place Music
All rights administered by WB Music Corp. *Used by permission of Alfred Music.* All rights reserved.

"The Highwayman"
Words and Music by Jimmy Webb
Copyright © 1977 White Oak Songs. Copyright renewed.
All rights controlled and administered by Universal-Polygram International Publishing, Inc. All rights reserved. Used by permission. *Reprinted with permission of Hal Leonard Corporation.*

"The Party's Over"
Written by Willie Nelson
Used courtesy of Glad Music Publishing & Recording LP, Heart of the Hills Publishing Co. and Pappy Daily Music LP. All rights reserved. Used by permission.

"The Songwriters"
Words and Music by Gordie Sampson and Bill Anderson
Copyright © 2014 Music Of Windswept, No Such Music, Sony/ATV Music Publishing LLC, Mr. Bubba Music, and Songs Of Southside Independent Publishing. All rights for Music of Windswept and No Such Music Administered by BMG Rights Management (US) LLC. *Reprinted with permission of Hal Leonard Corporation.* All rights for Sony/ATV Music Publishing LLC and Mr. Bubba Music administered by Sony/ATV Music Publishing LLC, 424 Church Street, Suite 1200, Nashville, TN 37219. All rights reserved. Used by permission. All rights for Songs of Southside Independent Publishing used by permission of Alfred Music.

"We Don't Run"
Words and Music by Willie Nelson
© 1996 Warner-Tamerlane Publishing Corp. and Act Five Music
All rights administered by Warner-Tamerlane Publishing Corp. *Used by permission of Alfred Music.* All rights reserved.

"What Would Willie Do?"
Words and music by Bruce Robison
© 2001 Tiltawhirl Mujsic (BMI)—Administered by Bluewater Music Services Corp.
All rights reserved. Used by permission.